Autumn 2007

# Griffith
# REVIEW

Divided Nation

Editor — Julianne Schultz

Griffith REVIEW is published four times a year by Griffith University in conjunction with ABC Books.

ISSN 1448-2924

Griffith Graduate Centre
South Bank Campus, Griffith University
PO Box 3370, South Brisbane Qld 4101
Australia

ABC Books
GPO Box 9994
Sydney NSW 2001
Australia

Telephone      (07) 3735 3071
Facsimile      (07) 3735 3272
Email          griffithreview@griffith.edu.au
Website        www.griffith.edu.au/griffithreview

Subscription (4 issues) incl postage and handling
$79.80 within Australia including GST (Recommended Retail Price)
A$120.50 outside Australia
Institutional and bulk rates available on application from the Business Manager at the Griffith University address above.

Opinions published in Griffith REVIEW are not necessarily those of the Publisher, the Editor, Griffith University or the ABC.
The copyright of all the material published in Griffith REVIEW and on its website remains the property of the author, artist or photographer, and is subject to copyright laws. No part of this publication may be reproduced without written permission from the publisher.

Letters to the editor should be sent to The Editor, Griffith REVIEW, PO Box 3370, South Brisbane, Qld 4101, Australia.
Alternatively they can be emailed to griffithreview@griffith.edu.au or by logging on to the website www.griffith.edu.au/griffithreview. The Editor reserves the right to edit letters for publication.

Publisher: Marilyn McMeniman
Editor: Julianne Schultz
Copy Editor: Sue Jarvis
Education Editor: Greer Johnson
Business Manager: David Mayocchi
Production Manager: Paul Thwaites
Production Assistant: Pamela Coyle
Marketing Coordinator: Erica Sontheimer
ABC Books: Stuart Neal, Brigitta Doyle, Lindsay Somerville, Liz White, Jane Finemore
Publicity: Amanda Balderstone
Original Cover Concept: Liveworm Studio, Queensland College of Art, Griffith University
Typesetting: Midland Typesetters
Printer: Griffin Press
Distribution: Allen & Unwin

---

Advertising in Griffith REVIEW

Each issue of Griffith REVIEW has a circulation of at least 4,000 copies. It's a direct and effective way for advertisers to reach individuals concerned with ideas, fine writing and debate. Its circulation is international.

Full page adverts are available for selected advertisers.

To book your advertisement, in the first instance please contact the Griffith REVIEW Business Manager by email: griffithreview@griffith.edu.au.

---

Cover image: 'Bomber' from the Vietnam Veterans series / Photographer: David Nielsen

Sir Samuel Griffith was one of Australia's great early achievers. Twice the premier of Queensland, that state's chief justice and author of its criminal code, he was a great, confident provincial who saw no reason why, as a Queenslander, he could not take a major role in the public life of the emerging nation.

Best known for his pivotal role in drafting agreements that led to Federation and as the new nation's first chief justice, Griffith was also an important reformer and legislator, a practical and cautious man of words – a legal draftsman, a poet and translator of Dante. Griffith, who died in 1920, is now remembered in his namesakes – an electorate, a society, a suburb and a university.

Ninety-six years after he first proposed establishing a university in Brisbane, Griffith University, the city's second, was created. Now Sir Samuel Griffith's commitment to public debate and ideas, his delight in words and art and his attachment to active citizenship have again been recognised by the university that bears his name in the publication of Griffith REVIEW.

This quarterly publication is designed to foster and inform public debate, to bridge the expertise of specialists and the curiosity of readers, provide the space to explore issues at greater length with more reflection, and offer the opportunity for established and emerging writers and artists to tease out complexity and propose new ways of thinking and seeing.

Each issue of Griffith REVIEW is devoted to a topical theme and includes essays, analysis, reportage, memoir, satire, fiction, poetry, photography and art. The range is deliberately wide. The complexity of contemporary issues cannot be adequately illuminated by one form alone – the who, what, when, where, how and why of events are all important, but the feel for what they mean may better be understood through a novelist's eye, the cacophony of current activities better comprehended with an expert's insight into competing theories or the rhetoric of public debate unpacked by detailed behind-the-scenes reportage. These forms and others will be welcomed in Griffith REVIEW as it attempts to capture the spirit of the times and build a bridge between literary, academic and journalistic writing and the reading public.

Like Sir Samuel Griffith, Griffith REVIEW will attempt to inform and advance public debate and understanding; it will also be iconoclastic and non-partisan, with a sceptical eye and a pragmatically reforming heart. ∎

# Contents

## INTRODUCTION

**7**    RESPECT VERSUS DIVISION
**Julianne Schultz** considers how politicians seek to exploit division

## MEMOIR

**59**    SYDNEY AND ME
**Lucy Lehmann** learns to love her home town

**121**    STRANGER IN A STRANGE LAND
**Phil Brown** suspects that he may never be a true Queenslander

**189**    THE FENCE
**Shane Strange** returns to his family home and the ghosts of the past

**227**    ON BECOMING A JEW
**Lee Kofman** finds that anti-Semitism cannot be simply wished away

## FICTION

**127**    I'M NOT HERE
**Dominique Wilson** traces a woman's troubling journey from Vietnamese village to the streets of Melbourne

## ESSAY

**11**    TRYING TO FIND THE SUNNY SIDE OF LIFE
**David Burchell** explores the way history, geography and policy intersect, and how the human spirit prevails

**67**    CRACKS IN THE VENEER
**Jago Dodson** and **Neil Sipe** start a conversation about oil prices, interest rates and the sustainability of the suburbs

**85**    THE EXILED CHILD
**Meera Atkinson** reveals the life long traumatic legacy of growing up in an abusive home

**99**    THE WORDS TO SAY IT
**Charlie Stansfield** examines the scarce options available for the homeless and mentally ill

**109**    BOOM! EXCURSIONS IN FANTASY LAND
**Julienne van Loon** explores the costs and challenges of life in a booming economy

**153**    THE GAP BETWEEN WORK AND CHOICES
**David Peetz** documents the impact of the new industrial relations laws, and finds them wanting

**167**    DESTINATION ADELAIDE
**Tracy Crisp** recalls why people leave Adelaide and what they find when they return

**182**    DISTURBING UNDERTONES
**Dorothy Johnston** finds a Gothic dimension to life in Canberra

*ESSAY continued:*

**197 THE ANTIDOTE OF MULTICULTURALISM**

**Geoffrey Brahm Levey** analyses the enduring legacy of multiculturalism and why the critics have distorted it

**209 BEYOND PITY**

**Robert Hillman** learns from two brilliant refugees that migration is mutually beneficial

**221 EXPLORERS, WRITERS AND OTHER CREATIVE STRANGERS**

**Joanna Kujawa** celebrates the Polish spirit and its lasting cultural, intellectual and political impact

**238 OF MIDDLE EASTERN APPEARANCE**

**Randa Abdel-Fattah** finds an identity that transcends the hyphens

**243 RETRO-ASSIMILATION**

**Anna Haebich** traces the political origins of assimilation and the campaign to sell it to a sceptical community

**256 ON BEING INVISIBLE**

**Anita Heiss** reflects on being a Wiradjuri woman and the invisibility of her people

**265 BLOW-INS ON THE COLD DESERT WIND**

**Kim Mahood** returns to a remote community to explain a new government policy

# REPORTAGE

**39 DOWN-AT-HEEL AMONG THE WELL-HEELED**

**Peter Meredith** respectfully documents the stories of poor people living in a rich neighbourhood

**145 VIETNAM VETERANS**

**David Nielsen** documents the lives of returning veterans and their families

**175 ON THE GROUND**

**Natasha Cica** reports from the most disadvantaged community in the most disadvantaged state

# POETRY

**81 SUBURBAN ARCHAEOLOGY**

**Anna Krien** embarks on a personal journey of real life in Melbourne's suburbs

You can keep your head and your beach house above water.

Invest in global cooling – energy efficiency and renewable generation from the sun, wind and hot rocks.

## australianethical
### investment + superannuation

**austethical.com.au**

Units in the trusts are offered and issued by Australian Ethical Investment Ltd ('AEI') ABN 47 003 188 930, AFSL 229949. Interests in the superannuation fund are offered by AEI and issued by the trustee of the fund, Australian Ethical Superannuation Pty Ltd ABN 43 079 259 733 RSEL L0001441. Product disclosure statements are available from our website or by calling **1800 021 227** and should be considered before deciding whether to acquire, or continue to hold, units in the trusts or interests in the fund.
Australian Ethical® is a registered trademark of AEI.

Divided Nation

## Introduction:
# Respect versus division
## Writer:
# Julianne Schultz

For some years, once upon a time, I lived in a little house on a cliff in a coal-mining village north of Wollongong. The spectacular views along the rugged coastline drew the eye to the industrial city's bustling harbour, the steaming and flaming chimneys of the factories that earned the city its "steel city" moniker. Million dollar views, guests would gush, as they lingered on the balcony, spotting albatrosses and sea eagles, dolphins and giant schools of fish just below the surface. Even the occasional whale.

During the resources boom at the start of the 1980s, the horizon was also dotted with container ships. Giant rust-encrusted vessels with utilitarian names from far-off ports waited to take the coal out, and bring the iron ore in. Ten, twenty, thirty ships could sit high in the water waiting a turn at a coal-loader that could not keep up with demand, just as they now wait off the coast of Central Queensland and Western Australia.

Once loaded, the ships would sink deeper in the water and we would watch them head north on the long journey to deposit their bounty and power the Japanese wonder economy.

Then one day it stopped. Where there had been scores of ships queuing to take away the dense black coal – which had provided just enough warmth and income for three or four generations of miners, and thousands of generations of Dharawal who found both physical and spiritual sustenance on the escarpment and in the ocean – all of a sudden there were none.

No ships waited to take the coal away, hardly any ships waited to deposit the iron ore destined to trundle along the conveyor belt and become girders and rooves and fences and pipes. The economy shuddered as the long legacy of the oil shocks of the 1970s continued to reverberate locally and globally. Steel and coal industries were in crisis everywhere – caught in the pincers of shrinking demand, under-investment, atrocious productivity, rigid work practices, poor planning and half-baked policy. The domestic market collapsed. As orders fell away, jobs went with them. Tens of thousands

Griffith REVIEW 7

## Introduction

lost their jobs, in the mines and factories and in the businesses that had grown up to service them. These were not glamorous jobs, but reliable, regular work that needed to be done, paid tolerably well and provided a constant stream of migrants with their first work in Australia.

The enormity of the crisis was clear and personal. My neighbour had the gruesome task of putting on his policeman's cap and investigating suicides of blokes he once drank with, who had found life unbearable.

Watching the disintegration of a community from a distance seemed inadequate, so I set out to write a book – *Steel City Blues* (Penguin, 1985) – about what was happening and why. Every day for months, I trundled down the highway, talking to tearful managers, a mayor (later murdered) with a vision, women who had fought for jobs in the steelworks only to be the last on first off, sons of men from Yugoslavia and Italy and England and a dozen other countries whose apprenticeships were cut short and who blamed the "slopes" [Vietnamese boat people], old men who had taught themselves English waiting in line in the steelworks canteen ("a milkshake please"), others who couldn't imagine what else they could do but go down the mines, kids who left school at fifteen and dreamed of becoming famous and successful, union officials with an agenda, management consultants with a plan, activists who wanted to foment revolution.

And there was a revolution of sorts. Those most affected fought to be taken seriously, to be treated with respect and decency. In October 1982, a group of miners stayed underground for sixteen days and won better redundancy payments. Thousands travelled to Canberra in a protest that culminated in breaking through the barricaded doors of Parliament House and flooding into Kings Hall. It was the beginning of the end of the government of Malcolm Fraser, who lost to Bob Hawke in March 1983.

As I said, this all happened once upon a time, in a distant age, when the notion of a million dollar view was a ridiculous joke. Now it is a statement of fact, the little house we built for $35,000 and sold for $110,000 has grown and is now actually worth millions. The view remains the same, but the neighbourhood is richer and tidier – a tourist destination; coal mines closed, steelworks beautified, a university the largest employer in the city.

Once upon a time, before the social reforms that encouraged cohesion, creativity, multiculturalism and reconciliation, before the economy was deregulated, the dollar floated, industry restructured and the economic framework that facilitated the long boom of the last fifteen years established.

For many years, the fruits of these policies were highly

contested and unevenly distributed. Pockets of high unemployment lingered well into the 1990s – despite spectacular growth, the transition from an economy underpinned by mining with a significant overlay of manufacturing to one where more people were likely to work in services was hard. Economic and social reform was the order of the decade from the mid-1980s, and it paid off for most people – but not without some resentment.

In his final speech to Parliament as Opposition Leader in November 1995, John Howard decried the damage that had been done by these reforms: "The worst legacy of this government ... will be the extent to which it has divided the Australian community, the extent to which it has put one Australian against another, the extent to which it has presided over the widening gap between rich and poor ... [Paul Keating] will wear the mark of dividing Australian society, of being a leader who has wounded and wrecked rather than healed and united, of being a leader who has seen partisan political advantage in setting one group against another."

Throughout his prime ministership Howard has been adept at managing division, and he has not shied away from fostering it. His government has been blessed with a buoyant economy and the flexibility this money provides.

The long boom of the past decade and a half has put paid to the old shibboleth that Australia cannot manage booms. Over the last few years, unemployment levels have fallen to record lows, the economy has continued to grow respectably without overheating, gross domestic product per person has increased faster than in comparable countries, and in the decade to 2003 income has increased by about 24 per cent for people living in both rich and poor postcodes.

Yet, over the same period, inequality has increased. The salaries of chief executives have increased from eighteen times the average wage to sixty-three times, conspicuous consumption by the affluent to some degree relies on the low wages paid to those in the hospitality, retail, childcare and agricultural sectors.

Generally we prefer to avert our eyes from those who have not done so well from the boom. Home ownership remains the key to economic wellbeing in this country, but as prices have increased it has become less affordable for many, just as others have made small fortunes from property speculation. Each year, more than $200 billion is collected and redistributed through the vast array of family and income support payments, yet single people living on welfare make do on $72 a week below the poverty line.

Former US President Bill Clinton once remarked that what a country does with its prosperity is as much a test as what it does when times are hard. The long-

## Introduction

term scorecard on Australia's performance in this boom cannot be written yet, but as the stories in this issue illustrate, it is not likely to be as uncomplicated or generous as many would hope.

In December 2006 in his first speech as Leader of the Opposition, Kevin Rudd echoed John Howard's earlier critique when he said: "This country is engaged in a battle of ideas for Australia's future ... In an absolute nutshell that is the divide between us – a view that says it is about me, myself and I and an alternative view which says that we are about an Australia which recognises that individual hard work, achievement and success are to be encouraged and rewarded, but at the same time we cannot turn a blind eye to the interests of our fellows human beings who are not doing well. That has been the divide between us for a century and remains the divide today."

Social and economic division is something that can creep up unexpectedly if you don't read the signs right. Like a southerly buster blowing up the coast, first there are a few white caps on the sea, then a dark line in the water, and before you know it a gale that drops temperatures and debris in its wake. At the beginning of 2007 two states were still booming, one was in recession and another was on the cusp of recession. The luxury of having more money and ideas looked set to expire.

Social division is a bit like that too, hard to predict, but impossible to ignore once it arrives. It can also be whipped up in a fury of rhetoric, ideology and spin, even in a relaxed and comfortable place like this. The naming and shaming of refugees, Muslims and Aboriginal people has proceeded with tacit, and at times explicit, political endorsement.

This is a tactic which has delivered for some politicians during the boom, but is at odds with the best of the Australian tradition. Egalitarianism and tolerance have had a tough time remaining the dominant values in recent years. The boom has softened this attack, but the corrosion has begun and if things turned bad, as they did in Wollongong in 1982, the repercussions could be considerable. The Sydney riots in 2005 demonstrated, in some communities a sense of grievance is not far below the surface.

The 2007 election campaign will be a test of how serious this is, and how resilient we are. A national survey by the Social Research Policy Unit at the University of New South Wales on the essentials for reasonable wellbeing reveals that everyone – rich and poor – considers being treated with respect by others as fundamental, more important than having lots of stuff. Respect transcends division and can be applied to all aspects of our lives. It is time to listen to the stories of those who have missed out, or been made invisible and try to understand, rather than turning a blind eye or reacting with a flash of fear. ■

Essay:
**Trying to find the sunny side of life**

Author:
**David Burchell**

*Image: Rioting in Macquarie Fields, 28 February 2005. / Photographer: Nick Moir / Source: Fairfaxphotos.com*

Divided Nation

# Trying to find the sunny side of life

When the historical datelines are being drawn up, the year 2005 may be marked down as the Indian summer of Australia's decade-long economic boom. Truly it seemed as if the sun might never set. Household disposable incomes, measured in dollars, were half as high again as they had been a decade earlier – a deluge of personal wealth we'd not seen since the halcyon postwar years. The dollar values of Australians' homes had more than doubled, while the interest rates they were paying on their mortgages were almost a third lower. Unemployment had fallen from almost 9 per cent in 1995 to little more than 5 per cent in 2005, and the average duration of that enforced leisure had roughly halved (from about six months to three). Housing extensions and renovations were making millionaires of builders across the major cities, while big-screen televisions and "home cinema" equipment were walking off the display floors faster than they could be ordered. "The economy" – that menacing couplet which had quickened the heartbeat of thousands of newspaper readers for decades – seemed to have become what the Romans would have called a *cornucopia*: a horn of plenty.

And yet the monsoon clouds were already gathering on the horizon. In Sydney – an increasingly fractious town wracked by drought, heatwaves and traffic snarls – the apparently weightless property market had begun to reacquaint itself with the force of gravity, and people were watching their real estate magic puddings unaccountably beginning to shrink. Housing affordability had already a hit a historic low, while over the decade from 1995 housing debt rose from about 40 per cent to about 70 per cent of households' disposable incomes. Almost two-thirds of private renters had fallen into a state the statisticians define as "housing stress". As if affected by the endless dry heat, a tone of rancour had crept over the city's baking streets. "Symbolic analysts" and "knowledge workers", those grand but dissatisfied beneficiaries of the boom, argued vociferously over their dinner tables about the nation's moral failings and our shrunken hearts. In the newspapers, there was increasing disputation about the city's status as the main repository for the nation's refugee and family reunion immigration programs. "Ethnic tension", that rough beast we'd associated with South Central Los Angeles or the tenements of Western Europe, seemed to be stirring. The airwaves hissed with anxieties around "home-grown" terror and Islamic extremism, while the dress habits of Arab-Australian women became matters of public notice. And, three times within the space of a year or so, young men – men with different causes, and from different backgrounds, it's true – took to the streets to throw things and words about, attack property and police alike, and generally raise the social temperature. For the first time since the days of the Rum Corps, Sydney had become a riotous place to live.

Late one Friday night, in the dying days of the long hot summer, three young men from one of the most stressed neighbourhoods of that stressed city acquired a late-model white Holden Commodore with a view to taking a joyride. Some minutes later, with an unmarked police car in hot pursuit, the car lost traction at a gentle bend on Eucalyptus Drive, Macquarie Fields, rolled several times and ploughed into a gum tree. Both passengers in the car, Matt Robertson and Dylan Raywood, died instantly. Robertson had been in jail so often his friends couldn't remember his age, but in two weeks he was due to start his first legitimate job, stall-holding at the Royal Easter Show. A year before, Raywood had been selected in the under-seventeen development squad for the Wests Tigers Rugby League Club, part of a program designed specifically to get troubled young players back on track. (The club's football manager admitted: "To be truthful, Dylan wouldn't have made the squad if it was chosen on merit. But the whole purpose of it is to keep kids off the street.") The driver, Jesse Kelly – himself a troubled young man with a precocious criminal record – survived, but he disappeared into the night. His aunt, Deborah Kelly, a formidable woman with a criminal record of her own, took charge of the situation.

According to a later police statement opposing her bail application, Deborah circulated a rival version of events according to which the police had rammed the car into the tree on purpose and then fled the scene. The Glenquarie Estate, a Housing Commission enterprise from the 1970s to accommodate troubled families and their children, is one of the toughest, most crime-wracked localities in Sydney, and relations with the police are generally fraught. Deborah Kelly's account of events sped up and down the laneways of the neighbourhood, and by the Sunday night hundreds of young people had gathered on the street, where they began launching missiles, fireworks and Molotov cocktails at police. The police responded with baton charges. For the next three nights, there were pitched battles along the broad bitumen curves of Eucalyptus Drive. The police donned helmets and shields, and deployed in lines reminiscent of the tactical doctrines of the Duke of Wellington. The local boys fought, posed for the cameras and took souvenirs of the battle. The television film-crews dodged and weaved as they strove to catch the best shots. Outsiders brought in deckchairs to watch the show. And the airwaves of Sydney radio ran fever-hot.

The so-called "law and order debate" nowadays has such a familiar, choreographed quality that it resembles those Balinese shadow-plays which are appreciated in stoic silence by Australian holiday-makers. In the aftermath of the Macquarie Fields riots, the little stick-figures had a busy time of it. The state opposition and the most popular radio personalities united in questioning how the police had allowed the riots to develop in the first place, and in calling for that hardiest of law and order slogans, "zero tolerance". (Exactly how zero tolerance was to be practised on a neighbourhood in which almost everybody seems to fall foul of the law before they reach majority was not explained.) The city's conservative-leaning tabloid, the *Daily Telegraph*, declared "Enough is enough". In sharp contrast, the city's liberal-minded broadsheet, the *Sydney Morning Herald*, offered the familiar "cry of pain" diagnosis: there were "deeper", "underlying reasons" for the riots than mere lawlessness, socio-economic disadvantage was the key.

Yet none of these responses ever seemed really to cut to the heart of the matter. Since, on the one hand, communities whose members routinely plunder and deface public property are rarely healthy places in which to grow up, the first set of responses (zero tolerance, tough love, where are the parents?) always seems inadequate and even perverse. Yet the reflexive incantation of the theme of socio-economic disadvantage – like some journalistic equivalent of a lecture out of Sociology 101 – often seems hardly more helpful. Solve disadvantage and you'll solve lawlessness and dysfunction, the slogan seems to say. And then – the tabloid-reading critic might well respond – why not go on to create world peace?

The events in Macquarie Fields, like those in Redfern before and Cronulla after, aroused such controversy in large part because rioting in suburbia seemed – at least prior to the overheated social temperature in Sydney of the last few years – to be strangely out of kilter with Australian mores. In Western Europe, public housing is almost synonymous with public disturbance. The classic tower blocks of inner south and east London, or on the outskirts of Paris – originally built as part of hopeful campaigns of slum-clearance – have defied attempts to foster civic pride. Instead, they have often become graffiti-encrusted, vandalised wind-tunnels, and have provided the cannon-fodder for tribes of neo-Nazi bovver-boys and jihadi-wannabees. In Australia, by contrast, the ambitions of postwar planners turned instead towards fostering private home ownership across the vast green-brown suburban expanses, and (despite the grand dreams of social radicals) inner-city public housing was aimed chiefly at the very poor and the elderly – who generally appreciated what was seen to be their privilege. For every wind-tunnel, there are probably two or three gatherings of neat inner-city window-boxes.

Yet, seen from the historian's point of view, the story of Macquarie Fields has the kind of irresistible logic to it which is often attributed to ancient Greek tragedies. It begins with the changing public housing philosophies of the 1960s and 1970s. As the waiting lists for inner-city public residences grew (and their tenants grew older), planners sketched out miniature suburbs of public housing across the outskirts of all the major cities. Often these neighbourhoods were given pastoral-sounding names like Green Valley or Ambarvale, and it was imagined that they could be designed and laid out like little country villages. At the same time, priority was increasingly directed to providing housing for those defined by new measures of disadvantage as being in crisis – meaning, in many cases, women with kids fleeing violent partners, parents with drug and alcohol problems, or those receiving counselling for behavioural problems – or all of the above. And so, without any explicit policy directive connecting these two movements, the new semi-rural estates became the chief repositories for families in crisis. In the early 1980s, my wife (who was then working in a women's refuge) dropped off an Aboriginal woman and her kids fleeing domestic violence to the then-new Glenquarie Estate, at a house which she recalls only as seeming to be in the middle of nowhere. It felt like dropping a pebble into the ocean.

Up until the mid-1970s, Macquarie Fields was little more than a collection of hamlets loosely following the curve of the Georges River, a half dozen or so kilometres south of Liverpool on the city's south-western verge. If you strayed more than three or four blocks east of Glenfield railway station (as a friend who grew up there recalls it), you'd find yourself wandering through the virgin scrub. Out of this frontier wilderness, the Department of Housing planners carved neat rows of brick-veneer bungalows and angular semi-detached "villas" for a brand-new suburb. But Macquarie Fields was to be more than an ordinary township. It was to be a public housing estate within a suburb: a little island of social experiment locked within the grand suburban sea. And when they came to draft the public housing estate on the suburb's eastern fringe, the planners called upon the ghost of William Morris. Rather than have the kids play on the streets, the architects shaped arcing drives with pastoral names like Eucalyptus, Rosewood and Cottonwood, and sculpted gum-strewn parks with wandering tracks and laneways, like the country lanes of an imagined bygone era. They called it the Glenquarie Estate.

In large measure, the experiment was still-born. Parents in crisis not infrequently reared children in crisis, and some of the children are now, a generation on, becoming crisis-ridden parents themselves. The jobless rate in the suburb is about twice the national average: on the estate it's higher again. Single-parent families are in the majority. Habits of domestic violence and substance abuse are commonly transmitted inter-generationally. It is possible to grow up on the estate nowadays and not know a single adult male who's unquestionably on the straight and narrow. For many, being burgled is a routine occurrence. In the 2564 postcode area in 2005, 114 cars were reported stolen, there were 227 reported burglaries, 457 cases of property damage, and 279 assaults. Given the prevailing relationship with police in the area, the reported figures are probably extremely conservative. Within a couple of decades of the first concrete-pours, the quaint laneways have become unsafe to walk at night, the paired semi-circular drives have turned neatly into amateur racing-tracks, and the paths through the parks make handy escape routes from the police. The neighbourhood has become a kind of monument to good planning intentions gone wrong. Building Jerusalem can hardly have begun more brightly, nor ended with so faint a whimper.

Like a number of my colleagues, I started receiving phones calls from journalists the morning after the first night of riots. My slim claim to expertise rested upon a small book on Western Sydney I'd written a couple of years before. I was inclined to be circumspect. Reporters from the *Sydney Morning Herald* and the ABC dutifully recorded my unremarkable views on the relations between youth, welfare dependency, dangerous driving and property theft. At the end of a *Herald* interview, I happened to mention that south-west Sydney was the national capital of the illicit car-rebirthing industry. Later that day it emerged that the fugitive driver on Eucalyptus Drive was believed to have taken up a career in the car-rebirthing trade. The next day I received a phone call from a television producer on *60 Minutes*, who seemed convinced – on this finest thread of evidence – that I must have the last word to say on the matter.

An appearance on *60 Minutes* is not something to be entertained lightly. The program distils all liberal academia's familiar loathings – low-brow entertainment masquerading as journalism, a knee-jerk conservative social agenda, and for many high-minded critics it provides an unwanted window into the regrettable cultural preferences of the working classes. Partly out of this anxiety, and partly because of a persistent sense that I was "not the right person", I proposed a series of other names, without evident effect. Eventually, with a sense of dread, I agreed to meet the crew early the following week at a house they'd decided – with true *60 Minutes* chutzpah – to rent a few hundred metres from the centre of the troubles.

And so my early morning rural ride down to Macquarie Fields was an unquiet journey. I wanted to believe I'd agreed out of a desire to speak my academic mind to a wider audience – to be the "public intellectual". Yet I struggled with the niggling fear that I was simply along for the ride. My restless mind cycled through the ways in which studious responses might be wrought by the alchemy of TV editing into inflammatory tirades, or absurd overstatements. I meditated upon the hapless Paxton brothers – two teenage boys who, some years before, had ignited an unedifying public debate on dole-bludging when they were filmed by its sister program, *A Current Affair*,

Trying to find the sunny side of life

refusing to cut their hair for a prospective employer. And, rather like the drowning man, I recalled in fast-forward every impulsive error I'd made since about the age of eight.

The unfurnished house rented by *60 Minutes*, 16 Cottonwood Drive, sits around the corner from Eucalyptus Drive. Except for the uncanny sense that everyone in the neighbourhood had their eyes fastened on a gap in the front curtains, it looked like a quiet backstreet. Outside Number 16, the show's star and presenter, Mike Munro, inimitably dressed in a button-down Ralph Lauren shirt, tight-legged jeans and shiny cowboy boots, was urgently pacing up and down with his mobile phone pressed to his ear. Inside, with the curtains almost drawn, the film crew sat on upturned cartons, tending to their equipment. After Munro read out his improvised questions (some rough outline of which I could see scribbled on an A4 writing-pad) I was shepherded into a Bundy-and-Coke doused Ford Falcon for the short drive around the block to the location. I felt a little like a suspect being led away by the police.

It's the stock in trade of *60 Minutes* to go straight to the emotional heart of things. As with Greek stagecraft and soap opera, the goal is to evoke catharsis in the speediest and most direct manner. They are not unaware of the risks inherent in such an approach – the common criticism that you simply heighten the preconceptions of your viewers, rather than adding to their knowledge. But they see this as simply one more hazard in a risky, no-time-to-stop-and-think kind of business. From *60 Minutes'* point of view, there are two worlds: the world of the participant-actor, and the world of the observer-commentator. They fell into the first category; I was there because I fell into the second. My job was to have scruples (or, if you prefer, to prevaricate); theirs was to act on raw televisual instinct. And so, of course, they conducted their interviews on Eucalyptus Drive, the interviewee posed in front of a notorious piece of graffiti that proclaimed, a tad vaingloriously, "Cops Kill Kids. We Will Kill You Cops".

The appearance of the *60 Minutes* star and his attendants in any small, tight-knit neighbourhood is inevitably a matter of great moment, and so our staggering progress was interrupted every two or three minutes by the blaring horn of a passing car, or the studiously inconspicuous hum of an unmarked police vehicle. Bus and truck drivers slowed and waved like old friends. Local mums watched from the front fence. ("It's not often we get stars here," said one, appreciatively. "Oh, surely I'm not a star yet," Munro replied, with a winning show of modesty.) The presenter's stage presence was impressive. One young mum with a stroller paused to watch the show from the street corner. When she'd had enough, she told Munro that she hoped they'd get the kids to stop the fighting, as it'd be nice to have a night's

David Burchell

sleep for a change. He gave her a serious, knitted-brow look that seemed to suggest that this, like just about anything else, was possible.

As we were winding up the interview, a familiar-looking pair of boys ambled up the street towards us, flashing gap-toothed smiles. Munro waved a greeting and called out brightly: "We've just been interviewing the professor here." One of the boys was Aaron Robertson, Matt's brother, the other was Matt's best mate. Each had been starring on the evening TV news. (Indeed, Aaron succeeded in getting himself arrested three nights running.) Both were about my height and build – which is to say skinny and shorter than average, as so many would-be street heroes are. Each was wearing the hip-hop uniform of baseball cap, baggy polyester tracksuit pants and runners, and an embossed polyester shirt – in the manner of an oversized ice-hockey jersey – with a different slogan. Aaron's best mate was particularly proud of his. Featuring a silver-embossed Uzi sub-machine gun in profile, it had the words "Class War" emblazoned in Gothic script at the top, and had a stirring slogan about resisting the state lettered across the bottom. "I'm against authority," he explained, rather grandly. As he told it, this was the uniform of the new neighbourhood gang, and wearing it was like an initiation rite. He was vague about the shirt's origins: I fancy some anarchist grouplet from the inner-city must have left its calling-card.

The boys seemed cheery enough and entirely at ease. They moved their shoulders jauntily back and forth and bounced up and down on their heels. As Aaron's mate put it, this was pretty much like being a Hollywood film star. They chatted about the events of the last few days, and about the details of Matt's funeral the next day. With a play of secrecy, one of them showed us some improvised firework-weapons – alarming the *60 Minutes* producer, who mistook one of them for a gun. It emerged that *60 Minutes* – which likes to spread money around among potential interviewees – was helping with the funeral costs. Munro asked several times who he should make the cheque payable to. Eventually Aaron angled his head and insisted the money must go directly to his mother. If it went through other family members, he hinted – with a slight movement of the eyebrow – it would probably disappear.

As the camera crew set up, so that Mike and I could be filmed casually strolling up the street, the boys intimated that they had some new business ventures on the go. Right now they had a brand-new stock of razor-scooters going for a song. "Thanks, but I don't have use for a scooter," said Munro, with a polite but firm wave of the arm. The rest of us demurred in turn. The boys smiled, waved and headed back on their way, hands in pockets, deep in conversation. It occurred to me that there was a curious synergy between the flying-by-the seat-of-one's-pants lives of these boys and the equally improvised *modus operandi* of the *60 Minutes* crew. Each lived for the moment; each chose their moments of opportunity on pure gut instinct; each had to keep moving lest their past catch them up. It might even be that this was one element in the *60 Minutes* formula for success: the show's stories of the badlands commanded conviction not because of any in-depth research or commitment to veracity, but because (unlike the ironic varsity voices of the ABC) they exude authentic street-smart themselves. "Ah, they're not bad kids," offered Mike as we watched the boys disappear up the road. "That's the worst of it." Then he reminisced, a little wistfully, upon his own youthful adventures in the suburban jungle. Accustomed by now to his talent for personal theatre, I took this meditation rather lightly. As it turned out later, however, this much at least of Mike's patter was the plain, unadorned truth.

After we'd wound up, the *60 Minutes* crew politely offered to drive me back around the corner. It was a five-minute stroll, but when I said I'd walk they looked alarmed. On the way back I passed Caley Park through which the mum with the pram had wheeled off homewards. You could still see the original town planners' bright intentions in the curve of the concrete track that wound through it. The sun was shining brightly through the leaves, there was a light breeze, and some birds in the boughs of the eucalypts were chirping. It was a beautiful autumn day, and strangely I found an old show tune was playing itself inside my head.

> Look for the silver lining
> When e'er a cloud appears in the blue.
> Remember somewhere, the sun is shining.
> And so the right thing to do is make it shine for you.

And then I was crossed by a sudden thought, like a flash of sunlight through the trees. It occurred to me that Matt's mates, far from being proper objects of solicitation and sympathy, actually must feel they had life sussed. They made fast money and paid no tax; they didn't have to queue at Centrelink, or fill out endless job interview forms; they were keeping out of their mum's hair (or maybe escaping her problems); they were high on adrenaline as much as dope or alcohol. So far from resembling welfare "dependants", the mournful passive beneficiaries of academic lore, their demeanour spoke of the adaptive small businessman, the eBay Powerseller, the itinerant entrepreneur. It was tough luck that a brother and a mate were gone forever. But then life here was a dangerous business: better to live it to the hilt than be cowed by it. In a decade or so, each one of them – like their fugitive friend Jesse Kelly – might well be doing some time in jail. But on Eucalyptus Drive you live for the moment, and a decade seems like an awfully long time.

> A heart, full of joy and gladness
> Will always banish sadness and strife.
> So always look for the silver lining
> And try to find the sunny side of life.

David Burchell

"It seems history is to blame," the Englishman Haines blandly observes of Ireland's "Troubles" in James Joyce's novel *Ulysses*. One way or another, it usually is. At the 2005 New South Wales Parliamentary Inquiry into the riots, the Liberal backbencher Charlie Lynn seized upon the testimony of senior staff from the NSW Department of Housing to blame a more recent historical culprit for the Glenquarie Estate's failings – the various "failed attempts at social engineering" which he associated with the social idealism of the '60s and '70s.

The NSW Parliament's Standing Committee on Social Issues is a gathering of larger-than-life individuals, and the inquiry's transcripts are a faithful enough representation of this. There was speechifying aplenty, so much so that expert witnesses sometimes struggled to get a word in. Among the committee's members is the inimitable Charlie Lynn, a former army officer, Kokoda Track tour organiser and Christian youth group activist – a man who takes it upon himself to be the spokesman for the "silent majority" of concerned citizens, alarmed at the dangers lurking on neighbourhood streets. As of November 2006, Lynn had delivered twenty speeches over his ten-year parliamentary career – each devoted to an aspect of the "law and order debate". In 2003 he accused a state government minister of taking sexual advantage of an under-age boy – accusations he subsequently had to withdraw. The chair, Labor Upper House member Jan Burnswoods – a veteran Labor branch and community activist with a fondness for flowers – seems to see her mission as being to demonstrate that Lynn is a fraudulent fool. Treatment which provides Lynn with ample opportunity to present himself as the hapless Mr Smith come to conniving, politically correct Macquarie Street. Chief among the other members is the euphonically named Democrat Dr Arthur Chesterfield-Evans, a former surgeon and anti-smoking activist who interrupted the evidence at various points to quiz witnesses upon the finer points of social policy theory.

In the course of its proceedings, the inquiry interviewed two senior administrators from the Department of Housing, Michael Allen and Clifford Haynes, about the history of the estate. The two men attempted to tell the committee – with all the heroic reserves of patience that only a career in public administration can provide – the tangled story of the estate's genesis in the 1970s and the various attempts to remedy its deficiencies through improvements to the physical environment in the decades since. Kitchens and laundries had been renovated; houses had been reoriented to face the street; funds had been provided to help around a third of the residents purchase their homes. The longer objective, they explained, was to create greater diversity of tenure and circumstance within the estate, to create a "more balanced community" with people from a wider range of social backgrounds

## Trying to find the sunny side of life

and more diverse sources of income. But this meant overcoming the legacy of large, relatively homogenous housing estates that had been entrenched in the planning of the New South Wales Housing Commission from the 1950s through to the 1970s. More specifically, it meant redrawing the estate to remove the numerous "access ways and cul de sacs" required by the "Radburn model" of estate in favour at the time.

At this point, the indefatigable, history-minded Charlie Lynn leapt up to attract an unsympathetic chair's attention. "I refer to the original Radburn model. When was it introduced? ... Who was the Rhodes Scholar who introduced it? ... Do you see it as a failed attempt at social engineering in the 1970s?" he asked, staccato-style, in a state of genuine agitation. And a jousting match followed between Lynn and Burnswoods as to which party had been in power when "Radburn's" experiment ("Radburn is not a person, it is a town in New Jersey," Allen patiently explained) began.

Lynn's instincts were not altogether misplaced. There is more to the history of the Glenquarie Estate than can be gleaned from government reports alone. But he was surely a little unkind to lay responsibility for the estate's troubles on the now-bowed shoulders of the "flower children". Indeed, if you really want to nab "history" for the troubles of the present, you need to travel a good deal further back than Lynn's historical vision allows. In fact, you'd need to travel back to the late nineteenth century, to the era of the classic social investigators, to the first dreams of slum-clearance and new working-class neighbourhoods studded with oak trees and festooned with flowers. You'd need to begin with a novel like *Looking Backward*, the 1888 time-travelling utopia of American Victorian social visionary Edward Bellamy – the book that pioneered the belief that the psychic wounds of modern industrial society could be healed by a new kind of built community, a city in which work and leisure, culture and industry, and even town and country could be seamlessly harmonised, supposedly combining the best of each with (in the best utopian tradition) the disadvantages of neither.

Bellamy's narrator awakes one morning to find himself in a recreated Boston of the year 2000, a city in which public and private goods intermingle. Want has been abolished, incomes have been equalised, and the mundane traffic in goods has been replaced by universal stores in which the best of everything is available at cost price. It is an image which fairly shimmers even today.

> Miles of broad streets, shaded by trees and lined with fine buildings, for the most part not in continuous blocks but set in larger or smaller enclosures, stretched in every direction. Every quarter contained large open

David Burchell

squares filled with trees, among which statues glistened and fountains flashed in the late afternoon sun.

Across the Atlantic, one of Bellamy's grandest enthusiasts was a sometime parliamentary reporter, Ebenezer Howard. Drawing upon Bellamy's bright vision, the enlightened factory-town experiments of Christian industrialists such as W.H. Lever and George Cadbury, and the aesthetic principles of the "arts and crafts movement", Howard gathered a movement of professionals and philanthropists to purchase land for the Garden Cities of Letchworth and Welwyn in Hertfordshire. Letchworth was a kind of commune (part Renaissance Florence, part Nimbin): all its citizens owned shares in the civic association, which leased the town's land back to them individually. (It's worth noting that Howard lived in Letchworth from 1905 to 1921, until Welwyn was built, whereupon he moved – and later died – there.)

While the actual Garden Cities varied markedly in pattern according to location (and readiness of funds, which were sometimes tight), Howard seems to have viewed them all as epiphenomena of a Platonic ideal he'd outlined in his 1904 book *Garden Cities of Tomorrow*. And indeed the diagrams there are organised on Hellenic geometrical principles, as a series of concentric circles. There is a central park (derived from F.L. Omsted's massive original in Manhattan) with grand boulevards leading outwards to the city's rim, criss-crossed with concentric-circular avenues of varying designs and functions. The private dwellings are to be "excellently built" in varying individual styles, but with common gardens and "cooperative kitchens". And the churches are "of such denominations as the religious beliefs of the people may determine, to be erected and maintained out of the funds of the worshippers and their friends". The industrial districts occupy the outer rim, where they intersect with the railway lines on which the city's products are conveyed to the wider world. And outside this grand circular gemstone lays a patchwork of private allotments, dairy farms and forests, fulfilling Howard's vision of uniting city and country into a single vision (albeit that, while the city is severely geometrical, the countryside remains illimitable).

Howard's notion was that cities of this kind could be assembled as a network of free-standing social islands, each sufficient to itself for basic needs, but engaged in commerce with others for the exchange of their industrial goods. When one garden city outstripped its bounds, Howard explained, the surplus population would skip over the surrounding countryside to form a new one some miles distant – much, he believed, as Adelaide had at once retained its urban parks, and established its new development in North Adelaide. The sea-lanes connecting this glittering archipelago of progress were the same railway tracks that already carried so many of the nineteenth century's other social hopes. The cities themselves, though, were without mechanical transport: citizens could walk to the central park, or the town halls, concert halls, libraries and museums that surrounded it, or to their workplaces on the periphery as if strolling through pastureland.

Howard's egalitarian democracy, like that of so many of his colleagues and acquaintances, was that of the religiously non-conformist, public-spirited urban professional – the doctrine of the spiritually, intellectually and economically independent. A little like the middle-class Bolsheviks a generation or two later, he envisioned a workers' paradise where the soul was nourished by cheap classical concerts and shapely yet severely functional domestic furniture, where conspicuous poverty and "shoddy" were the twin scourges of humanity.

For this ideal to flourish across the Atlantic – where visions, after all, had more room to flourish, and urban allotments were easier to obtain – it had to be enlarged to cater for less high-minded products of industrialism such as the private motor-car. And so, when a group of similarly minded professionals founded the Regional Planning Association of America in the 1920s, they both drew on the Letchworth model, and reimagined its basic geometry. Clarence Stein's 1929 Radburn Estate in New Jersey, the first Garden City in the United States, resembled a complicated root-system: motorways spawned side-roads, each of which branched off in multiple rootlings towards the rear-facing garages of private villas, which looked outwards towards an encircling tree-lined footway. The car had been accommodated – as, in the new demotic era of motor-transport, it had to be – but only, as it were, through the back door. This pragmatic modification of the Garden City geometry – the harmony of the spheres reduced to a kind of inelegant maze – became the basis for some of the grandest and most fateful experiments in (private and) public housing after World War II.

Australian planners and visionaries had been abreast of the Garden City movement from its early stages. In the interwar years, a prototype public housing Garden City was built on reclaimed land near Port Melbourne, though it failed to bear fruit. At the end of World War II, in the more propitious heyday of nation-building, Walter Bunning was assigned the task of creating a new munitions complex at St Marys, on Sydney's western fringes. Bunning – the main author of the Commonwealth Housing Commission's 1944 report into the country's impending postwar housing needs – was a modernist architect and Garden City enthusiast. Most of the munitions site's workers commuted to the factories by train, but Bunning also constructed some temporary housing across the tracks. And then – as if by way of a casual afterthought – he added a small experimental village, rigorously drawn up on the Radburn model, on the site's eastern fringe. The St Marys

David Burchell

Permanent Cottage Area – now heritage-protected for all its few meagre blocks – still stands today, a few kilometres away from the campus on which I work. Within its slender geometric curves lies the strange seed that, thirty years later, blossomed in Macquarie Fields.

Some years earlier, a new private housing development was pegged out in a semi-rural outer western glen by a canny North Shore building firm with the then-chic name Homes De Luxe. It was called Green Valley. The site was later bought by the New South Wales Housing Commission in the wake of nation-building pride, and developed in the 1960s to become the largest public housing estate in the Sydney basin, designed especially for the poorest and most welfare-dependent families. (The Housing Commission commemorated the occasion with a promotional booklet hopefully titled "Estate of Tomorrow".) Public planners and bureaucrats ("never complain, never explain") leave few records of their governing philosophies, and so we're forced to guess at the process whereby the tidy-town blueprints of Letchworth and Radburn – carefully designed to be self-contained urban entities, each with local factories and processing works – were transmuted into Australia's grandest laboratory experiment in all-commuting-public-rental-accommodation, with no nearby employment, limited public transport and few amenities. According to 1960s researchers at Sydney University, two in five of the original settlers there had no car, while only one in ten could afford a telephone. Once you'd moved there, you were – quite literally – on your own.

Over the course of the 1960s, the phrase "Green Valley" entered Sydney's comic lexicon. The joke lay in pretending that this was indeed a pastoral paradise, as its name seemed to suggest. And, like all the geographical put-downs that litter the folklore of the most unforgiving of Australian cities, this was thought to be irresistibly funny. (In the same idiom – though less maliciously – it's become popular in recent years for Sydneysiders to wear t-shirts claiming "I climbed Mt Druitt" – another of Sydney's "struggle-towns".) By the end of the decade, the estate had already become famous enough to draw sustained comment from the otherwise slightly parochial Adelaide academic Hugh Stretton in his classic *Ideas for Australian Cities* (Georgian House, 1970). Contrasting the still-pristine Green Valley with the unfashionable but striving blue-collar dormitory town of Elizabeth on the northern fringes of his home city, Stretton acknowledged that, of the two:

> Green Valley looks better. Its land undulates pleasantly under some mature native trees. Its street planning is more imaginative … its school buildings are better, it has some attractive pedestrian ways and better and safer pedestrian planning … and you can't tell its owned from its rented houses.

## Trying to find the sunny side of life

Here, though, Green Valley's advantages ended. A journey to the beach was a day trip, and most of the residents didn't have cars. There were few jobs in evidence, and poor access to health care. The shopping centre closed early, and the local pub was inhospitable. Unlike Howard's Letchworth, neither doctors nor politicians chose to live there, and the few stories of personal success were "not enough to shake the steady, intelligent desire of three-quarters of its residents to get out of the place". In short, the problem wasn't poor planning, still less a shortage of services (which would "wilt there, for want of paying custom"). Rather, Stretton observed:

> All Green Valley's poverties spring from the poverty of its people, hand picked ... for their comparative incapacity to get on, or get tough, or get well, or get rich, or get things moving; then dumped outside the city walls all together and all alone without work, allies, entrepreneurs, exemplars or defenders.

Substitute the words "Macquarie Fields" for Green Valley in Stretton's choleric judgement, and you may find that you don't need to change a single word. There are still quiet, orderly families on the estate, people who've nurtured their gardens with care, and who still cleave to the bricks and fences bequeathed by the citizenry all those years ago. Jenny Pel, who has lived on the estate since 1977, told *The Age* she was sick of the rioters' endless excuses for bad behaviour. "I love my street. But I'm scared they're going to bulldoze our houses now." But they are outnumbered by those whose "steady, intelligent desire" is to get out of the place. The poor transport, the social and geographic isolation, the resident-body made homogenous in their incapacities by the zany logic of humanely intended social policy – it's all there, with the single signal difference that while Green Valley was meant, in the planners' minds' eye, to be a stepping-stone to a happier and more prosperous future, the Glenquarie Estate seems to have been conceived with no coherent image of the future whatever.

It's a curious fact that, of all the antipodean imitators of the Radburn model, it's the Glenquarie Estate – the last built – which most faithfully adheres to the contours of the original. You can superimpose a projection of Radburn from the 1920s onto the central hub of the Glenquarie Estate – the hub bounded by the now-famous Eucalyptus Drive - without too much violence. The curves and the cul-de-sacs have stayed the same; only their purposes seem insensibly to have changed along the way, a little like the shrunken wings of a flightless bird. The encircling pathways which at Radburn were supposed to mark out each of the neighbourhoods as distinct, and save them from the impending tyranny of motor-transport, have on the Glenquarie Estate mutated into the encircling bitumen curve of Eucalyptus Drive – arguably the city's busiest street-racing circuit. The central "motorway" of the Radburn model, which in the original was meant to serve as an artery to the neighbourhood houses, has been stripped of its pulmonary function, and serves chiefly as a short-cut from one side of the racing-circuit to the other. And the stumpy bucolic "places", meant to provide rear exit-ways from cottages to the street, turned in Glenquarie into back-alleys, quick exit-routes for the apprentices of the neighbourhood academies of property-theft.

Brenton Banfield, the Mayor of Campbelltown City, grew up on the Glenquarie Estate, and he can still recall the optimism with which the earliest residents greeted their spick-and-span new homes: "Back then it was a place of hope and opportunity. People were living in affordable accommodation. They could save up for a deposit and move out." Over time, those who were well-resourced enough or severely disciplined enough in their family budgeting did indeed move out, creating a perverse process of unnatural selection of those who stayed behind. They were the ones without the capacity to move on, and they felt trapped. In the meantime, the priorities of public housing shifted further, so that few if any of the later arrivals had a realistic hope of escape. As the department's Michael Allen explained to the parliamentarians, when the first concrete was poured at Macquarie Fields, about one in two of the state's public tenants received rental assistance; today, the proportion is close to nine in ten. Back then, seven in every ten public renters were couples with dependent children; today only one in ten is a couple with children – most of the rest are single-parent homes, and more than half subsist on pensions of one kind or another. If you conducted this kind of experiment with laboratory rats, there would be animal activists on hand to demonstrate.

At the same time, the mere existence of 1970s-style public housing estates does not necessarily denote social disaffection. Another witness at the Parliamentary Inquiry was Gary Moore, Director of the NSW Council of Social Service (and alumnus of the tough mid-western Sydney suburb of Lakemba). Asked where he thought Macquarie Fields stood in an imaginary league-table of public housing stress, he surprised many of the committee members by rating it fairly low. After all, there are free-standing estates in parts of Sydney's outer-south west – such as at Minto, a few kilometres further south – with concentrations of public renters as high as nine in ten. Compared with those, the travails of Macquarie Fields (where almost six in ten residents of the wider suburb are home-owners) may seem relatively small. Yet there are no signs of rioting, or even of widespread lawlessness, there.

Doubtless there is no single explanation for this seeming paradox. Yet it is worth observing that, while Minto is an island of public housing, sufficient unto itself, Glenquarie Estate is effectively a public housing colony within a larger suburb. And in that wider suburb, it sometimes seems, all the good citizens take care of their front lawns, and dearly wish that the troublemakers would simply go away. On some accounts, the hardest aspect of growing up in Green Valley in the 1960s and 1970s wasn't the personal problems of the local community. Rather, it was the opprobrium you carried when you went in search of a job. To be a poor colony of a republic of growing affluence may in its own way be the cruellest fate of all.

The redoubtable Charlie Lynn is himself a social idealist of sorts. He works with Father Chris Riley's "Youth Off the Streets" program – the same program which plans to build a new youth centre on the Glenquarie Estate – and in the parliamentary recesses he leads groups of "troubled kids" up the Kokoda Track, in search of those equally intangible entities, self-discovery and national spirit. Like Mike Munro, perhaps, he seems to view this kind of activity as a street-smart, pragmatic alternative to the unworldly social visions of the welfare-sector left, which must appear to his agitated eye to be inscribed into the concrete of Glenquarie's meandering lanes. In this his instinct may not be entirely misguided. After all, while grand welfare strategies wax and wane, the humbler rituals of self-help and community food-baskets seem to go on forever. Over the march of a century, the maxims of Samuel Smiles seem to have mutated insensibly into those of Oprah Winfrey. But, when all's said and done, Lynn's combat against the mythic Mr Radburn is really a sparring match of idealists, rather than the rhetorically satisfying collision of dream and reality.

In any case, in the end the Garden City model was less unworldly than its historical legacy may suggest. Cadbury, Lever and the rest – like the pragmatic, unromantic founders of Stretton's Elizabeth – had been solid, worldly men, men who just happened, by virtue of their various minority faiths, to be gnawed at by a particular species of Christian conscience. They built their experimental estates around their own factories, and they possessed the power to provide health and retirement entitlements of a level and kind of their own choosing. (This was, after all, the golden age of the benign planner.) Howard, being a man of more modest means, had not been blessed with all these powers of beneficence, but he was still always canny enough to ensure that his new garden cities possessed an adequate complement of well-paid factory jobs, and that they were gifted with fast and effective transportation links with nearby commercial centres. Likewise, Radburn was built in a long-standing industrial area, with a solid mix of employment types, and a strong leavening of office workers with bank accounts. In this sense, the spiritual descendants of Welwyn and Radburn aren't the denizens of Green Valley or Macquarie Fields, but rather the tidy-town citizens of Glenmore and Harrington Parks in Sydney's outer west – and of all the other so-called "gated communities" that are springing up in the more upwardly mobile reaches of our outer cities. Except that nowadays the tastes of our cultural arbiters have tacked one hundred and eighty degrees, and what would once have been celebrated verdant little private utopias are now decried in the big-city broadsheets as havens of "white flight".

In this respect, the problem wasn't the "Radburn model" as such, but rather the application of a model, founded in the controlled-experiment utopianism of another era, to the circumstances of an entirely different mix of human subjects – not orderly factory workers and their families, but a new class of welfare beneficiaries created out of a new and different world of family chaos, social dislocation and greatly increased substance-dependency. The factory workers of the late nineteenth and early twentieth centuries were a constituency in the process of acquiring serious political and industrial clout, and they had to be reckoned with (by state and employer alike) as potentially dangerous social actors in a new demotic social order. In our era, on the other hand, we've managed to fill our little would-be utopias with a new class of public beneficiaries distinguished by their almost complete dearth of political, financial and televisual leverage of any kind. Howard delighted to reside in Letchworth and Welwyn, the creations of his own mind's eye. And, as Stretton noted, sports stars and other notables were lured by various pecuniary incentives to live in Adelaide's Elizabeth. But no serving politician or planner, then or now, ever went to live in Green Valley or Macquarie Fields. The locals there can't strike or stop work, or lobby local dignitaries. Forming precinct committees would impress no one. Instead, like the urban "mob" of pre-franchise English cities, they have to throw bricks and break things to make themselves heard.

It's worth noting that, even today, Letchworth Garden City is a busy going concern, choc a bloc with earnest-minded public sector employees, organic food stores and sensible, low-fuel-consumption cars. (Heeding the siren-call of "globalisation", the local factories have mostly moved on, but the equally international tourist industry has obligingly taken their place.) And, even today, the tidy-town residents of Radburn take a proper civic pride in the history of their peculiar burg, where the autumn leaves fall on curving walkways and arrow-straight "motorways" alike. These are towns through whose veins flow money and hope, and whose hearts still tick with that instinct for "community activism" so often found in communities which are thriving, and so rarely in those which logic (and the dreams of radical historians) might suggest should need it more. If things went badly in Radburn or Letchford, you can be sure there'd be tertiary-educated folks hammering down the door of local mayors and government ministers. Neither is ever likely to need the missionary-style community activism of Father Chris Riley

Trying to find the sunny side of life

or the Salvation Army's food parcels. There may be a sense in which "history" is indeed to blame for failed experiments like Green Valley and Macquarie Fields. But if so, it may be less a matter of commission than omission, less a story of grand folly than of the casually lazy betrayal of good intentions, less the execution of an inexorable vision than of innumerable small-scale instances of amnesia and neglect – all because the people to whom the administrators were ministering were effectively of no political account.

Of all the grand moral disputes of the times, of all the awesome gulfs within our political imagination, that over crime and criminality is perhaps the most primal and profound. It raises, after all, the elemental questions of justice, order, personal accountability and responsibility – the moral touchstones of personal competence and public order beloved by ordinary striving Australians. And it invokes the moral weight and grandeur of our primal human impulses towards caring and interpersonal sympathy – those ramparts of the liberal moral imagination, and the religiously and professionally driven individuals who form its garrison. Among a generation of citizens for whom the Bible is little more than a childhood echo, it pits the Old Testament against the New, Jehovah against Jesus. Should I love my neighbour as myself? Am I my brother's keeper?

And so, in the days and weeks after the riots, the Glenquarie Estate achieved a strange kind of mythic glamour. According to your allegiance, this little republic of misery became either a vessel for the discharge of elemental human sympathy or a repository for good-citizenly revulsion. Academic social scientists and earnest broadsheet journalists alike shook their heads sadly and asked how it was that boys could be reduced to such a state, and how the acute problems of the area could have been neglected by governments for so long. As it happens, they haven't. As one government minister angrily pointed out, at least forty-five million dollars has been spent on public infrastructure for an estate of four and half thousand souls in recent years, including a technology centre and a swimming pool, while policing the neighbourhood requires the organisation of a minor military campaign. Since the riots, further public money has been committed to the area, and church groups have plans for a new three million dollar youth centre. At the same time, Sydney's inimitable high-octane radio commentators asked what kind of parenting these kids could have received for them to have gone so bad so early. Where parental discipline had failed, they concluded, youngsters like Jesse Kelly would have to learn the lessons of personal discipline the hard way – through the court system.

Jesse Kelly's biography reads a little like the life-story of the estate. According to newspaper reports, Jesse's birth father disappeared early, his

David Burchell

mother found herself incapable of caring for him, and his step-father refused to acknowledge him as a son. When he turned twelve, Jesse's grandparents took him in to their house in Macquarie Fields, but by this stage he was simply too hard to control and they were forced to send him to a special school. (They have nevertheless kept in touch with him throughout his travails.) Like many kids in the area, it's been suggested, Jesse started stealing cars as a form of borrowing; pretty soon he may have moved on to disguising and selling them. As he graduated, he offered a role-model to other young boys in the area for the imagined glamour of the outlaw existence. During the fortnight he remained on the lam after the fatal car-crash, Jesse Kelly's surname was routinely invoked in echo of the much more famous outlaw Kelly – who had of course also hailed from a semi-rural "glen". No doubt this appealed to him. Through friends, he explained cockily to journalists that he was on the run because the police, if they caught him, would show him no mercy. A few days after the fatal crash, a neighbour rather incautiously suggested to the TV news that Jesse should turn himself in. According to the police, Kelly and a group of his friends appeared at the neighbour's house after dark, took apart the man's face with a broken bottle in front of his children, and disappeared back into the night. Yet Jesse's outlaw spirit has the brittle toughness of the lifelong gang member. When, a fortnight after the car chase, he appeared in court charged with two counts of manslaughter, his shoulders dropped and he wept like a lost child.

Thus told, Jesse Kelly's life – like that of so many other boys in the area – is little more than a vessel for the discharge of human sympathy, or else a repository for revulsion. For commentators of all persuasions, he serves – like the monster of the youthful Mary Shelley's imagining – as an exemplary figure. Against his measure, we can find society's claims to inclusion wanting, or lament the waste of a precious life – or else we can use his example as a glass through which to apprehend a decline in societal and personal responsibility, self-discipline and values in parenting. Like refugees from distant lands or the victims of distant wars, his example serves either to rouse our sense of personal conscience, or else to stir our sense of indignity, either to soften our heart or cause us to close it. Such is the power of the personal case, the face with a name to it. Mary Shelley's monster passed solitary hours in the company of Goethe's Romantic tales and pondered his existential plight. It would no doubt make for excellent journalism could Jesse Kelly be persuaded to do the same.

When we debate the fates of communities in crisis, these familiar and even ritualised responses seem to have led us into a series of policy cul-de-sacs. On the one hand, the case for a "zero-tolerance" solution can probably be summarily dismissed. Nothing less than the wholesale evacuation of the estate would be required to bring a "law and order" solution here. That may indeed be a solution – there is an argument that the remaining welfare enclaves like the Glenquarie Estate ought to have been broken up and dispersed years ago. But if it is, it will be one born of the Departments of Housing and Community Services, not the New South Wales Police Service.

On the other hand, liberal-minded sympathy often serves to provide an equally stylised range of responses. Too frequently, there seems to be an almost unbridgeable gulf between the moral imagination of sympathetic journalists and commentators and the actual life situations of those with whom they sympathise – those ingenious, inventive, sometimes malevolent, sometimes fellow-spirited young men of the back streets who make their living as best they may, given where their lives seem to have taken them. Young men who have been selling hot electronics equipment on the streets since early adolescence are soberly advised to take up a trade. Boys who have been disrupting classes for as long as their teachers can recall are earnestly enjoined to stay on longer in school. Kids for whom violence is the indispensable glue of their self-image are guided painstakingly through anger-management counselling.

Military historians have pointed out that, in many cultures, if you want to have a satisfactory battle it's necessary for both sides to agree tacitly on where and how to hold it. Likewise, many of our most bitter political controversies involve a strange kind of conceptual complicity among the warring parties. Defences and critiques of economic deregulation in the 1980s, for instance, alike turned on the assumption that a modern economy could be deregulated, and that the resultant entity would bear a resemblance to the "free market" universe imagined by nineteenth century industrialists. Supporters and opponents of the War on Terror insist upon treating it as a rerun of the Cold War, a kind of ghostly Brezhnevian Groundhog Day. Members of the so-called "welfare lobby" and their opponents too often seem determined to moralise the treatment of poor and dysfunctional communities, so that those who live within them are almost necessarily viewed (according to your preference) as helpless, demoralised and irresponsible, or simply out of control. Jesse Kelly can be enlisted with equal vigour to support any of these interpretations.

No one should under-estimate the corrosive effect on the human spirit of a cocktail of the "stress factors" identified by diligent social investigators such as Tony Vinson. All too often, to be born into an area with (in Vinson's words) "high rates of low birth-rate babies, high levels of sickness and disabilities, shorter life expectancy, lower school retention rates, low incomes" – all the usual suspects, in other words – is a debilitating experience, draining the self-confidence of those who already lack it, and undermining the life skills of those with a fragile grasp on them.

Commonly, though, people do emerge out of these circumstances with their confidence intact or even lifted by the survival instinct, and their life skills hardened into a kind of granite through long usage. Nor should we trivialise the impact of these success stories. The current Mayor of Campbelltown – which administers the Glenquarie Estate – grew up there, while Labor's "lost leader", Mark Latham, defied at least one of Hugh Stretton's predictions by emerging – with the aid of his local community – as a single "exemplar" from the unforgiving streets of Green Valley.

Sometimes the fact of these success stories is tossed back at the much more numerous non-successes as a mark of reproach: if they could get out of there, why didn't you? (The New South Wales Premier and Police Commissioner both made liberal reference to their own humble upbringings when criticising the Glenquarie rioters.) Yet the harshness of this response simply serves to mask a wider point. On the whole – contrary to some versions of pop psychology which have entrenched themselves as a kind of scientific orthodoxy in liberal opinion in recent years – humans are resilient, resourceful, adaptive, ingenious creatures. Given a chance – all else being well – they'll strive to rebuild their lives after even the most trying experiences. Nor do you have to have your life in perfect order in order to escape cycles of "welfare dependency" or personal dysfunction. Depending on how you measure these factors, tens or maybe even hundreds of thousands of Australians have alcohol and drug dependency problems or mental health issues, but mostly they still strive to raise families responsibly and hold down paying jobs. Given half a chance, they commonly succeed.

In the 1990s, American sociologists – attempting to cut through the familiar moralising debates on welfare "dependency" – strove to measure empirically the responses of welfare recipients to varying policy signals. The results were complex, but their general direction seemed clear. Given a choice, even the poorest and most troubled welfare recipients generally choose to escape their lot by the most reasonable path open to them. Provide single parents with a viable path back into the workforce and they'll take it. Remove "welfare trap" obstacles to accepting unskilled but paying jobs and most people will take those jobs instead. For all but a bohemian few, welfare isn't so much a "way of life" as a pause in life's struggles. Recently, the Australian Housing and Urban Research Institute adopted a similar approach in investigating the relationship between the receipt of housing assistance – which nine in ten public tenants now get – and workforce participation. They found that those receiving rent assistance were significantly less likely to be in paid employment – mostly because it would not make sense for them to take the work. Probing further, they asked unemployed renters how much extra it would cost them to sustain a return to work once their lost entitlements were factored in. The answer was an average of $188. It turned out that the average additional income those renters would have received from taking a paid job was $189 a week. Had they taken those jobs – from their view at least, if not that of taxpayers generally – they would effectively have been donating their labour.

In short, public renters in places like the Glenquarie estate, like welfare beneficiaries more generally, may be as able as anyone else to do the sums when it comes to making life choices. Turning to petty crime in Macquarie Fields probably makes more sense as a life decision (at least in the short term) than taking a low-paid legitimate job. Only idealists and forward-thinkers would see things differently – and they tend to be in short supply in struggle-towns. Indeed, welfare recipients arguably are more able than most people to make such short-term decisions accurately, since for them the margin between success and failure is narrower, the financial calculation are immediate, predictable and small-scale – unlike the speculative projections of soon-to-be-retired Baby Boomers or mum-and-dad Telstra investors. As in the days of the Victorian social investigators, it seems very likely that "financial improvidence" is a lesser obstacle to poor people's self-advancement than the simple lack of a capital base. (This may well be why Green Valley's most famous son, in his time as opposition leader, chose to champion "micro-finance" schemes for poor families.)

It's tempting to see contemporary Sydney – like the country more widely – as an ocean of affluence studded with small islands of "disadvantage", such as Macquarie Fields, Claymore or Minto. The problem then becomes one of attending to these poor castaways, stranded in would-be garden suburbs, remote communities or regional cul de sacs. And yet, while emotionally gratifying (it appeals, after all, to that old instinct of *noblesse oblige* which still suffuses the outlook of the concerned professional classes), this is a deceptive vantage-point. To borrow from the terminology of medicine, "treating" disadvantage is rarely a matter of applying a cure – far more often it's the application of a therapy, the aim of which is to soothe the symptoms rather than preventing them. It's not simply that, in our rush to achieve, we've left the poor strugglers behind. The problem is more fundamental than that.

The decisions that created the welfare suburbs which stud our major cities were specific acts of policy, and many of those policies have long since been abandoned. Yet our welfare islands owe their continued existence not to those original decisions alone, but to an entire architecture of policy misdecision which continues to this day. Indeed, you could argue that, rather than having learned from the past, over the decade of our long boom we've simply been reproducing old policy errors on a much larger scale. An historically unprecedented number of those on our welfare rolls today are there not because they are incapable of working or unwilling to work, but because of a series of obstacles placed in their path – often by the same governments which claim to be trying to help them. Employers today demand of those applying for jobs of even limited skills "pieces of paper" – often of decidedly limited practical value – which too many individuals are incapable of acquiring because they fail to complete school. Young men leaving education today without some form of qualification will be condemned to a kind of workforce twilight zone for much of their adult lives. At the same time, benefits and rent assistance are still too often calibrated to taper off as people – often trying to escape from them – start to do better for themselves, so that those who fall out of the mainstream find it hard to drag themselves back in.

Sole-parent benefits and child-care costs sometimes still seem purpose-designed to discourage tens of thousands of mothers from returning to work, and have made unwilling "welfare mums" of thousands of independent-minded divorcees. Economist Bob Gregory has pointed out that female single parents – whose most common life goals are to find new jobs and new partners – don't seem able to find either nowadays, while among married women rates of full-time employment have actually been growing. Meanwhile, as Gregory has observed elsewhere, sanctioned changes to employer behaviour, labour relations and unemployment benefit provisions in recent decades have forced tens (or maybe hundreds) of thousands of older but able-bodied men to recreate themselves as perpetual state dependants and invalids. Indeed, these trends have actually worsened over the course of the ten-year boom. In 1995 the combined total of those on the sole-parent pension and the disability pension was roughly equal to the number of people on unemployment benefits. By 2005, however, the two groups outnumbered those on unemployment benefits by a factor of five to two. And while unemployment rolls have shrunk at an impressive rate (by about twenty-two thousand a year between 1995 and 2005), the sickness benefit roll has grown faster (at twenty-five thousand a year). It's possible that a majority of all those who dropped off our unemployment rolls haven't become employed, but rather have become (at least officially) sick. These are not small, isolated, pitiable fragments of the community. Put together, they add up to an absolute majority of all those on our welfare rolls, and a very considerable proportion of the entire citizen body.

Our contemporary schooling debacle accentuates these difficulties. Until relatively recently, graduates of solid local state comprehensives had a respectable chance of doing better in life than their parents. Increasingly, as ambitious and better-resourced parents defect to other parts of the system, this opportunity seems to be melting away, and with it much of a proud national tradition of self-betterment. In 2002, the Vinson Report into New South Wales state schooling quizzed principals from "low socio-economic status" areas like Macquarie Fields. One principal in outer western Sydney reported that, over the previous two years, no fewer than four-fifths of their existing teaching staff had successfully sought placements elsewhere. Out of the senior staff, the only survivor was the principal himself. Of the current staff, forty-two of the forty-six were in their first teaching appointment. In its final report to the state government, shortly after the Glenquarie riots, the New South Wales Public Education Council examined the placement of beginning teachers in schools across the state. The report noted that one-third of the new teachers who found first jobs in state schools in New South Wales in 2004 were drafted into just 3 per cent of the state's schools – each of which, on average, will have been required to digest at least seven first-time teachers each year. If these schools were the same size as that unnamed western Sydney school documented in the Vinson Report, each one of them would turn over its entire staff every six years or so. As educationist Richard Teese has observed, this is a veritable production line of social incapacity.

Too much of the debate over Australia's new "age of affluence" has been moralised unhelpfully – or, perhaps more precisely, it has been moralised in the wrong way. Our key problems aren't the supposed "time-poverty" of busy knowledge-workers (in any case, as researchers at the University of New South Wales recently pointed out, the most "time-poor" are actually single parents on the workforce's fringes), or supposed enslavement to poor tastes in housing design or "conspicuous consumption" (that old reliable stand-by of disgruntled aesthetes). Those who've achieved high levels of personal and financial independence may mostly be left safely enough to exercise that independence as they see fit. (And if the exercise of that independence causes them psychic trauma, they have an historically unprecedented variety of therapies and spiritualisms of which to assuage it.)

The greater problem is that the new tide of affluence doesn't seem to have brought with it a comparable widening of this experience of personal independence. Australians have always hankered to be able to fend for themselves, but too many are still condemned to hankering. Our incomes may have doubled since the 1970s, but the numbers of those stuck on welfare has stubbornly refused to fall. Unemployment – at least as officially recorded – has halved over that time, yet the numbers of people excluded from the workforce have arguably risen, as the labour market for the unskilled has dwindled. Self-employed tradespeople and contractors nowadays may seem to live in a land of milk and honey, but too many waged employees endure fearful working existences. If we're dissatisfied with our national achievement, this may not be on account of some kind of intangible *ennui*. Rather, there's a promise there that lies unfulfilled, and the riots in our struggle-towns may only be the most violent indications of it.

David Burchell

Still our debates over work, incomes, tax and welfare continue to roll along the same well-signalled rail lines laid down for our ideological traffic thirty, forty or even fifty years ago. On the left, the size of our welfare outlays, or of our public housing stock, is still too often treated as if it were a marker of our degree of civilisation – as if tending to incapacity were an act of humanitarianism. Clearly, welfare recipients should have the right to a dignified standard of life. And in a society where most citizens aspire to own their own house in their own name, there is no particular electoral incentive for government to care too tenderly for those who cannot, unless others call them to account. Yet it's worth remembering that the advocate's outlook is a partial view. The measure of a civilised society ought not to be the size of its welfare outlays, or of its public housing sector, but rather the success of individuals and families in achieving some stable lifestyle and accommodation which can give them self-reliance and self-respect. To treat the body of public renters and welfare beneficiaries as foot-soldiers in an imagined global war between market and state provision is unfair to the hopeful, if struggling, households who inhabit that "stock" or collect those funds. They don't want to become trophies of a social vision – mostly, they just want to move on.

By contrast, conservatives have always liked to trumpet their rhetorical and ideological commitment to personal striving and independence. Yet in practice this instinct – which is no doubt sometimes sincerely felt – generally loses out to the right's more visceral revulsion against the power of state agencies, even where they can play an active and constructive role in encouraging personal independence, rather than stifling it. If the current federal government leaves behind it a single significant initiative in social policy, it will be the Job Network. In theory, the Network is supposed to "empower" jobseekers by providing with choice of job-search providers, and granting them the status of a customer rather than a supplicant to public bureaucracy. In practice, though, it serves in good measure to create and then entrench different categories of the jobless, divided by how expensive (which is to say how unprofitable) they are to help. And since few self-respecting businesses would get into an industry ordered along these peculiar lines, the experience of job-seeking under the Job Network often seems to involve less a change in customer status than a transfer of dependency, from being the supplicant of a government bureaucracy to being the recipient of Christian charity. This is hardly a monument to personal independence. Rather, it is a memorial to the ideological impasse of our times.

On the right, it's been convenient to measure the economic successes of the last decade by the flood of cash they've brought in their wake. The left – as is far too often its wont – has reacted to these claims in a negative, call-and-response manner, either by decrying Australia's affluence as a triumph of poor taste, or seeing it as a kind of financially induced hardening of the moral arteries of the nation. Yet both of these positions, viewed from the wider historical perspective, look myopic. A century ago, Australia's quest for nationhood was measured by the extent to which the entire nation was integrated into a common public life and culture – a life and culture which had been designed, up until that point, chiefly for the enjoyment and satisfaction of the propertied classes. On this measure, the last decade has been a conspicuous historical failure in our national life – a failure made more egregious by the numerous opportunities the wealth and tranquility of the times have offered us. If full citizenship resides in possessing a secure stake in the nation and its culture, we may well have more non-citizens now than we did half a century ago. And their travails may well continue to haunt our midsummer nights.

In October 2006, after eighteen months in prison for other offences and a turbulent relationship with his warders, Jesse Kelly pleaded guilty in Sydney's Downing Street District Court to two counts of aggravated dangerous driving causing death. This time the newspaper reports made no mention of any crowd of well-wishers outside the court. In his summing-up, Justice Brian Knox SC observed that Kelly seemed to have viewed his long-running cat-and-mouse relationship with the local police as a kind of game – noting, with true judicial sententiousness, that "if it was a game, it was a particularly deadly one for his two passengers". Kelly was sentenced to a maximum jail term of seven years and nine months, with a minimum sentence of five and a half years. In handing down the sentence, Justice Knox concluded: "I do not find there are strong prospects for rehabilitation." After the verdict, Jesse's loyal grandfather, Peter Parker, spoke to reporters outside the court: "I think Jesse accepts the sentence as it stands. But who knows what lies down the road." ■

David Burchell teaches in Humanities at the University of Western Sydney. He is the author of *Western Horizon: Sydney's Heartland and the Future of Australian Politics* (2003) and numerous essays on contemporary politics and culture.

Reportage:
**Down-at-heel among the well-heeled**
Reporter:
**Peter Meredith**

*Image: Norma by Sara from the 'Tenant by tenant' series / Source: www.keithsaundersphotography.com*

# Down-at-heel among the well-heeled

The Southern Highlands of New South Wales is a rural region with a reputation for city-style affluence. Most visitors, and a significant number of its residents, see it as the happy hunting ground of the very rich and the ordinarily rich. It's up there with Sydney's Double Bay, Melbourne's South Yarra and Brisbane's Ascot in the status and desirability stakes.

This view has a historical basis. Since 1867, when the railway reached the district, it has been not only a cool-climate tourist destination but also a popular bolthole for those able to afford large country homes and estates among the rolling green hills.

Today, the trappings of affluence are as conspicuous as ever: the multi-million-dollar mansions, the Mercs, the spotless SUVs, the plethora of restaurants, cafes and boutiques, even an offshoot of Jones the Grocer. And while the image all this creates of a wealthy enclave may be unintended, there's no doubt it helps fuel tourism as well as economic and population growth in the district.

But beneath the glitz lies an unacknowledged reality, and you don't have to dig far to find it. Tucked away out of sight in the three main towns – Bowral, Mittagong, Moss Vale – and some of the outlying villages are areas of housing that resemble down-at-heel big-city suburbs. Here live people who have been stricken by a whole Pandora's box of misfortunes, from illness to domestic violence, that have forced them into hardship. More difficult to spot, but prevalent nonetheless, are what might be termed the genteel poor, people who have known better times but who now suffer unseen behind closed doors. And, like any inner-city zone, the district has its share of vagrants and substance-abusers.

In 2006, geographer Ian Bowie lifted the lid, if only a little, on poverty in the district. In his book, *Wingecarribee Our Home* (U3A Southern Highlands/Wingecarribee Shire Council, 2006) he uses statistics from numerous sources, including the 2001 census, to paint a portrait of the Southern Highlands that demolishes long-held myths.

Some figures stand out. One is that a third of households reported incomes below the Henderson Poverty Line for the average family. Others are that more than 40 per cent of individual incomes were below the poverty line for a single adult and three-quarters were below the median average weekly ordinary full-time earnings level, which in 2001 was $700.

Bowie warned that these were slippery figures, but behind the statistical fog lie a few solid rocks: "Thirty per cent of standard households under the poverty line suggests there's got to be very real poverty here."

Another revelation (although again the figures are slippery) was that there were very few people who could be termed truly rich. At the time of the 2001 census, there may have been as few as 1,250 people with incomes of more than twice the median average.

"So the perception of this part of the world being rich, affluent, is simply not right," Bowie said.

I set out to find the faces behind the poverty that the statistics alluded to. First I talked with people (individuals as well as the representatives of organisations) dealing with poverty and the poor. They quickly confirmed the message of Bowie's stats – that there were indeed many financially stressed people living amid the affluence. Family counsellor Francine Bartlett added a relevant twist: "Research shows that it's the relative gap between rich and poor that is more destructive than the actual degree of poverty ... People who are poor here actually feel it more acutely because there is relative wealth around them."

Anne-Marie Kennedy, project manager for Interchange Wingecarribee Inc., a non-profit community-based organisation, created a striking picture: "One of my first client visits was to a very elderly woman who had an outside toilet and no sewerage. She just used to dig her waste into the ground. That, juxtaposed with the images of the region of great estates, people playing polo and cashmere jumpers, was bizarre."

Early in my investigations, I hesitated to use the words "poor" and "poverty" for fear that such blunt instruments might hurt or offend. It was easier to crouch behind anodyne and thoroughly correct terms like "strugglers", "battlers", "people doing it tough" and "financially challenged".

But one of the battlers set me right. I'd circulated a carefully worded letter among the clients of one organisation calling for volunteer interviewees. A woman phoned me.

"I hear you're looking for poor people to interview," she said.

I baulked at her directness. "Ah, um, yes, I am indeed after people experiencing financial distress," I said.

"Well, I'm poor. You can interview me."

So I did. Her story and those of a number of other people follow. Just as much as they illustrate the theme of this article, they reveal how unique, rich and astonishing are the lives of all individuals. Even the poor.

The names of interviewees, and the names of the people they mentioned during interview, have been changed.

Peter Meredith

Jake, 15: I dropped out of school when I was thirteen after I got arrested for assault with a deadly weapon on my mum. I had ADHD [attention deficit hyperactivity disorder] and bipolar [disorder] and now apparently I'm paranoid-schizophrenic too.

It was my third time getting arrested, but I got let off. The times before it was for the same thing. I dunno why I did it. Just one day she had a go at me and I snapped.

I didn't like school at all. Everyone used to pick on me, maybe because I looked weird and had weird hairstyles and stuff. I've always been different, and I like it like that.

I was living in Wollongong then, with my mum and my sisters. My dad had left and was up here. I have four sisters, no brothers. My father had me and my older sister; two of my other sisters were by a different dad and the third one was a by different dad again.

I got into drugs when I was ten. My first smoke was when I was ten and my first cone was when I was ten. Same day. I've tried a knock-off version of acid; I've had ice, speed, heroin (only a little bit – when I bought pot laced with heroin), and a couple of home-made things and mushrooms. I like pot, but the rest, well …

After I got arrested and let off, I came up here to live with my dad on a farm. He used to be a biker and was a maintenance fitter, a mechanic, and used to fix machines for big companies and do up old cars and sell 'em. He stopped work six or seven years ago when he had his first heart attack. After that he got really sick and fat and had more heart attacks and was on a pension.

Up here it was just me and him in an old run-down cottage with rats the size of cats. There was another house on the property, which belonged to the owner, my dad's friend who was eighty-six, and there was a farmhand. That's all the people there was on the property. And it was about a thousand acres.

On the property I helped my dad out. I grew a real massive garden with all different herbs like oregano, and vegetables. That's all I did most of the day, or I just watched TV. Well, as much as I could on the black-and-white TV attached to a battery. We had no power, see, and no hot water in the cottage. For showers we had solar hot water bags we put in the sun on top of the bathroom.

There was power in the shed, which was a kilometre down a driveway. We were allowed to put a fridge and microwave there. We had a gas stove and me and my dad took turns cooking. Spaghetti Bolognaise, or those Coles heat-'n'-eat lasagnes, or big stir-fries, with chicken, vegetables and rice and

## Down-at-heel among the well-heeled

stuff. We cooked mad things. I used to cook my own omelettes, two-egg omelettes that were that fat ...

After I moved in with my dad I had no friends at all, no one to talk to except my dad and his friends. It was okay with my dad except when he started hitting me. He did that because I used to be uncontrollable and he couldn't control me so he just hit me and just kept on hitting me and then finding excuses to hit me. He was all right other times. He used to grow pot and smoked it but wouldn't let me.

I got bashed by my dad for about two and a half years. Sometimes I used to run off when he tried to hit me and disappear for like two or three hours and then come back. One day he was bashing me and yelling at me and I just went, "The hell with this" and I started walking and never went back.

I went to the cops and they took me to a refuge and I stayed there about three months. They charged my dad and he was brought to court. I never found out what happened about it. I used to see him sometimes after that. He used to sit out the front of Coles nearly all day. He died two months ago of a heart attack at the age of forty-six and I ended up with his bong, but I got rid of it.

I got kicked out of the refuge three times, got suspended. The last time was for attacking one of the staff while I was speeding off my head. I got very violent, threw a chair.

I left, stayed in a friend's house for one night, lived at another friend's for two weeks and then I was in Goulburn for four months. I got a job working trolleys, but I got sacked for swearing. I had a couple of other jobs and I was getting my life right and then a couple of kids across the road, all pot-smokers, got me in trouble and I got arrested for shoplifting, which I didn't do – I did it for someone else.

Then I came back up here. Been living here about a month now. I've been happy ever since. I live at a house with a couple of friends. I just pay $50 a week rent and buy a bit of food and my own smokes. The money comes from Centrelink, $170 a week, and I take the rent out of that. And I'm looking for a job.

Haven't been getting myself in too much trouble. Well, a little bit but not much. Like buying pot off a dealer. Also I was doing favours for people, running drugs to other people and selling them. I was getting free pot for that.

I don't really know where I go from here. Probably end up dead soon or ... I dunno. I'll try and get a job doing fireworks, letting off fireworks for people or blowing stuff up for the army. Sounds like fun.

My other job was going to be drug dealing but I got out of that one 'cos I've done it before. When I was thirteen I used to grow pot and sell it. If you can grow tomatoes you can grow pot. It's that easy. Just plant the seed, get the right fertiliser, the right light, or outside, though I grew it better as a hydro set-up.

I used to draw. I keep all the pictures. But I can draw excellent like. I make weird characters, like weird devils and goats and different creatures and evil symbols like upside-down crosses. I drew a grim reaper on a motorbike once. I actually sold one of me pictures to someone for $300. It was just a pencil drawing.

There's tons of kids living like me. Most ain't as young as me. I stopped hanging around with younger kids 'cos I know a bit more about drugs and shit than them. So I hang around with older people that just relax and smoke cones all day.

You're better off not even starting into drugs. Try it, and if you like it, keep going with it, but don't get yourself in trouble with it. You always have to be in control of the drugs; the drugs can't be in control of you. I used to think that it was in control of me. I'd rather have just a little bit occasionally, otherwise I'm too hyperactive. That's why I started smoking in the first place.

**Vera, 72:** I was born and grew up in Sydney. During the war my parents sent me to Frensham [an exclusive girls' boarding school in Mittagong] because they thought Sydney might get bombed. After school I wanted to travel, so I went to England, lived in London, worked like hell and saved money for wonderful weekends in Paris or Spain or somewhere.

Then I was in Africa on and off for about eleven years. I was a bit of a travel writer, got a few stories in *South African Tatler* and a magazine called *Travel and Trade*. I covered Botswana's independence, was there on and off for about five months before independence and went back afterwards to see how things were going.

After I came home to Sydney, I bought a lovely unit in Mosman and in 1988 I had a mortgage and got on with living and enjoying my life. But then I developed empyema, an illness that nearly killed me. I took about a year to recover, during which time I couldn't pay my mortgage because I'd lost my job. I temped for a while but I could see I wasn't making it and my mortgage payments were going backwards.

I sold the unit and bought a little house in Launceston, Tasmania, and was there for four years. But Bass Strait really cut me off from things, so eventually I sold and came back to Sydney. I was back to renting again but I had no job and was living on my capital. It was then that I put my name down with the Department of Housing. At the same time I decided to get out of Sydney and started looking around.

## Down-at-heel among the well-heeled

About seven years ago I came to stay with a friend in Bowral. He took me around to the agents and that's how I found a place in this part of the world. I got little jobs here and there, knitting and sewing and walking dogs and babysitting for a spare dollar. Everything was fine until I broke my leg. It happened in Sydney where I'd gone with a group of friends for lunch. I hadn't drunk much but just tripped on a small step. If the break had been a little higher I would have needed a hip replacement, but it was lower, so I've got a pin down there.

After that I really couldn't cope financially very well at all, so when the Department of Housing contacted me a year ago to say they'd found me a cottage, I jumped at it and moved in, and now I'm as happy as a sand boy.

Financially I'm coping – just. My rent is deducted from my pension, my water rates too, and then I have to pay electricity and gas on top of that. I have difficulty with those, particularly in winter, and I have had to turn to the Salvation Army and St Vincent de Paul. They've been extremely helpful and I'm terribly obliged to them, so I try to buy from their shops and donate things as well.

Material things don't bother me. I just want a bed, a chair, a cup, a saucer, a handful of friends, some good wine and a good book. I want to enjoy this lovely part of the world, our safety from unhappiness and the upheavals of war-torn countries. To me that's what life's about.

I'm not terribly well at the moment. Last year I suddenly lost a lot of weight, and I went in and had day surgery and they found a lot of polyps, two cancerous. I am on the waiting list to go back to hospital to see if there are any more.

I can say it makes me slightly embarrassed to be poor. In the seven years I've been here I've got to know a lot of people. I think some of them know I live in Housing, but not many. They're a wonderful group, and I get invited out a lot, but I can't always repay that hospitality, because on $350 a fortnight you can't exactly spread it around like horse manure. I just have to make excuses. I'll go and pull weeds, dig a hole in the garden, plant a plant, because that is my way of overcoming that. In winter I probably cook more and may have three or four people around for dinner with lots of grog and a laugh and it's fine.

I don't resent it at all that people have more money than I do. Because they've put so much effort into making that money, I think they deserve every penny of it. I've just been too lazy, spending so much on enjoying my life and travelling that I haven't put anything away for a rainy day. I do regret that, but I don't regret my good life.

I talk with my neighbours over the fence. I babysit sometimes, or in exchange for fresh vegetables from their garden or eggs from their chooks I do a bit of sewing. That's a nice way to be, a nice way to live.

Peter Meredith

Gregor, 82: When I came to Australia in 1949, I was very proud to say I was Australian. I shouted it: "I'm Australian!" But now I look around and I just whisper it because in my lifetime the change I have seen here is absolutely unbelievable.

When I came, there were ten thousand rich and ten thousand poor and the rest were middle class. Now you have dirty rich and dirty poor and nobody in between. The middle class has died out.

I was in the motor trade. When I arrived, I wanted to start my own business. I went to the bank to borrow money to buy a wrecked car which I was going to fix up and sell, right? I borrowed £150 and when the car was finished I got £500 for it. So I had a chance as a newcomer to borrow money.

We've got five children, one son and four daughters. Our son wanted to start a business. He went to the bank, got a loan and I acted as guarantor.

I had my own service station and a beautiful house, absolute waterfront [on the NSW South Coast]. We were planning a big party on New Year's Eve 1980 but I ruined it by having a heart attack that morning. I went back to work for another two years, but the heart started to play up and in 1983 I went on the pension.

After I retired, my wife was a passenger in a car that crashed and she had a very bad chest injury. One lung was pierced and her sternum was smashed. At the same time we found out that our son had gone broke and the money he borrowed was lost. As guarantor, I had to pay it off and we had to sell the house. It nearly broke my heart.

But we still had enough money to buy a block of land up here. The breeze [on the coast] was salty and my wife's lung didn't heal. The doctor recommended we move to somewhere high for fresh, clean air.

So we came up here in 1986. We didn't know at the time, but one daughter was hooked on the pokies. Her wages just went into the pokies, and next thing she and her husband lost their house. Because now we had a half-acre block up here where we were going to build a two-bedroom place for us for our old age, the daughter said to the mother, "Why don't you build a big house and we can move in there with you?"

We worked out how much we occupied of that house, and the daughter and our son-in-law borrowed money from the bank to buy their share. With the property in our name, we were responsible for it.

But we found out too late that the daughter had been hooked so badly and got so deep into debt that she and her husband couldn't pay their share of our mortgage. So we had to sell the house. We got $110,000 for it, and after paying the bank we had nothing left.

Down-at-heel among the well-heeled

We rented a two-storey townhouse in Mittagong in 1989. By then my wife had had two heart attacks and a kidney stone and while we were in the town house she had a stroke. So we had to move again. My wife suggested we apply to the Housing Commission. We did and we got this place as soon as it was finished, which was very nice. We've been here six and a half years.

We are both on pensions. We used to be able to afford to go out to dinner at the club two or three times a week. Then it went down to two times, then one time. Now we can't afford any times.

My health is not good. I have this bad circulation problem. I have an eye problem too. I have only one eye. The other is artificial – I lost it in an industrial accident. Well, then I started seeing foggy in the good eye.

The hardest part of being sick is paying for all the tests. When I went to an eye specialist, he said: "Public or private?"

I said: "Public."

He said: "See you in twelve months."

So twelve months later I went back. By then I couldn't cross the road because I only saw the cars when they almost hit me. He did tests, and I paid and paid, and they found out what we already knew: it was a cataract.

Then the specialist said he wouldn't operate on a person with one eye. "When you can't see, come back and see me."

I said: "Doctor, if I can't see, how can I come and see you?" [Chuckles]

He said: "Sorry, an operation is not recommended."

So I went to my doctor in Moss Vale, and he said he knew a specialist in Goulburn who was like Fred Hollows, you know. I went to see him, he did the operation, put a lens in, finish! When they took the bandage off they put a patch over the eye and told me to go. I said: "Go where? I can't see anything. Other eye is artificial!" [Chuckles heartily]

Now the wife, she's eighty-three, and she can't walk, she puffs a lot. When you're getting old and get all this sickness, today everywhere you pay. Where do you get the money from?

As pensioners, we haven't got the power to change things. What could we do? Who listens to pensioners? Nobody. Nobody cares about lower class people. When people learn we are living in the Southern Highlands, they say we're lucky, we are rich. We're rich all right – rich in debt.

Michael, 28: I went into the relationship feet first. Should have thought about it a bit more.

I met her through the internet. We chatted over the net for a few weeks and then I met her in person. After that she came and stayed with me for six months. During that time she fell pregnant, and when she was four months pregnant I left my job here in the Highlands and went back to her home town with her to become a father.

She already had a two-year-old daughter from a previous man. She told me she'd finished with him and all this kind of jazz before I came into the picture. So she got her daughter to call me "Dad".

My girlfriend had our daughter, Milly, in 2004. I used to look after her, change her nappies and do the housework. I got a job at the local hospital looking after aged residents. I got a second job in a hostel looking after ten residents, giving out medications and feeding.

A year ago my girlfriend told me to go. Like she put it straight to my face: "Get out!" That kind of thing. It hit me for six because I didn't see it coming. I was suicidal; I rang Mum and Dad and said goodbye and then cut my wrists. About five minutes later the police and ambulance turned up and took me to the hospital, and then Mum and Dad came and got me and took me back down here. After I moved back here, my girlfriend got a new man who's fourteen years older than her.

I was born in the Highlands and I grew up in the house where my parents have lived for thirty-odd years. At school, I struggled with pretty much everything, though I enjoyed rugby union, where I was hooker and prop. I left school at seventeen, did a basic personal carer course in Sydney and then worked in nursing homes. You do the showers and the feeding and make the beds and that kind of stuff, general care.

So I was in Sydney for a couple of years and then I moved back home with Mum and Dad and got a job here, same kind of work, and I was here for two or three years until I moved up to my ex-girlfriend's place.

I didn't see little Milly for three months after we broke up. I had to go through court and all that kind of nonsense to see her. I've been seeing her for eleven months. She comes here and I take her to playgroup. That's very rewarding. She's got little friends to play with and I see other mothers to talk to and I have friends there.

Milly's two and a half now. I've got a very close relationship with her. She clings to me, and on handover she cries because she doesn't want to go back to her mother. I have her for five days a fortnight. I pick her up on the Wednesday and take her back on the following Monday. Well, it's dad that does the driving because I don't drive. And she's really only three days here because there's two days of travel. I'm not working but I've applied for a job working every other week so I can be free for when she's here.

I've found a house through a charity and I'm going to move out of my parents' house and live there on my own. It's a semi with two bedrooms,

## Down-at-heel among the well-heeled

close to shops and general area. I'm on Centrelink benefits and they'll take the rent out of that.

When Milly's old enough to understand, I'd like her to come down and live with me and be happy. That's all I can hope for. My lawyer told me that because she's got a sister they try to keep the siblings together. I don't know how I'll get over that, but I'll just have to.

I don't go out to clubs or pubs by myself. I just find it a bit more relaxing at home. I chat to people on the computer. That's the only hobby or interest I have, apart from when I've got Milly.

If I had more money I'd be able to spend a bit more on her. When she's here I try to give her treats. I get her ice-cream, go to the park or the lake, or Mum and Dad take us down to Shellharbour to the beach. I try to do something different with her every day. She loves the water.

**H**elen, 56: This is crisis housing and, as you can see, it's perfectly adequate. I'm not a refugee in Chad or anything. It's part community housing and part charity housing, and I've ended up here on an extremely low income inasmuch as I'm on a disability support pension.

My background is as a successful singer-performer. I moved up to the Southern Highlands from Sydney in 1989. Circumstances had conspired against me: I'd reached the age where the phone stops ringing for female performers. The wonder that was the Australian arts in the 1970s and early to mid-1980s was, thanks to successive governments, pretty well destroyed.

I didn't have the money to buy property. I found a dear little farmhouse to rent on a property about fifteen to twenty minutes out of Bowral, in a beautiful valley, owned by good old-time farmers. I was still doing some performing around the place but then I developed Chronic Fatigue Syndrome and my stamina went right down.

Then I got lung cancer and had a lung removed and ended up with what they call pain syndrome, which is body pain, most acutely in legs, feet and arms. I had really nothing to fall back on, no family. I'd been married for six years, but he decided when I got the cancer that it was time to leave. So it was all a little bit grim.

I'm in remission, as the expression goes, and they say if you haven't died within the first five years, your chances of surviving are pretty good. So with me it's living with disabling pain, which isn't constant but it's extreme when it's happening.

These weren't my only problems, however. Last year I had major accommodation problems too. To cut a long story short, the farm and my little farmhouse got sold to a rich Sydney couple who'd already bought a neighbouring property and I was given my marching orders.

Peter Meredith

So I've ended up in "the system" at probably the worst time in the history of our country's social welfare. I'm paying $80 a week in rent here but I'm also paying $60 a week to keep my belongings in storage. The rent is deducted from my income. I don't pay electricity, and the phone is a ring-in only; I can't ring out on it, but fortunately friends got me a mobile and I just get a pre-paid [card].

Having come from a background in the arts, where if you're in work you have fun, if you're out of work you don't, I guess poverty has been a serial event in my life. It's a bit like taking vows as a Franciscan monk: you dedicate yourself to your art and accept you'll be poor.

I have a good medical support team here and that's pretty damned important. Most doctors up here don't bulk bill. I'm fortunate to have a doctor who has seen me through near-death and who is wonderful, incredible and who bulk bills me. God forbid that anything should go wrong with my teeth because there would be a six-month waiting list with an impacted tooth or something. I believe all this is so unnecessary. I mean, how many million dollars a week are we spending on troops in Iraq?

I think it's the insecurity that gets to me, the spectre of ageing without any likely alleviation of that insecurity. Unfortunately, government assistance is getting sparser. Before July, if you were in government housing, you were secure for life. But Howard has now brought in a system where people in government housing get two-year or five-year leases, or ten-year leases if they're over sixty-five, after which time they automatically get an eviction notice and the onus is on them to show why they shouldn't be evicted. So people are going to be living in terror. At seventy-five are they going to be asked: "Have you trained as a brain surgeon? Are you self-supporting?" It's a thoughtless and very cruel system.

I write and I paint. What you see on the walls are just prints of some of my paintings. I've written and painted a kids' book, and feedback is that my text is far too dense and static. So I haven't been able to get an agent or a publisher for it and I'm wanting to hand it to a writer to put a bit of oomph in it.

I have three bedrooms but as I'm alone I'm only allowed to use one. The others are closed. How weird is it that at fifty-six you are not allowed male visitors, alcohol on the premises or to smoke. There are visits every fortnight when they come to see if you've pawned the television. It's a bit Gestapo-like and invasive.

Paying bills is terrifying. If it weren't for friends … I mean thank goodness for the fraternity in the performing arts. I am fortunate to get a little help with that sort of thing.

Bowral is now full of the sort of people that I left Sydney because of, the vicious, greedy CEOs of this nation, the so-called first-world greed mongrels.

## Down-at-heel among the well-heeled

I feel gratefully different from them. Do I feel like a sub-species? No, I don't because I know I'm not one. It is only when I am actually dealing with people who work within the welfare system that I feel outraged. There are only a few within the system that I've dealt with who have superior intellects. Perspicacity is not high on the list of requirements to work in community housing, government housing or charity welfare organisations. One has to pay more for that. And as the government withdraws more and more money, less and less appropriate people are working in the system.

This is a beautiful area where the Baby Boomers who've done good want to end up. It seems to me that they're changing other people's lives dramatically for the worse as they move in. They want to turn thousands of acres of the best growing land in New South Wales into pleasure parks and little Xanadus. It is a mindless takeover of good farming country which is going to disadvantage them or their offspring in generations to come. But the first to go, the first to be massively disadvantaged, are people like myself, and we are feeling it and seeing it directly.

Rita, 50: I've had custody of my eight-year-old grandson since he was six months old and I've been fighting the government ever since to get payments to help me to bring him up. He's the son of my eldest daughter. She was fifteen and heavily into drugs when she had him and she tried to look after him as best she could but she got herself into a hell of a situation.

I believe my role is to try and keep the family together as best I can, not just for my grandson's sake but for her sake as well. I love her very dearly and I will bend over backwards to try to make sure she's okay.

I come from a violent background, from my parents to my ex-husband, whom I left in 1992. I had a Department of Housing house in Sydney, and three years ago I did a swap with someone for this one. I'd always wanted to live in this area. I felt like I belonged here, for some reason.

My grandson has Asperger's syndrome, which is high-functioning autism. Asperger's kids are very obsessive, very active – and very tiring because it's a twenty-four-hour-a-day job looking after them. If he wakes at one o'clock in the morning, he won't go back to sleep. This morning it was half-past four. You think: "Oh, just give me some peace, please!"

But I take it all for granted because I've been doing it for so long.

School was a challenge. The first year I had to sit in the classroom with him the whole time. He doesn't go to the local school. It had a class for children like him or children with ADD [attention deficit disorder], ADHD, this that and the other, and I thought he had enough problems without having to cope with all those other kids as well. So he goes to one of the village schools and I have to drive him there every day.

He's doing really well. I'm so proud of him. He got an end-of-term award last term. The school is very proud of him too, because when he first started they said he would probably never learn to read or write. Well, he's reading now. He had his IQ and everything tested when he was seven, and he had a reading age of eleven years and nine months, with comprehension too.

As a grandmother raising a grandchild, you don't fit in with younger parents, because they all talk such nonsense – they go on about make-up and perfumes and shoes and dresses and everything. But then you can't mix with grandparents either, because they don't have little babies tagging along with them.

I do go without a few things, but my main priority is him. A couple of months ago we didn't have enough food in the house, but I made sure he had a nice hot meal every day. I told myself I could do without food until the next day, and I'd just have a cup of tea or whatever. I buy him new clothes but I can't afford new clothes for myself. I don't go to the hairdresser either; I cut my hair myself.

I had cancer and about three weeks before I got him I had a total hysterectomy and ovariectomy and lost a part of my bowel. So we've been through all that together. I'm in remission at the moment but I still have to go for a check-up every three months.

Up to now I've been getting the sole parent pension but now I've been classified as a foster parent, so from this week I'll be getting a payment from DoCS as well. It's taken me eight years to get that. I asked if they could backdate it but they said no!

There's also another advantage now because if anything happens to his health all his medical expenses will be paid for by DoCS. When I first got him, all his internal organs had shut down and he needed an emergency operation and I had to pay for it. You should have seen him. He hadn't been breast-fed; he'd just been getting cow's milk and water. He was skinny, malnourished and had never been fed formula.

I had to give up work when he came to live with me. I did try at first to work but the babysitters I got for him didn't know how to cope with him so it was impossible to work.

My father was Polish, my mother Irish, a very beautiful mixture. About four years ago I found out that he wasn't my dad, that I was adopted. It was the biggest shock I'd ever had in my life. My mother was an alcoholic and very abusive. My father – well, my stepfather – was beautiful, gorgeous, the most beautiful person, but my mother was the aggressive one. She wouldn't think anything of breaking a brush over your back. She had fourteen kids altogether.

### Down-at-heel among the well-heeled

I grew up and went to school in Liverpool [UK], then put myself through college and got qualifications in typing, shorthand, commerce. Then I trained as a psychiatric nurse and worked as that in Liverpool. After I married my ex-husband (he's English), we went to live in West Germany. He worked for NATO and I learnt German and got a job as a translator for the British Army and did that for five years. After that we came over here.

If you're in my situation, people do look down on you and I get so cranky about it. I get it sometimes when I'm shopping. I might be a dollar short or something and the shop assistant looks down her nose at you and you feel like saying: "Hey, come on! Haven't you done it tough in your life?"

I pay my big bills off monthly. If anything unexpected happens we're sunk because I've got no reserves. I did have once: I used to have some gold antiques, but last year I needed money desperately and I sold the lot. I didn't realise they were so valuable! That's all gone now. But still, we're managing. We have to.

Shirley, 43: Before I came to this meeting with you, someone said to me: "Why don't you go in your trackies and runners?"

I said, "Just because I'm poor doesn't mean I have to dress like that."

I had a look in my cupboard this morning and found I've got extra tea, coffee and sugar. This means I'm not as poor as I was the other month.

I was born in Murwillumbah. Our family weren't tribal Aboriginals and I'm still trying to work out what we are. Grandfather, or one of them, was brought over to do the sugarcane. They were probably Kanaks.

I went to a Catholic school at first but when I was eight I was made a ward of the state. I couldn't understand then why they took me away. Yes, there was five of us living in a garage, but we had it all partitioned off and we all had separate rooms. Officially I was taken away because of neglect and improper guardianship. To my mind, they separated black children from their families, especially girls – who were sent further afield – so we would lose interest in our families. It worked in my case.

After they took me away, I came down to Bidura [Children's Court, Sydney] and then here to Renwick [school for underprivileged children, Mittagong]. I was there seven years, which I call my sentence.

I did fifth and sixth class at Mittagong Primary and then I went to Bowral High. I didn't really stand out at school. I'd heard that black people excelled at sport but I didn't want to be that good – I just wanted to be average. Not that that would make me any less black!

I didn't do years eleven or twelve. I left when I was about sixteen and went back to my family in Murwillumbah, but that didn't work out, so I decided to go to an aunty in Mildura. At seventeen I was working for Community Welfare in Mildura as a girl Friday. I think they needed a token blackfella and they didn't have too many to choose from there!

I was nineteen when my first child was born, in 1982. I met the father at a party in Mildura. When my son was two years old, I came here for a Renwick reunion and I haven't left! I wrote to the Department of Housing in Goulburn and said I was moving to Bowral and I'd really like a house. And they said there was a three-year waiting list. A friend put me up during that time and I worked for the police as a clerk. I'm a clerk by trade. I worked quite a lot before my next child was born. I went back into youth work, then I did cleaning at Renwick, and for about two years I worked for the CES.

After I had my first child, I said: "No more children." Well, the CES sent me on a developmental course where you plot the rest of your working life, a longevity line. Halfway through it, I said to the instructor: "This line made me understand that I want more children."

The father of my second child is an ex-ward [of the state] who is nine years my junior. He is white, a redhead, which is about as far away as you can get from having black in you! When I decided to have children through him, I told him I wanted four. I never legally married him because he was in and out of jail.

When we first got together he said he'd never be a drinker or a druggo. But then I found him stoned one day and said to him: "Time for you to go, brother." So he went out to the pub and rang the police and said: "Get over there before I do, or bring body bags." The drugs in him made him want to kill me. That threw me in such a spin that I've only been coming out of in the last few months. I was so scared for my kids and took out an AVO on him.

My cousin, who's four years my senior, sleeps by the back door now just in case. With him here, I've been very fortunate for eighteen years not having to pay a babysitter.

After I'd had three kids, I was out of work and technically I haven't worked for twelve years. I'm here with four kids, two girls and two boys, and there's my cousin. My oldest, who's twenty-four, moved out. It's a three-bedroom house, but the safety of my kids is paramount, so we've all been sleeping together in the lounge room for three years.

My depression was bad. I wasn't leaving the house. But I'm getting things back together because I don't want to be useless before my time. I'm not uneducated; I'm going into law, hopefully next year, and because of my experience with family issues, that's what I'll specialise in.

We don't go to the pictures, we don't go to the pool, we don't do holidays.

There's been times when I've kept the kids out of school because I didn't have anything to give them for lunch. I can't afford school excursions, but I'm not real fond of sending my kids on them anyway. My twelve-year-old is a big girl and I can't get a standard uniform for her from the shop and I don't have the money to have one specially made. I buy shoes once a year, but they only last three to six months. Too bad. We have to rely on hand-me-downs.

I don't regret having children, but with hindsight maybe I shouldn't have had children with the man I did. I wanted thirteen children. As it turns out, my first beau – who was a ward of the state, too, and who I knew when I was twelve – has eight. Add that to my five, that's thirteen!

**P**enny, 29: I have osteoporosis and the bone density of an eighty-three-year-old. And I was told the other day I have no kidneys left.

When I was ten years old a doctor found I had Fanconi Syndrome [a kidney condition that can affect bones] and said I had brittle bones, which is why I've had lots of breaks. I've broken this wrist four times, this twice, my ribs, my knee, my ankle, my thigh, my hip, my big toe. But that's life. Shit goes on.

I'm on peritoneal dialysis, which means I've got this tube permanently sticking out of my belly and it plugs into that machine at night and it runs for eight hours while I sleep. I work, you see, and I don't have time to do that shit at any other time of day. It's a big hassle for me to have kidney failure at the moment.

If I didn't do dialysis I would die in two days. I'd kind of welcome death, but it doesn't ever seem to want to take me, so it's not an issue for me.

I found out today I'll be able to get one of my brother's kidneys by February, which is a bit daunting. A new kidney will mean I won't be attached to that machine any more but my bones won't improve.

I have bipolar so you'll have to stop me if I go on a bit.

I had a religious upbringing in Canberra – my parents were Mormons – and I was very sheltered and very naïve. My dad left my mum when I was twelve. My mum married again when I was thirteen and they went on a honeymoon and the shit started after they came back. I remember the first time it happened. My mother's new husband ripped us all out of bed in the middle of the night. I have two stepsisters and there was my brother. My mother's husband lined us up and said that apparently we'd seen his naked bum or something, and he lectured us for hours. Then he ripped me out of the line and flogged me until I fell on the ground. Then he picked me up and shoved me back in the line and I had to wait until everyone else had their turn.

Peter Meredith

When I was fifteen I couldn't take it any more. I left school in the first week of the first term of year ten and stayed with a friend for several months and moved out when I was sixteen. I'd had sex with two people by then and when I was fifteen I fell pregnant and miscarried. I never went to the hospital and it was a pretty fuckin' horrible experience.

After that I didn't have sex with boys but I got real hardcore into the alcohol and pot. I didn't get into speed till I was seventeen or into relationships really till I was seventeen and a half. By that time I was on a disability pension for my osteo and my kidney problems.

I met Jed after my nonna set me up in a flat with a friend of mine. He was dealing speed and that's when I started getting into speed. The others would put the needles in my arm because I'd never learnt how to do that. I ended up having sex with him and after three months I fell pregnant with my son.

When I told him I was pregnant, he said I had to quit speed, alcohol and cigarettes but could smoke as much pot as I wanted. I argued with him about it and then he slapped me about the face and hit me again and again. That's when it began. He broke this wrist, my ribs, nicked my neck with a knife, gave me black eyes, pulled my hair out so I thought I was going to go bald.

I left him when my son was eighteen months old and I came up to the Highlands, stayed with a friend and then was in a refuge for about six months until my nonna organised for her church to pay for the bond on a flat. I'd go down to Canberra once a month to visit my doctor for my kidneys and on one of those visits I met up with a friend of my brother's. He promised me everything, white picket fence, everything I wanted. Being stupid and naïve and lacking in self-esteem – I'm a lot stronger and more hardcore now – I believed him. I got pregnant and when I was six months pregnant I found him shooting up in the bathroom and I told him I would leave him if he continued it. Well, he continued it and then got into the alcohol and gambling.

I have to tell you I never wanted to have two kids on my own but I promised myself I would never be with a man who was an alcoholic or a druggo ever again. He never laid a hand on me, but I left and moved in with a friend. I had my daughter when I was twenty-three.

I don't have any family up here, or friends. I had friends here once, but I got into the alcohol and the pot real bad, so when I moved into this flat two years ago I cleaned myself up. This place is subsidised by the Housing Commission but because I work – part-time as a youth worker – I'm paying $200 dollars a week rent.

I did a welfare course at TAFE part-time for two years at night and I graduated in March 2005 with six distinctions, five credits and the rest were passes. I'm so proud of myself. And I'm very fuckin' proud to be a working woman.

## Down-at-heel among the well-heeled

I'm as well off now as when I was on benefits. The only thing that's changed is that when I was on benefits I only had $50 a week for food for the three of us and now I have $100.

My daughter's six and my son's eleven. People are that snobby and stuck up themselves here that as soon as they find out I'm a single parent or that I'm the mother of my kids, my kids don't get invited to other people's houses. I write notes inviting other kids to play with my daughter but no one ever replies.

I have a ten-year plan which is now seven years gone. I want to live on a hobby farm, just half an acre, in a rundown house, with my kids and one sheep, one chook and one duck. I want my kids to have friends so that on weekends they can go over to their friends' place and can come home and tell me all the fun things they did. I want their friends to come here so that I can show them that even though I'm a single mum, I'm not that bad a person and I still have a normal life. I want my son to be happy every day at school and not be bullied. I want my daughter not to be bullied by kids who pick on other kids because they're short. I want my son to grow up into a really, really, really good man and I want him to appreciate things. I never ever want my kids to complain that they were hard done by in life. I grew up in a povo household and I never got spoiled. I never got anything and I had to work damn fuckin' hard for it. I want my kids to grow up with the same respect that I have. I want them to appreciate people from different walks of life. I don't want them to ever discriminate. I don't want them to be arseholes and I don't want them to take shit. I want them to stand up for themselves and not get walked all over like I did a lot of my life. I don't give a fuck what happens to me in my life, but I just want the best for them. And most of all I wish this stupid Southern Highlands would pull its finger out and realise that there are people here like me and that we're not bad because we don't have money and can't afford big fancy flash cars and can't afford to eat out at fancy restaurants every night. We're normal people and I'm damn sure we have bigger hearts than them, because we know what it's like to suffer.

That's what I want. ∎

---

Peter Meredith is a freelance journalist and author who lives in the Southern Highlands. His essay "The ugly cousin's visit" was published in Griffith REVIEW 10: Family Politics and his memoir "My ten Cadillacs" was published in Griffith REVIEW 12: Hot Air. He would like to extend his heartfelt thanks to all those people and organisations whose help made this article possible.

Memoir:
**Sydney and me**
Author:
**Lucy Lehmann**

Image: Pio Carlone / Sirius on Paddington / oil canvas, 70 x 47 cm / Courtesy of the artist

# Sydney and me

From the beginning to the end of my twenties, I hated Sydney. It was a city whose high prices dictated the terms of its inhabitants' lives: a week of fast-paced, stressful labour, ending with a short bout of frenetic spending. I was trying to be a writer, an occupation that gradually consumed more and more of my time until there was scarcely any left for work that earned money. At my desk, I knew that what I was doing had value; away from my desk, in my capacity as, for example, a job-sharing receptionist at a disposable nappy delivery company, I was worth approximately one hundred times more than I was as a writer – though it soon turned out that I was not worth even twelve dollars per hour, and I was sacked, either for incompetency or for not wearing deodorant, or both.

In a relationship, especially one that is turning bad, certain trivial events or exchanges can come to represent everything that had previously been formless, though unsettling. In a moment of apparent clarity, something all but material is born out of the swirling miasma of nameless emotions – a boyfriend sits in the driver's seat without asking whether you would like to drive, proving his latent male-chauvinism; a girlfriend – proving her self-absorption – buys a block of Old Jamaica, although you have often told her how, ever since the year 12 after-formal party, you can't stand the flavour of rum. These pieces of anecdotal evidence are recounted for the edification of a close friend or a psychiatrist – a partisan listener only for, although these pieces are supposed to conclusively reveal the truth about a third party, they ultimately provide insight into no one but the speaker.

I collected a catalogue of evidence that, I believed, strengthened my case against Sydney. Here is one commonly cited piece: the state of vacant lots and abandoned houses in Glebe. While I was growing up there, an abandoned house had lurked in every second street, a cause for crossing to the opposite footpath if it were dusk or, if it were a bright day and you were with a friend, a cause for an explorative expedition dissolving, on discovery of a dead cat or a used condom, in a squealing, giggling retreat. A pianola had stood immovably in the front room of Hereford Street's abandoned house, a ghost had been sighted in Boyce Street's, junkies in Bridge Road's, and an ancient man or woman, practically a ghost, had stood unseen in each of the numerous houses that just looked abandoned.

Then there were the vacant lots – the city child's equivalent of bushland – where the growth of castor oil, fennel, asthma weed and pampas grass catered for every activity from building a cubby house, to finding gay porn

## Sydney and me

magazines and playing spin-the-bottle. For years, there was a vacant lot – this phrase having a similar sinister, bureaucratic ring to it as "terra nullius" or "reclaimed land" – in the middle of Glebe Point Road, so spacious that in season a pond appeared, complete with bull-rushes, frogs and waterbirds. Needless to say, eventually it became a shopping court, and the other vacant lots became expensive apartments, while the abandoned or derelict houses were – my most hated word – renovated.

I would appeal to my listener: "Can't you see?" It was clear that this attitude towards land – that earning potential must be fully exploited – would soon be applied to me. A passing developer would cast a merciless eye into my own overgrown and ramshackle landscape of thoughts and ideas, and peremptorily level out this unprofitable mental space to make way for a full-time job and a craving for car and a new kitchen.

My hatred for Sydney exploded with the approach of the Olympic Games, as the last vacant or forgotten public spaces, like the man-hole on the corner of Liverpool and Pitt Streets in which, on bending down and peering through a broken glass brick, you could see a large fern growing, were hastily cleaned up. I moved to the central west of New South Wales, where I could find land that was free – free to carry something as unremunerative as a temporary frog-pond or a cubby-house or a tree. Abandoned houses, unthreatened except by possums or an escapee sheep, rotted peacefully in paddocks everywhere, including ours.

To those I had left behind in "Sydney 2000", I declared: "I'll come back when they have a ticker-tape parade down George Street for an Australian who's just won the Booker Prize."

Living away from Sydney didn't soften my stance against it. In rural New South Wales, where inhabitants were vigilant against the pull of the capital that we revolved around, partisan listeners abounded: "When I was in Sydney last month, I got a haircut and it cost me seventy dollars!" The drivers were angry, and everyone was always in too much of a rush (country people are always busy, but without rushing) to talk to you on public transport or smile as you passed each other on the street. Cities didn't have to be that way; take Melbourne, for a moment – strangers there were always starting up conversations on trams.

After a few years in the central west, I moved to Melbourne, via a sojourn of two months in Sydney where I was victim to such outrages as spending $10.50 in Watson's Bay on a takeaway sandwich, so excessive that I could only eat half of it, and was forced to leave the remains behind on my rock ledge, hoping that some hungry animal would not let it go to waste. Melburnians talked to me on trams and, judging by their clothes and hairstyles, expected to spend their weekend in small galleries or discussing, in a friend's lounge room, a provocative comment posted on mono.net, rather than on a schedule of activities that started in a nearby café with the Big Breakfast plus coffees and juice, progressed to a yoga class, then a bikini-line wax, accommodated unscheduled sallies into incidental shops, took for granted petrol and sundry parking meters and the odd bottle of cold water – the type of weekend that, in a couple of hours, would exhaust my entire weekly budget. And even when, after nine months, my excitement over this new city was tempered by a few episodes of disillusionment, my affections didn't begin to wander back to the place of my birth; only on two points did Melbourne's shortcomings illuminate Sydney's advantages – water and hills.

"You have to understand," I would say apologetically, "I'm used to going for a walk and coming across a sudden view over a dozen suburbs." I had come to expect those panoramic views that are regularly produced for Sydneysiders in all sorts of unlikely places – layers of hills visible from the train to Hurstville, North Shore buildings and the moon rising in an surprising direction at North Bondi, and even, crossing George Street at Central and turning my head to the west, the wide and occasionally trafficless curves, up and down, one of the city's most well-worn thoroughfares. And although the only event at school swimming carnivals that I'd ever had a chance in was the cork scramble, Sydney's muscular waves and its tidal bays that emptied twice a day to a floor of silky mud and oyster shells had still always been part of my life. In Melbourne, I kept it to myself that in the gridded CBD I had walked all the way down Swanston Street only to feel vaguely bewildered when it hadn't ended with a choppy blue harbour.

So I further condensed my personal possessions and boarded a plane to the northern hemisphere. I got to know other cities with water and hills. I could have started a life in any one of them; home was no longer a unique relationship that bonded me to a single place, but it was the book that I was reading, the album that I was listening to, my guitar, my diary, my writing. Home, like marriage, was just the chair you chanced to sit down in when the music stopped. We look back in wonder and gratitude, some time later, on all the apparently random steps that were incrementally leading us to our destiny, unwilling to consider that it was but one of a million scenarios which, had another eventuated instead, would have seemed equally fated. You could just as well be living, in a comparable state of happiness, irritation and loneliness, with your husband's brother, or his friend, or his Icelandic pen-pal from whom he hasn't heard since Fifth Class.

## Sydney and me

And so, arbitrarily, I didn't extend my stay in one of those European cities, but returned at the end of the year to Sydney, which I found, as I stepped off the plane, that I hated as much as ever.

My hatred was now compounded by the fact that, after living away from it for five years, I had only two remaining Sydney friends, had forgotten the names of all the streets, and didn't know anywhere, apart from the perennial chew-and-spew food courts in Dixon Street, that would provide a dinner for less than ten dollars. The footpaths that I had trodden for the first twenty-five years of my life were familiar in the most tedious way, yet barren of the fruits that such familiarity is supposed to bear – going to the right place without having to think about it, and finding your friends there without having to organise it.

I was unhappy in Sydney, so went as far away from it as I could – to Pittwater – and took to coming back only when my groceries and pleasure in my own unrelieved company were exhausted. Filling up my basket from the aisles of the Glebe IGA, I at least acknowledged that it was an improvement in my life that the only stressful moment of grocery shopping was waiting for approval of my EFTPOS transaction. Memories were still vivid of requiring food in locations such as the island of Rügen, and the mild trauma of first finding shops, second identifying the supermarket, third translating, with the aid of a dictionary, the words on the packets and, after ten or twelve other mini-crises, including avoiding any banter that would publicly uncloak my imbecilic grasp on the German language, attempting to distinguish *fünfzehns* from *fünfzigs* and responding in time with the appropriate Euro. I could see how taking things for granted, which is generally considered a crime – especially when that thing is the person with whom you're having a relationship – was actually an essential element of a productive life. Mental exertion that is not spent on figuring out whether you're looking at a packet of rolled oats or a packet of kitty litter can be directed at more lofty endeavours, such as writing novels.

In Sydney, I could speak the language, it was true. I could find water and hills all over the place. And having two friends to meet up with wasn't so bad after you've spent time in places where you have no friends. If, as I had concluded, home was just a matter of sitting down, then why didn't I sit down in the chair marked "Sydney"?

I felt incredibly depressed at the prospect, as though I had made the first major compromise of my life. I fled back to Pittwater, safely separated from the city by a two-hour bus ride and a ten-minute ferry trip. When I wasn't writing, I was applying for arts grants that would involve relocation, or falling precipitously in love with anyone who didn't live in Sydney. And yet there was another project which, without conscious intent, was beginning to take shape; a second body of evidence was slowly amassing – this one in Sydney's defence.

An aunt moved from the north-west to a flat in Glebe. I visited her with my family, and we admired the view from her balcony – in the foreground were gum trees, and across the low, former mangroves of Wentworth Park was a view of city buildings, their windows reflecting the late-afternoon sun. She pointed to the right: "You can see the clock-tower of Central Station."

"Oh, how nice!" I had always loved the country trains hall at Central, possibly because I associated it with journeys to places that weren't Sydney.

She realised that I had missed her point: "But, you know, our father had his office in the top-left-hand corner of the building there."

The view from her balcony altered. The city skyline was no longer dominated by the tall, glassy structures, but by the shorter buildings of brick or stone. When she turned to speak to her brother, she could have been addressing the boy with whom she had once shared the family home, rather than the sixty-year-old he had grown into. I thought of the house in Hereford Street, whose owners must see its heritage colours and low-maintenance, landscaped garden while I, walking past, see only a defunct pianola standing in an otherwise empty front room.

Now, at the beginning of my thirties, I found myself in conversations with people who embraced Sydney rather than rejected it. After speaking to a historian, I saw Sydney in terms of its bridges and its five remaining functioning vehicular ferries. After meeting an elderly woman on a bus – perhaps, in my twenties, my face had worn on public transport a certain belligerent expression that repelled all friendly advances – and ending up with her at a Starbucks, selected by her for the outdoor tables which lent themselves to a cigarette, I caught a glimpse of Sydney as it was at a quarter of its present size, when it was possible to find a mutual acquaintance or a family connection with every member of a crowd. I talked to Glebeites who wouldn't live in any other suburb, and Bondi boys who rarely even stepped out of theirs. I saw Sydney in terms of its fishing spots, its surf, its potential for kayaks and for party-girls and graffitists. I saw Sydney from the top floor of the Four Seasons, and from the tunnels – now the domain of the light rail – bored through Glebe and Pyrmont. There are four and a half million inhabitants here; there are four and a half million different Sydneys, its meaning simply the result of what one inhabitant chooses to see and not see.

Sydney and me

My set against Sydney had been dismantled. The city no longer exerted a force over me that I had to resist or succumb to; it was, at last, just another city, where every characteristic was negotiable except its topography.

If I were looking for a fixed truth, perhaps I didn't need to look further than water and hills. I was standing at the end of the wharf at Palm Beach, looking across Pittwater to the sharp, dark-green hills that were my destination. On the wharf with me were children burning their mouths on hot chips, adults strolling in casual clothes licking ice-creams, a family frantically unloading a week's worth of camping provisions, their disorganisation increasing as the wooden ferry approached.

There are so many changes in just one human day. The ice-cream is eaten, the children are rounded up, the mood turns from Edenic to quarrelsome as dinnertime is nigh sometime around the traffic jam at the Spit, the sun sets, the night is grey under streetlights, the children go to bed, the house is quiet, a book – enjoyable last night – is picked up, only for one page to be read in fits and starts, the mind unengaged, jerking instead between subjects that leave a melancholic emptiness, until the bed lamp is switched off and blinking eyes close at last.

After a decade, we have been through so much change that a few carefully selected memories are all we have left of who we used to be. But when I am standing at the end of the wharf, I know that time is an experience so different as to be an entirely other, unimaginable substance for the water and hills in front of me. A couple, holding hands, steps up to the white-painted rail at the end of the wharf and looks out across the water. The man licks his ice-cream then says, as though it is the first remark that he has made in the past hour, and possibly even his final word – why not? – on the whole afternoon, "This is a nice part of the world." ■

Lucy Lehmann is the author of *The Showgirl and the Brumby* (Vintage, 2002).

Essay:
**Cracks in the veneer**

Authors:
**Jago Dodson and Neil Sipe**

*Image: Rick by Bill from the 'Tenant by tenant' series / Source: www.keithsaundersphotography.com*

# Cracks in the veneer

Fedele Franzoni is on the edge. He lives with his family in Hoppers Crossing, in the outer tract of Melbourne's rapidly expanding western growth corridor. It's a place like many on the fringes of Australia's cities, where hopeful households have flocked in recent years chasing the promise of a better life enriched by the Australian dream of home ownership.

But Fedele Franzoni's dream is souring. Escalating petrol prices and mortgage interest rates have pushed him to take on a second job to keep his family's budget in the black. His edgy neighbours are slashing their spending to make ends meet. Holidays, entertainment, new appliances and health insurance have all been cut. "It's just getting so hard," he told the *Herald Sun* in May. "They say we live in the lucky country but that's crap when people have to live like this."

Meanwhile, in Sydney's outer north-west, house prices are plummeting. One house in the fringe suburb of St Clair sold for just $260,000 in August 2006, leaving its mortgagee former owners with a capital loss of $190,000 on their 2003 purchase. Such woeful tales are increasingly common in Australia's metropolitan areas. Mortgagee repossessions tripled in Victoria and doubled in New South Wales between 2005 and 2006. By August 2006, real estate agent Ray Dimarco had a growing list of default sales on his books, according to the *Sydney Morning Herald*. "It's very, very sad," he sighs. "We've had some cases where they've handed the keys over and they're still wiping the kitchen down. They're still proud of their home."

In the growing suburb of Cashmere on Brisbane's northern fringe, developers hawking new house-and-land packages are resorting to giving free fuel to home buyers to make a sale. The promoters of the Cottage Garden Estate were having trouble selling their new homes and so offered $10,000 worth of free fuel with every house bought in October 2005. The costs of travel in Brisbane's sprawling northern suburbs are now looming concerns in households' home-buying decisions.

As interest rates and petrol prices rise, the auctioneer's hammer falls on ruined mortgagees in Australian suburbs and Prime Minister John Howard proclaims the virtues of our urban "sprawl". Housing affordability, he claims, demands that the long march of the Australian suburb must continue outwards. It is the price we must proudly bear, he claims, for the standard of living we expect. Yet among the sprawling landscape of suburban Australia, new cries of pain are being heard.

## Cracks in the veneer

What is happening in Australia's cities? Home ownership is the great aspiration. But the sunny dream is darkening. The cruel winds of rising fuel prices, rising interest rates and stagnant housing prices bring a chill to financially overburdened families. Cracks are showing in the veneer of the Australian dream. There is now great vulnerability in our cities. Why, in the lucky country, must so many live on the edge?

A national conversation is now emerging about the ways we organise our neighbourhoods, suburbs and cities. Ordinary households and policy commentators alike are questioning whether the model of suburbanisation followed in recent decades can be sustained. This debate is long overdue. It must now be had because the model is currently unravelling. We cannot risk our futures by ignoring how our suburban dreams are dependent on cheap fuel and debt. We need to begin rethinking how we build and manage our cities, and change to protect our lifestyles and livelihoods from instability and risk.

The making of Australia's recent suburbs has increasingly relied on household borrowing. Historically low interest rates have produced the apparent miracle of affordable suburban home ownership and its unexpected consequences: the hyper-inflation of housing markets, supersized new housing, over-geared mortgage debts and outward expansion. As well as cheap mortgages, government policies have shaped housing markets through negative gearing, metropolitan plans and stamp duty. We need to appreciate this complexity to comprehend how our suburbs can become more resilient to the painful pattern of boom and bust.

The second critical part of the new suburban conversation is the state of transport in Australian cities. Transport underpins suburban living; it links our homes to all the things we do beyond the front gate. Our transport systems also reflect the choices we have collectively made about how we will travel – whether on foot, by bike, bus, train or car. These choices are important because how we get around has a cost in fuel, vehicles and road space not only for individuals, but also for businesses and governments.

Our ability to travel depends on cheap and available fuels – petrol for cars, diesel for trucks, gas for buses or electricity for trams and trains. Costly fuel disrupts suburban lifestyles and has dramatic impacts on our cities. As fuel prices rise, suburban transport systems face unexpected shocks. Accelerating fuel costs threaten to compound the growing mortgage risk for households who depend heavily on cars to traverse the spreading suburbs.

The condition and prospects of Australian cities – namely, the reliance of our suburbs on private motor cars for transport and on private debt for home purchase – have made our cities immensely vulnerable to oil and credit shocks. There are strong indications that Australian suburbia will be shaken further by rising fuel prices and mounting financial constraints. It is essential that, as a society, we recognise these vulnerabilities and identify their origin so that we can begin the urgent rethinking of the Australian city to avoid these threats.

We should begin this conversation about Australia's suburbs by recognising that their creation has also been one of our greatest national achievements. The provision of high-quality, affordable housing has been the basis for Australia's living standards. But because they are so central to urban life, our suburbs are places of great risk and danger – not just because of their physical form, but because of the inherent social and economic dependencies upon which they are founded.

Australia's cities rely on cheap oil. Residents depend overwhelmingly on cars for transport and access to widely dispersed employment, education and community services. More than 70 per cent of all journeys within Australian cities are by automobile.

Fuel prices have almost doubled over the past two years, driven by geopolitical tensions, weather events and accelerating demand from growing global economies. Last year petrol prices touched near-record highs. The Prime Minister fears the hikes may be permanent. In the background, a spectre looms in the form of "peak oil" – a geological theory which suggests that global oil supplies will soon hit a peak beyond which they will decline forever.

The shocks have been slow in hitting, but households are altering their behaviour to cope with increasing fuel costs. Reports have flooded in of households driving less, cutting back spending on non-essentials or using public transport more. But car-dominated planning means that budding estates like Glenmore Park in Sydney and Caroline Springs in Melbourne lack the good-quality public transport found in central areas. Walking and cycling facilities in Australia's newer suburbs are poor. Retail and other services are widely dispersed throughout the suburban landscape, making access difficult.

The Chivers family of Kellyville on Sydney's north-west edge exemplifies the sense of shock. "It is ludicrous," Chris Chivers told *The Daily Telegraph* in May 2006, as his family's monthly fuel bill rose by $80. "Living in Kellyville we have no public transport, so it is very limited. Something has to go. We can't just absorb it." Like the Chivers, many in Australia's suburbs are utterly dependent on their cars. So far, there has been little attention on the very suburban impacts of the recent oil shocks. Horror stories of outer suburban households crippled by rising fuel costs have made headlines, yet there has been barely any public debate of how we got to this point. Who allowed the suburbs to get so risky? More importantly, what are we going to do about it? Such huge questions now confront our cities. As a nation, we need to start understanding how we have created oil-vulnerable households and suburbs, and start debating the necessary planning and community steps needed to insure our cities against the rising oil threat.

The second great modern suburban vulnerability is private household debt. Debt is utterly essential to modern suburban life. The past decade has seen huge growth in household housing debts, whether owner occupied or for investment. The proportion of Australian households with mortgages jumped from 29.6 per cent in 1995 to 35.1 per cent in 2004, and the total value of mortgage debts ballooned. Australia's housing debt in 1996 totalled around $125 billion but by 2006 had reached over $350 billion. The binge was made possible by historically low, stable interest rates and receding unemployment.

Cheap debt has also boosted purchasing capacity relative to household income. House purchasers have borrowed more and bid higher for their housing. The average first home mortgage rose 132 per cent from $90,000 in 1995 to $209,600 in 2005. The credit flood created a king tide of house prices that has washed across Australian cities. Median house values grew from $180,000 to $485,000 in Sydney between 1993 and 2003, an increase of 169 per cent. House prices in Melbourne and Brisbane grew 149 percent and 131 per cent respectively over the same period. Perth boomed later but has overtaken Sydney due to rapid economic growth in Western Australia.

The boom not only primed housing prices, but produced a wonder economy of imagined wealth and aspirations. The amount of housing consumed has soared as low interest credit grew into square metres of floor space. The modesty traditionally shown by Australian home owners vanished. In the past, modest income Australian households bought simple dwellings and added to them over time as wages rose, with renovations and extensions. Now the full house is bought upfront.

Low interest rates loosened the spending reins and cheap credit provided the illusion of instant wealth. Why wait years down the track for the third bathroom, walk in robes or a rumpus room? A little more on the loan upfront adds only a fraction to the weekly payments, so let the rumpus rip was the message. Thus, in New South Wales, the floor area of new homes spread by nearly a third between 1993 and 2003 and by a quarter in Victoria. Cheap debt remodelled the form of Australia's new housing, exemplified in the rise of the so-called "McMansion", reflecting how access to low-cost debt has enabled big borrowing to buy big dreams. Cheap consumer credit made these houses, and also allows aspirational splurging on domestic "bling".

This spending binge probably wouldn't have happened if not for the low cost of credit. Australian households have now amassed a mountain of debt, mostly for housing and the shiny gear inside. Debts must be repaid. The house price boom and its huge debt burdens make any interest rate rise chew deeper into household budgets in far-flung places. The mortgage misery could easily escalate. Outgoing Reserve Bank chair Ian McFarlane last year forecast the end of the cheap credit cycle and predicted that interest rates will soon swing back up to their "normal", higher levels.

Few complained as interest rates fell in the mid-1990s and many celebrated as rapid house price growth brought a glossy veneer of wealth and security. The lonely critics of the property debt party were ignored. But the chorus of mortgage pain has finally stopped the great suburban barbecue. The revelry is ending and our cities are tottering. The hangover leers.

We urgently need a new public debate about the condition of our suburbs because they affect the entire economy. The consumption of debt has grown the economy by creating a legion of new jobs in construction and services. These jobs have also provided work for many mortgage holders, as dog washers, pool cleaners, appliance salespersons and carpet layers. But the suburban debt-consumption economy has also primed inflation, and the Reserve Bank is ratcheting interest rates upwards. As rising interest rates contract millions of suburban household budgets, this web of housing-based employment will also begin to fray. Reports suggest the Sydney construction sector is already in recession. Shrinking finance, construction and retail sectors could cause shivers across the whole Australian economy. Shaky housing choices may yet unsettle work choices.

Paul Kelly has argued that Australia's remarkable political stability since Federation is effectively the result of a "settlement" between capital and labour. The result has been described by historian Frank Castles as the Australian "wage earners' welfare state". Under this pact, industry conceded more of the profits accruing from private ownership of capital to workers and in return retained rightful ownership of private property and enterprise.

The idea of settlement helps us to understand Australian cities, because it evokes not only an agreement completed but also an enduring state of dwelling. Indeed, the Australian settlement was as much about accommodation – ensuring everyone could afford a dwelling – as it was an industrial contract. In a culture that now celebrates home ownership, settlement is the rite that marks a point of personal, social and economic becoming – the last sacrament in the mass ritual of owner-occupation. Settlement defines our national aspiration.

## Cracks in the veneer

The "Australian accommodation" came literally, throughout the twentieth century, in the form of the progressive delivery of modern housing by expanding the suburban realm. The nineteenth century Australian city had not produced the horrid slums found in other industrial metropolises, but was nonetheless a foul place for many residents. The huddled masses began their flight to new spaces. Under the Australian accommodation, industry provided the wages and finance to make home purchase affordable and governments ensured access to a supply of adequate land upon which good-quality housing could be built.

This model has endured many shifts in political fashion and ideology. The Whitlam government, for example, used state control of land release and infrastructure to plan suburbs. Howard's suburban toolbox includes interest rates and private land developers. While their methods of provision and delivery differ, the two sides of politics are unified in their support for the Australian dream. Every government's attempt to expand suburban home ownership is a version of the aspiration inherent in the Australian accommodation. In challenging and debating our cities, we must appreciate these experiences and the lessons they hold for our suburban future. But dreams are built in material worlds.

Paul Keating once remarked that the "tyranny of distance" that characterises Australia's contrary global geography is almost a national obsession. The Australian accommodation involves an inverted tyranny of distance within our urban land markets. This minor tyranny is found in the trade-offs forced by land prices that are high in the city centre and slope gradually away with increasing distance from the CBD. Central city properties have historically been of highest value because of the close access they provide. In the outer suburbs, land is cheaper but services are sparse and infrastructure is poor.

In the early industrial period, most industrial activity occurred near the city centres and required a workforce that in turn demanded housing. Initially, workers lived within walking and cycling distance of their employment. The competition for land created high residential densities and crowded living conditions. Many rented their housing from slumlords. The tiny terrace cottages of Melbourne's Fitzroy and Sydney's Surry Hills reflect this cramped early-urban period.

Technology broke the tyranny of suburban distance and enabled the Australian accommodation. The advent of the trams and trains in the late nineteenth century sped the outward expansion of Australia's early suburbs by providing access to cheaper land far from the rotting cores. Land speculators encouraged the growth of rail lines and land sales around stations. Governments, many of whose members were implicated in speculative ventures, provided the public capital to support the rail schemes.

In Sydney and Melbourne, new suburban villages with vibrant commercial hubs sprouted around each city's suburban rail stations at places like Malvern and Ashfield. But distance again imposed its tyranny in miniature, limiting the expansion of suburban villages to little further than walking distance from the rail station. Beyond the station, land prices quickly fell away and landscapes remained semi-rural. Only in those areas criss-crossed by tramlines did continuous development prevail.

In the golden weather of the post-World War II economy, Australia's suburbs grew apace. Affordable access to motor vehicles further relaxed the tyranny of distance. At the end of the war, only half of Australian households owned their homes, but with strong government subsidies home ownership grew rapidly, reaching nearly three-quarters over the following thirty years.

The postwar decades marked the advent of the period of the private automobile. This drew patrons away from public transport, and motor vehicles crowding suburban streets came into conflict with the trams. As traffic growth clogged arterial roads, state governments began to dismantle their tramways, replacing them with diesel buses. Sydney's trams ended in 1961 and Brisbane's in 1969. As a result of historical accident, only Melbourne's trams survived.

The early postwar period also coincided with growing national interest in cities and the first real attempts at their large-scale planning. Rapid growth allowed the testing of new planning ideas and models. From the late 1950s, Australia's urban planners embraced the motor car and new models of suburbanisation drawn from an ascendant and newly prosperous America. American road consultants were invited to draw up freeway plans for Australian cities. Melbourne's 1969 road plan sought to superimpose a lattice of intersecting freeways across the city. Similar plans were created in Brisbane, Sydney and Perth, and were implemented over the following decades. Melbourne's South East Freeway opened in 1967; Sydney's first freeway was completed in 1971.

The freeways were a double blow for public transport. Cars draw patrons away from the rail routes, and roads took large amounts of government finance that might otherwise have gone to public transport. Australia's public transport systems have languished ever since. Patronage bottomed out in the late 1980s and has, at best, only matched population growth since then.

The motor car permitted a previously unknown degree of mobile freedom that conquered the tyranny of suburban distance. Suburbanites were no longer tied to the radial tram and rail routes, and could traverse the city. The car became a tool of housing policy by helping to open up new, cheap land for housing. Commerce and industry followed the workers to their new suburban locations, and also became detached from the train and tram systems. Shopping centres drove this process – Melbourne's Chadstone in 1962 was the first to break the link between rail and retail.

The freeway era has created two city types within the Australian metropolis that are marked by differences in design and location. The first "rail city" is the pre-World War II area previously accessed by the tram and train networks. This zone tends to be of higher dwelling and commercial density, often involving mixed uses, and is well served by the remnant public transport with high rates of public transport use, walking and cycling. Eastern Sydney's Randwick and Bondi or Melbourne's Richmond and St Kilda exemplify this. Only 20 per cent of the journeys undertaken by residents of inner Sydney involve private motor vehicles; the rest are by bus, train, bike or foot.

The second city type is the freeway city that grew beyond and between the public transport networks. Doncaster in Melbourne's east, Baulkham Hills in Sydney or Brisbane's North Lakes exemplify them. The differences between the two cities are marked, and are clearly due to the divergent relationships between transport and land use and the lived experience of their populations. Thus, while residents of Sydney's Marrickville, Crows Nest or Woollahra travel on average less than twelve kilometres each day, those in outer western suburbs such as Camden and Penrith cover four times that distance.

Cheap fuel has produced not only car-dependent suburbs but an evolutionary growth in the species of vehicle on which suburban residents depend. Australia's passenger vehicle fleet in 1963 burned 11.4 litres of fuel every hundred kilometres. Despite four decades of technological improvements, occasional oil panics, environmental doubts and the advent of smaller cars, the best the Australian passenger vehicle fleet could achieve by 2005 was 11.7 litres per hundred kilometres. Australian fuel efficiency is worse now than it was in 1963.

Just as low interest rates make housing consumption more attractive, so increased motive efficiency translates into greater fuel consumption through increased engine size, bulked-up vehicle frames and luxury extras such as air conditioning, electric windows and fancy electronics. These qualitative changes have simply absorbed the efficiency gains while the total fuel cost has effectively remained static.

The two-cities geography of the Australian metropolis is now a brittle fulcrum around which the question of oil vulnerability hinges. Rising fuel prices are likely to have much less impact on the first city type than on the second because residents of this area have access to and use public transport more than their more mobile cousins. Dependence on petrol now poses one of the most significant risks to Australian suburbs. These risks are spread differently depending on local conditions.

The freedom and mobility provided by the automobile are entirely due to the availability of cheap petrol. The decades-long campaign to overcome the tyranny of urban distance in Australia's cities has largely been backed by easy access to cheap oil. Our suburban armies march on their petrol tanks. But nothing lasts forever, and there is a significant and growing body of science and commentary that suggests the age of cheap oil will face major challenges over the foreseeable future. If oil is finite, so is the Australian suburban model.

As if interest rates weren't bad enough, Channel Nine's *60 Minutes* recently announced "two of the scariest words in the English language". These weren't the usual bogeys of global terror, bird flu or even climate change. The words formed the bland and innocuous phrase of "peak oil". This unremarkable but consequential term has emerged over the past few decades from being the niche interest of a few petroleum geologists to becoming a major issue for businesses, governments and policy-makers.

Peak oil theory is drawn from the production patterns of individual oil wells. In the early life of an oil field, extraction accelerates quickly – often exponentially. As the pumping increases, the field's pressure subsides and the rate of extraction slows, providing a "peak" moment of maximum flow. Production then declines and output falls away.

The theory is increasingly being proved right. Oil production in the United States "peaked" in 1971. The North Sea oil region peaked in 1999, Australia in 2000. Many observers believe the theory also applies to the entire world's oil reserves. Peak oil has enormous implications for the Australian accommodation and our "oiloholic" cities. Our oil-driven escape from the tyranny of suburban distance may prove illusory in an age of uneasy oil.

Even without the spectre of peak oil haunting the suburban accommodation, new and troubling pressures are already being felt. Global oil prices have risen markedly in the past two years, from just over US$30 per barrel in early 2004, to more than US$70 in mid-2006. Wars have raised global strategic oil concerns. Tensions in Nigeria and Venezuela have also heightened oil anxieties, while malevolent meteorology and shoddy Alaskan pipeline maintenance have also shaken global supply confidence. The future of oil-reliant Australian outer suburbs now depends on the fractal geology and tensions of unstable foreign lands.

Security fears would be only minor worries if the global thirst for oil were not so great. Global demand for oil will likely continue to put pressure on

Cracks in the veneer

world supplies. The world consumed about eighty-four million barrels of oil in 2005 and this is projected to increase by about two million barrels annually. Where this new supply will be drawn from remains unclear and partly explains the current level of speculation over oil futures. The rising global price of oil has translated directly into rising Australian domestic fuel prices. By mid-2006, the cost of petrol in Australian cities was around $1.30 per litre, close to a doubling of the mid-2004 price. The rising fuel prices have seen much public complaint and consternation as motorists find their wallets thinner and their tanks less brimming than before.

Household budgets have been pressured, especially for those in the outer suburbs where a car is the basis for almost all aspects of social and economic life. Many newspaper articles have described the grim theme of families struggling to accommodate rising fuel costs within debt-burdened household budgets. Formal reports are shedding light on the trade-offs that households are making to cope with rising fuel prices. The Commonwealth Bank Research Unit has reported that Australian petrol consumption is plummeting. Sales of petrol in 2005 plunged 8 per cent compared with 2005 – the steepest fall in twenty years.

Market research agencies such as ACNielsen and Sensis have revealed that rising petrol costs have had two major effects on households. Families are avoiding driving by making fewer trips, combining journeys and travelling shorter distances. Simultaneously, they are abandoning discretionary spending, with "entertainment and going out" featuring at the top of the list of arrested activities. Holidays and private health insurance have also been cited in reports of changing spending habits due to high petrol prices. Sales of 4WDs crashed in 2006 and resale values are crumpling.

The public transport flame has been rekindled in Australian cities as the costs of motoring end the love affair of recent decades. Most major cities have reported bus and train patronage growing beyond their planners' expectations. In Brisbane, a bus shortage has led to crush loading on many routes and spawned a bitter political fight between the Labor and Liberal councillors over who is to blame for the crowds of irate passengers left stranded at bus stops. Adelaide, Melbourne and Sydney have also reported jumps in patronage. The scramble back to public transport is one way to soothe the petrol sting. But for the many who lack this option, there is little relief from the beating at the bowser.

A crucial factor that is much overlooked in the public flapping and squawking over fuel price rises is the way that the historical development of Australia's cities is shaping and determining how households experience the impact of rising fuel costs. Where you live in Sydney, Melbourne,

Perth, Adelaide or Brisbane can greatly determine the fuel pain you're feeling. As our empirical research shows, those in the post-World War II cities where the car dominates and public transport is weak are at greatest risk from rising fuel costs because these are also the areas where mortgage debts are greatest and incomes most modest.

The legacy of public transport investment is now set to create winners and losers from the suburban oil shocks. Perversely, the localities that currently display some of the highest rates of public transport use in Australia are also among the country's wealthiest. Melbourne University academic Chris Cheal has described these areas as "transit rich" because of the high quality of their public transport services. The legacy of public investment means that the risks of rising fuel prices for the affluent residents of these areas are largely socialised, backed by history and ongoing public subsidy.

Beyond the historic middle- and inner-city tram, bus and rail lines, Australia's public transport services are typically infrequent and poorly connected. In Melbourne, 85 per cent of the city's households were found by Cheal to be "transit poor", stranded in a suburban desert. Their inevitable resort to private motor vehicles means that the risk of high-cost oil is largely privatised, yet they have limited alternatives should petrol price rises continue.

While public roads comprise a public subsidy that far exceeds that for public transport, the upfront costs of private vehicle travel by road are much greater than for public transport. Yet even the direct public subsidy for mega-roads has been surpassed in recent years as Australian cities have seen the emergence of private tollways. Melbourne's City Link and Sydney's twisted grid of tollways exemplify this phenomenon, but even Brisbane is hurtling headlong down the sinkhole of private tolls with the $3 billion North–South Bypass Tunnel.

Sydney's chaotic toll roads have become highly contentious, with the Cross-City Tunnel sparking major controversy over its parasitic presence among the city's tangle of private and public motorways. Motorists in Sydney now face seven different toll regimes, each creating a bewildering array of potential travel prices and costs. Some reports suggest that households may be paying hundreds of dollars each month simply to access employment and services on Sydney's roads. For many, there is no viable alternative and, as fuel prices grind upwards and mortgage interests escalate, the costs of private mobility may easily become a toll too far for Australia's car-dependent suburban residents.

Australia has spent the last half-century investing heavily in the suburban accommodation. The suburban oil and debt economy is interwoven with and buttressed by entrenched political dynamics and imperatives that seek to sustain the pairing of land, automobile and debt. Land developers, automobile manufacturers and their workers, road user lobbies, construction companies and unions, energy companies, banks and even government agencies all have their fingers in the suburban pie.

This national economic dependence on the production of Australia's suburban realm is a major reason why political leaders have historically celebrated the expansion of Australia's suburbs, even in the face of some of the environmental impacts this brings. Prime Minister John Howard remarked in 2006 that suburban "sprawl" is the price worth paying for the Australian accommodation.

But the geography of the Australian accommodation is also political. Many of the nation's most marginal political electorates fall within areas that exemplify the contemporary vulnerabilities of car dependence and indebtedness. These zones pose a substantial conundrum for political parties. Rising fuel prices are putting oil vulnerable suburbs under significant social and economic anxiety. The volatility in petrol prices could quickly translate into electoral volatility among those observing their private suburban nirvana transformed into an equally private nightmare. George Megalogenis has argued that the debt-boom economy has softened political thinking on housing and cities. Both sides of politics may soon be scrambling to offer urgent therapies for post-traumatic petroleum syndrome.

Prime Minister John Howard faces the greatest challenge from the new electoral geography of oil and mortgage. Howard has basked in the glow of the overheating housing markets and owes much of his success to his ability to appeal to suburban dwellers. His political strength has been the ability to convince them that he supports their aspirations to personal material wealth and offers the best policies to assist that acquisition. Yet Labor has built strong state governments by providing public services funded by massive stamp duty revenues. Very little of this gain has flowed to the new suburbs where oil and mortgage risk is greatest.

A public conversation must now be held about the sustainability of the contemporary Australian suburban model and its multiple vulnerabilities. What will the consequences be for politicians who have sold their electors a suburban dream whose illusion has become all too painful? The coming months will no doubt see this conversation unfold as the political tradesmen line up to plaster the cracks in our suburban veneer. ∎

References available at www.griffith.edu.au/griffithreview

Jago Dodson and Neil Sipe work in the Urban Research Program and School of Environmental Planning at Griffith University. Their most recent publication is *Shocking the Suburbs: Urban location, housing debt and oil vulnerability in the Australian city*.

# Suburban archaeology

*Anna Krien*

Living on a stable plate
while others tumble into the sea
you would think that maybe
we're special
or chosen
to stay alive while everyone else
is swallowed by the sea.
Or maybe
because we're so brand new
like freshly shorn marines
we're not quite ready to see the seams
of the earth
split open like a mouth.

And in this strange
cookie-cutter of a country
where waves flick like some girl's hair,
clouds scuff against a faded denim sky
with its LCD ticker tape of highways,
there are
only wells.
Holes that shriek
like baths being drained.

Sometimes
you see them slowing down,
drifting across a four-lane highway.
The night careening with cross-eyed cats' eyes,
and the sky,
yellow and piss-coloured,
spits warm into the bay.

Seal-skinned swimmers freestyle between buoys
bobbing like bloated goldfish.
Goggles glint orange as the sun sinks
behind the smokestacks and empty apartment
blocks
with the lights left on by real estate agents.

You can hear the blink of ships
as they slip under the Westgate,
the soft plonk of fishing lines
and tinny rambling of AM radio.
The clicking and cracking of the magnet factory,
silver discs spilling towards each other
across the Williamstown warehouse.
Dreams here are black,
except for the solitary flashlight of abalone
poachers.

And at night,
lumps grow.

They grow up
out of the local football field
that used to be landfill,
a suburban grand canyon.
The under 18's have to dig out car wrecks
that rise to the surface between seasons.
And in the cancer ward at Geelong's Mercy,
a hundred women wait
like oysters to be shucked,
hands over their breasts
feeling for pearls.

We drive through Little River,
past the toilet block where my grandma
once found a finger,
a small bloodied pinkie,
black hair still on its knuckle.
My grandma stood there
next to the pinkie
and strewn paper towels,
waiting for the police.

\* \* \* \* \* \*

I run.
I never jog.

I fill the days
with cups of tea,
checking on my laundry across the road
and visiting the painter downstairs
who does canvases for Ikea
to match lounge settings.
He hears voices, mostly of the shrill variety.
It's like a pair of macaws in here,
he once said, pointing to his head.
Sometimes it gets so bad
he shrouds the windows
with bed sheets he must have saved from when he
was a kid,
teddy bears and ET and racing cars
shield him from the light.

The painter asked me not to turn on the TV or the
radio
when his world was solitary and unused
– silent like a held breath –
under sheets like deceased estate,
because the voices travelled through
the goose-pimpled walls.
So I read the newspaper
to the sound of a giant moth's paper-wings turning.

A frat boy is found dead
post-initiation night,
his throat clogged with Hawaiian pizza.
They say his body was covered in thick black texta,
I take it up the arse
nigger lover
I suck cock
eat shit and cum.
The ink sunk in like rigor mortis
and the parents had to bury him like that,
covered in the haiku of a fucked-up generation.

But still
when the sheets come down,
the painter exits,
a little thinner and spooked.
I can't help
thinking of the girl on the news
who called out of my clock radio
at exactly 7am
– I'm drowning –
when she was being raped
in her basement.

\* \* \*

When I met him,
his leather bat-winged jacket flapping,
standing in the service lane,
smoking hurried limp cigarettes,
ghosts coming out of his mouth,
I knew I was going to take to him
like lightning to a lake.

He had said, striking another match,
that before matches were red,
they were yellow.
And the factory workers in London,
they used to glow.
The phosphorus got into their hands and faces.
People watched them coming home,
bright yellow in the night.

His tongue flicked out the corner
of his mouth as he talked,

wetting a patch of dry skin on the curve of his lips.
Treads from trucks lay about us,
rubber flanks restless like horses in the starter box.
And his three-legged dog named Jack Farley
hopped up and down the service lane
barking at the cars.
Later he swore to me
that sometimes he could see a fourth paw print
when looking back at his and Jack Farley's tracks
along a beach.

For an entire week he stood on a chair,
neck bent like Michelangelo's,
mapping out the southern hemisphere
with 38 packets of glow-in-the-dark stars.
He copied everything straight from a map
except for the Milky Way.
That, he said, as we camped out in my one-
bedroom flat
he traced from the freckles
spilt across my nose.

When Jack Farley and I slept,
the dog's phantom leg twitching,
the stickers fading,
he worked.
He would stay up all night
zooming in on strange pixelations
and wispy formations.
A police scanner read out the sites of ordinary
crimes,
homicides and suicides.
He mapped out each ghost religiously
on his free tourist map of Victoria.
He collected life's leftovers,
and had installed hundreds of web cams
across the state and beyond,
trying to catch the rah-rah skirts of the dead.

In the dark
my hands scrambled towards him
like spiders across the bedroom floor.
Sometimes he would take me half-in
half-out of sleep. I would come
with a film of moon over my eyes.
In between bulbs igniting like cars in the distance
was a deep underwater tug,
a fishhook caught on my insides,
dragging plastic bags full of sea.

And a jogger
– it's always the joggers that find them –
he would tell me in the morning,
clutching their iPods
white rubber sneakers squeaking,
and a house key on a bit of string under their
t-shirts.
They would find the night's bodies.
Creaking overhead in the mottled morning
under bridges covered in birthday banners,
pink bloated pendulums swinging
over concrete footpaths inscribed with teenage
love affairs.
Strewn like dreams coaxed to the surface.

Sometimes
the joggers note the small
squeezebox
of a heart.
A little bit of night
dragged into the day.
A cat with blood on its whiskers.

Out the window
I watch as the owner of the Laundromat
pushes each machine back against the wall
after they spent the whole night
shuffling forward on spin.

\* \* \*

In summer the flat is too hot.
The stickers on the ceiling peel off.
He laughs and says
Falling Stars.
Jack Farley barks and tries

to catch the glowing stickers on his tongue.

In just a t-shirt I can see
on his arms the tattoos he had done with another
girl.
They had been rubbed out.
Like faded mistakes I can still see them
under his new artwork,
lingering in the way
only an ex can do.

I feel gangly around his ghosts.
My arms thick and legs like pylons.
Boobs like water balloons.
I close my eyes and smell our way out of the city,
past the vegemite factory,
the car rattling like an old Luna Park ride
up over the Westgate bridge.
The Vicks distillery, the treated pine yards
and treated shit farm.
We pass the toilet block where my granny found
the finger.

I can smell this place.
The secret blimps in the sky,
the paused kangaroos,
and the ink in my fingers.
Perhaps this country's fault lines
are not so big and obvious like San Francisco's
cracks,
or shuddering
like the earthquakes of Indonesia.
Maybe at the bottom of all the seas,
the place where letters land,
we are just a yellow canary blowing out
underground.
A little bird,
eyes like poppy seeds.

Wrestling a jammed cassette out of the tape player,
I unravel the shiny brown tape
that once somehow sung
out the window.

Black streamers pouring out the car,
catching on the fingertips of ti-tree.
Tomorrow the crows will line their nests
with the river water tears of Johnny Cash.

At the pink marshes
where my mum and me used to wade out,
bare feet and holding empty jam jars,
scaring off the egrets like miniature storks.
For cooking, my mum would say,
as we scooped up the crusty top layer of salt,
and the cuts on my feet stung.

Just past the crisp white bulldozed mounds of salt
where models pose for snow season fashion
spreads.
In goggles, puffy jumpsuits and beanies,
they crouch with skis poised and ready to go,
but all that's ahead of them is a dirt road,
the last length of powerline,
and a soap factory where his most prized webcam
is on the blink.

I wait for him
beside an open container of rose-scented soap,
while Jack Farley leaves a fourth paw print on the
dusty concrete floor,
and he hunts for ghosts
that stink
like potpourri.

Anna Krien is a Melbourne-based poet and writer. Her poem "These are wobbly days" was published in Griffith REVIEW 13: The Next Big Thing.

Essay:
**The exiled child**

Author:
**Meera Atkinson**

Image: Hannah Evans / Domestic and family violence. See the signs. Be the solution / Highly Commended: StART Thinking Poster Competition 2006 / Courtesy of the artist

# The exiled child

Our battle with the twenty-one-year-old party girl next door over her top-volume dance music came to a head one evening. Having tried the friendly, then friendly-yet-firm route, my husband and I decided to show we were serious. We'd called the police before and the music had promptly been turned down, but the cop who came that fateful night heard the doof-doof blast from downstairs and took it upon himself to issue a twenty-eight-day summons to cease and desist, even though she'd turned the music off on her way out a moment before he reached her door.

As he pulled out his pad, we listened from behind our door, exchanging triumphant smiles. Then all hell broke loose. We opened the door to find our neighbour, dressed to go out, screaming at the cop to get out and trying desperately to shut the door on him. He stood firm, one leg holding the door open, demanding the information he needed for the summons. When she realised she had no retreat, she became wild, kicking at his shins and throwing a live cigarette at him, her eyes wide in confusion, rage and terror. He warned her he would arrest her for assaulting a police officer. I appealed to her to calm down.

Suddenly his back-up arrived, and six or seven officers surrounded her in the hallway. She flailed like a trapped animal; her breast fell out of her dress. She cried out: she couldn't breathe; she was having a panic attack, a heart attack; she wanted her doctor, her mother; she couldn't believe this was happening; she had a party to go to. As the cops descended to make their arrest, her heels made skid marks on the walls. It was obvious that they viewed her as just another methamphetamine loser or, worse, a lunatic cop-hater. But for the first time since I'd met her, I saw her as a kindred spirit.

There have been many times in my life when people have come to negative conclusions about me, and many terms applied: juvenile delinquent, alcoholic, drug addict, drama queen, borderline personality disorder, self-destructive, hysteric, depressive, neurotic, phobic and hypochondriac. But I've discovered a new one, and according to the literature it may be at the heart of all the others: *chronic trauma survivor*.

I realised some years ago that I was a traumatised person, but it wasn't until I read *Trauma and Recovery* by Judith Herman (Pandora, 1998) – a book my therapist refers to as "The Bible in the field of trauma studies" – that I came across this phrase and finally understood the true nature of trauma. Many who have grown up in an environment of domestic violence, where trauma has become the norm, come to this realisation after decades of suffering. Most, like me, will have collected a hefty sack of labels along the way, labels that all too often only succeed in describing symptoms. The hardest thing about being a chronic trauma survivor (and it has no end of hardships) is the crushing loneliness of being misunderstood.

The simplest definition of trauma is that cited by Elizabeth Waits in *Trauma and Survival: Post-Traumatic and Dissociative Disorders in Women* (Norton, 1993): "Injury to mind or body that requires structural repair." I have known for the best part of two decades that growing up with domestic violence damaged me, but I used to think of that damage as a vague, amorphous influence on my equally vague and amorphous emotional life. Until recently, I didn't know that this damage occurred at a concrete level on the actual structure of my developing brain, and that this "structural damage" explains why the process of recovery for those chronically traumatised as children is such an enormous challenge.

Researchers from the University of South Australia, in their 2002 report *Children and Domestic Violence*, describe children as "the 'silent', 'forgotten', or 'invisible' victims of family violence". They outline the problem of the traditional division between domestic violence and child protection – when child abuse is viewed as a health and welfare matter and domestic violence is referred to the police, courts and women's refuges, children fall through the cracks. The researchers conclude that domestic violence *is* a child protection issue: "There is now increasing recognition that these are not separate phenomena and that children's exposure to domestic violence is a form of child abuse."

My parents divorced when I was five. After that came "the boyfriends". My mother had three live-in relationships between the divorce and the time I left home at fifteen. It was the second, a man I dared to love and came to fear, who proved to be the most *traumatic* – the man I'll refer to as Arthur. He earned the dubious title of "the worst" partly because he was probably sociopathic, and partly because he let me down so badly; I had desperately wanted him to be a loving partner for my mother and a father figure to me.

For the first few years after my parents' divorce, I clung to the hope that they would reunite. I interrogated my mother about why they'd parted. Though there must have been tension between them and in the home, my memories of early life are tranquil. The most damning thing I could say about my father was that he seemed distant and was often absent. During the late '60s and early '70s, I felt the stigma of being a child of divorce keenly. I absorbed the images of happy television families, and suffered from a constant sense of inferiority for failing to belong to one.

I was nine when my mother and I moved into a new apartment and I started at a new school. Stacey was among the first children I befriended. She was my age, the daughter of a single father. It didn't take us long to hatch a *Brady Bunch* plan. We decided that Stacey would come to my place after school one afternoon and stay too late to walk home. In between the idea and the execution, we each primed our respective parents about the availability and charms of the other. Arthur arrived at the appointed hour and lingered late into the evening, talking with my mother on the sofa while we girls giggled excitedly in my bedroom, plotting our deliriously happy future as sisters. Arthur and Stacey moved in quickly and the four of us enjoyed a blissful honeymoon. My mother, who was an indoor person and an avid reader, was lured out of doors on a seemingly never-ending string of adventures. We took boats out on the water, enjoyed long country drives and even went on holidays.

Not long after I'd started calling Arthur "Dad" and Stacey started calling my mother "Mum", my newfound happiness gave way to mayhem. Home became a place of increasing fear and secrecy. "If the idea of 'home' implies physical and psychological safety and security as well as shelter," as Jill Astbury wrote, "then a child, adult or older person affected by domestic violence experiences a hidden 'homelessness'." For a child – who needs a safe environment to develop – this homelessness can be a kind of lifelong exile.

Even after years of therapy, I am unable to map out a reliable and linear timeline of events, or to articulate a cohesive reconstruction of the disintegration of their relationship. All I know is that one day they seemed content and the next they were fighting. I have no idea whether I witnessed ten, fifty or 150 violent fights. All I have is a collection of random memories without their broader context. This is, the experts assure me, completely normal for someone with post-traumatic stress disorder. Judith Herman describes how it works: "Traumatic memories lack verbal narrative and context; rather, they are encoded in the form of vivid sensations and images. Robert Jay Lifton, who has studied survivors of Hiroshima, civilian disasters and combat, describes the traumatic memory as an 'indelible image' or 'death imprint'." These are among the most vivid of my "indelible images":

- A fight has started on our way home from a wedding on a Saturday night. Arthur is in the driver's seat and he has pulled over so that he can strangle my mother. I'm sitting behind him in the back seat, leaning out the window screaming for help so loud my throat hurts. Three or four people pass by and look at us, but they keep walking and do not help. I'm watching my mother gag and I reach out and pull on Arthur's hair with all my might. His hands release my mother's throat; he twists around and belts me in the head.

- We are camping in a tent pitched at the top of a hill. They've been fighting all day and Arthur and Stacey appear to have abandoned us there.

## The exiled child

My mother and I are sitting in the tent. The air is thick with apprehension and tension. Suddenly we hear the car revving up the hill. We emerge from the tent and start running. I turn around and am blinded by the headlights coming towards me at full speed.

- I'm running up to the police station in my nightie in the dead of night.
- My mother and I arrive home to find slurs scrawled all over the walls in huge, mad letters.
- My mother lies on the floor in the kitchen. I think she is dead.
- My mother sleeps on the sofa in the living room with a knife under her pillow.

Elizabeth Waits explains why these memories still feel like a bad dream from which I can't quite wake, rather than reality: "The shock of trauma produces states that are so different from ordinary waking life that they are not easily integrated with more normal experience. As a result of this discontinuity, the traumatic state may be lost to memory or remembered as a dream is sometimes remembered, as something vague and unreal."

The younger a child is, the less easily they will be able to articulate the trauma, but it is a mistake to equate this with a lack of registration. Judith Herman points out that among twenty children with documented histories of early trauma studied by psychiatrist Lenore Terr: "None of the children could give a verbal description of the events that had occurred before they were two-and-a-half years old. Nonetheless, these experiences were indelibly encoded in memory. Eighteen of the twenty children showed evidence of traumatic memory in their behaviour and their play. They had specific fears related to the traumatic events, and they were able to re-enact these events in their play with extraordinary accuracy."

She describes the difference between people who experience a one-off traumatic event and those in "captivity" who are subjected to repeated and inescapable trauma: "People in captivity become adept practitioners of the arts of altered consciousness. Through the practice of dissociation, voluntary thought suppression, minimisation, and sometimes outright denial, they learn to alter an unbearable reality." The person who experiences a one-off trauma from the basis of an already stable personality suffers differently from someone whose selfhood has formed in its chronic presence. Herman says: "People subjected to prolonged, repeated trauma develop an insidious, progressive form of post-traumatic stress disorder that invades and erodes the personality." Because chronic trauma survivors do not fit the classic description of "simple" post-traumatic stress disorder, she calls for a new category – "complex post-traumatic stress disorder"– that can better describe the complicated picture with which chronic trauma survivors often present.

Chronic trauma is, literally, unacceptable. Even now, after all these years, a memory will flash up – like the image of me jumping on to Arthur's back and clawing at his giant shoulders to pull him off my mother – and I tell myself I must be mistaken, this cannot have happened. These images cannot possibly belong to me and my life. And while trauma is trauma and "the severity of traumatic events cannot be measured on any single dimension", Herman says certain "identifiable experiences" increase the probability of harm, including "being taken by surprise, trapped, or exposed to the point of exhaustion". Each of these "identifiable experiences" is typical for the child of domestic violence. Days that started out as joyful excursions whose sunniness seemed sure to continue would, in a second, cloud over and become a publicly humiliating storm.

The most common time for fights to erupt was late at night after I'd gone to bed. I would lie awake for hours stilling myself so that my breath was almost inaudible – the better to monitor the sounds from outside my door for any sign of discord – but once started the fights went on for hours. Adrenaline would keep me from feeling tired, but I passed countless sleepless school nights trying to referee. No one is more trapped than a child who cannot survive without the adults on whom they depend. When those adults are also their prime threat, they are trapped in a double bind. In some ways it might have been easier if the discord had been constant. But the contrasts were extreme: the highs the highest I'd known – our home was wonderful when the adults were happy – the lows unbearable. I dared to relax into pleasure and security only to be jolted out of it by the all too familiar signs of a fight.

Children in violent families are on the classic domestic violence rollercoaster. Everyone is familiar with the cliché of the woman with the bruised face softening at the sight of a repentant abuser. Without the benefit of a fully developed brain and life experience, children are particularly susceptible to the magical thinking that the cycle of domestic abuse demands. My mother didn't fit the mousy victim stereotype: she was an outgoing, modern working woman who owned her own apartment and was not economically dependent. And yet she stayed in a relationship in which control, jealousy and intimidation were routine, vulnerable time after time to the sweet words of remorse and promises.

If at first I too believed these words, I soon grew familiar with the devastation of fairytale faith giving way to bitter disappointment and despair. In the shadows of this devastation, a child develops certain beliefs in an attempt to make sense of the cycle of trauma. As Elizabeth Waits explains: "Trauma is not merely experienced but interpreted ... A child's perception of *what* happened is frequently quite accurate, and vivid veridical memories often persist long after a terrible event, but understanding *why* is harder."

# The exiled child

Irrational interpretations can themselves distort developmental processes and complicate recovery according to Judith Herman, and I've uncovered a number of my core beliefs, including: Don't hope for the best because the worst will always happen; Don't trust happiness because the rug will always be pulled out from under you when you least expect it. And most detrimentally, a belief that is so deeply embedded as to almost evade consciousness: You will be annihilated any minute now. These are the thought patterns that trigger the anxiety and panic so endemic among chronic trauma survivors, and they inform a dazzling array of symptoms and behaviours, most of which have eluded correct diagnosis for centuries.

During her 1990s reign as queen of daytime therapy TV, Oprah Winfrey liked to say that child abuse *changes who you are*. Neuroscientists now confirm that this is exactly what happens to a developing mind exposed to abuse and trauma. Louis Cozolino, Professor of Psychology at Pepperdine University in Malibu and author of *The Neuroscience of Psychotherapy* (W.W. Norton, 2002), describes how the systems of the brain link up to create experience: "When we reach a certain level of traumatic experience our brain does a number of things that don't enhance our ability to integrate experience. And that really is what dissociation is, it's a cutting off, it's a disconnection of different neural networks." In other words, trauma causes a profound split between the language-producing conscious part of the brain and the non-verbal, more primitive regions. In a "war zone", change takes place at the structural/neuronal level as an adaptation to relentless stress. When the "war" is over, the brain doesn't shift out of its now-programmed, fill-tilt limbic response; it gets stuck there and fires up even at minimal stimulation – real, metaphoric and metonymic. Therapy aims to heal this split between thoughts and feelings by encouraging speech connected to the traumatic event – activating cortical areas that allow a person to reintegrate neural networks dissociated by trauma.

Herman cites three categories of symptoms of complex post-traumatic stress disorder: hyper-arousal, intrusion and constriction. Hyper-arousal includes irritability and restlessness, impulsive and risk-taking behaviours, hyper-vigilance, sleep disturbances, and psychosomatic complaints. Intrusion comprises the flashbacks and nightmares typical of war veterans. And constriction entails various avoidance strategies: shutting down or out, surrender and psychic retreat, fantasy, numbing, trances and dissociation, in which the traumatic experience may "lose its quality of ordinary reality".

My hyper-arousal symptoms included asthma attacks during our time with Arthur. They stopped as soon as he left and have never reappeared. Traumatised people are also prone to "real" illness and impaired immune function as a result of inescapable stress. Waits cites several studies in which the experience of trauma "has been found to be associated with increased susceptibility to infectious diseases, autoimmune disorders, and cancer". I recall the surreal sense of derealisation that would descend on me during fights – they always felt like film, not quite of this world. In its most extreme form, this detachment presents as Dissociative Disorder (previously known as Multiple Personality Disorder, the condition made famous by films like *The Three Faces of Eve* and *Sybil*). This usually only develops in children subjected to early, severe and prolonged abuse. Most people who dissociate do so in less elaborate ways – amnesia for certain memories, absent-mindedness and a lack of clarity. As a teenager and young adult, I experienced almost complete amnesia regarding the violence. When a drug counsellor asked about my early life I told him I'd had a "happy childhood". I wasn't lying – I believed it; I couldn't remember.

But even (or maybe especially) in an amnesiac survivor, complex post-traumatic stress disorder can manifest as eating disorders, self-cutting, addictions, compulsive sexual behaviour, anxiety and/or panic disorder, phobias, obsessive/compulsive behaviour, perfectionism and over-achieving. Exhibiting lots of symptoms is no guarantee of diagnosis, though. Survivors suffer first from the condition, and second from a lack of understanding of it. As Judith Herman notes: "Because post-traumatic symptoms are so persistent and so wide-ranging, they may be mistaken for enduring characteristics of the victim's personality. This is a costly error, for the person with unrecognised post-traumatic stress disorder is condemned to a diminished life, tormented by memory and bounded by helplessness and fear." People often get frustrated with survivors and counsel them to simply "let go" of their anger or fear, failing to realise that: "The survivor is continually buffeted by terror and rage. These emotions are qualitatively different from ordinary fear and anger. They are outside the range of ordinary emotional experience, and they overwhelm the ordinary capacity to bear feelings."

Domestic violence has an undeniable effect on a child's self-esteem. In order to preserve faith in their caregivers, a child must reject the obvious conclusion that something is wrong with them. Instead, they will assume responsibility – and a belief in "innate badness" or "wrongness" is born. In an attempt to "construct some system of meaning that justifies it", the child "seizes upon this explanation early and clings to it tenaciously, for it enables her to preserve a sense of meaning, hope, and power". My sense of culpability was heightened by my belief that I had brought them together. Poor self-esteem can manifest as anti-social behaviour or it can be masked by an abused child's "persistent attempts to be good".

I was not an outstanding student, but I did excel at dance school. During the Arthur years, I threw myself into dancing with unprecedented zeal. I

## The exiled child

went to classes after school and all day Saturday. I pushed myself to the limit in one class after another – classical, jazz ballet, acrobatics – and it wasn't long before I was chosen to be part of an elite group of students who performed professionally on television and in shopping centre showcases during school holidays. I absorbed the showbiz ethic – "the show must go on" – and no matter what torments might have kept me up the night before, I would turn up and dance my heart out with a smile frozen on my face. But by early adolescence, I had given up both dancing and trying to be good.

Women aren't always the victims of violence, and men aren't always the perpetrators, and even when they are it's not always as clear-cut as many would like to think. My mother often provoked Arthur. At times it seemed she thrived on the chaos. If this reeks of "blaming the victim", to my child's mind it looked like "asking for it". I could never understand why, just when Arthur seemed to be settling down, she would slam doors, throw objects and revive the drama.

I bristle at the coupling of "women and children" when people speak of domestic violence, as if they were equal in their capacity to confront their circumstances. I hold my mother accountable for failing to seek help. However economically, emotionally, or otherwise trapped an adult may be by their abuser, whatever fears they hold for safety, they have power that a child does not. Perhaps this is what remains of my rage toward my mother: part of me says: "I don't care how much he broke you down, you were the mother and you should have protected me."

According to Judith Herman, the final step in the psychological control of the victim is not completed until they are forced to violate their own moral principles and betray their basic human attachments. The moment Arthur succeeded in forcing my mother to betray me is burned in my mind. He made no secret of the fact that he beat his daughter. He believed that whipping Stacey with a belt was an acceptable form of parental control. My mother had never hit me nor allowed anyone else to do so. But there came a day when Arthur decided that Stacey and I were equally guilty of some childish wrongdoing and that we should both be beaten with "the strap".

Stacey could take the beatings and she rarely cried, but I cowered and pleaded with my mother not to let him hit me. As the strap came down on my flesh, blow after blow, I screamed in anguish. She sat on the sofa and watched, her face twisted into a grimace of pain and guilt. I could see in her eyes that she knew she was violating us both, and my howling as she looked on is my "indelible image" of betrayal to this day.

We later lost many years in estrangement when my incomprehensible wrath was too great to stand being in the same room as her, and we reconciled only shortly before her death. My already troubled relationship with my father was also a casualty. In my child's mind, I reasoned that if he loved me, he would have known and done something about it. My relationship with Stacey, too, was shattered. We were not only no longer sisters; we weren't even on speaking terms. By the end of their stay, Stacey mimicked her father's abuse of my mother by writing barbed slurs on all of our belongings. The literature discusses the business of identification – a child will identify with one or the other of the adults. I identified with my mother, Stacey with her father. She slept through the fights. I rushed out of our bedroom fearing for my mother's life. I had no one with whom to share the terror. She had lived with violence all her life and accepted it as normal, having known no other reality, but to me it felt life-threatening every time.

It ended, finally, not with a bang but the whimper of my exhausted challenge. I told my mother that she had to choose: him or me. She took out an "apprehended violence order" and they left. I thought that was the end of the story, but it was just the beginning of my life as a traumatised person.

Like many trauma sufferers, I abused substances. I started smoking and experimenting with drugs at thirteen, by fifteen I was drinking heavily and consuming drugs recklessly. I over-ate and was depressive as a teenager; as a young adult I lived on the edge in an addiction to drama that I now know is commonplace. I had a volatile relationship that had its own share of violence, followed by others that kept my stress levels high. I started mainlining speed at twenty, and then turned to heroin. I was never tough and I was never cool – I was a messy addict, and not fussy. I'd take anything in any combination.

Sometimes, traumatised people are suicidal. I remember waking up from yet another heroin overdose and realising with absolute clarity that I was trying to kill myself. This realisation brought with it a sense of eerie comfort. But when I continued to survive overdose after overdose, I decided instead to live. Living in a non-self-destructive way was not something I knew how to do however, and quitting drinking and doing drugs was only the first of a series of necessary major changes.

I lived on mania and cigarettes and after the shock of adjusting to sobriety subsided, the trauma surfaced in dysfunctional and now painfully unanaesthetised relationships and as anxiety, which Judith Herman describes as a "major symptom of post-traumatic stress disorder". I was afraid of flying, tunnels, home invasion, the night and physical attack. I arranged my world so that these fears were rarely confronted and the disorder did not impinge on my life. Over the years, I developed new phobias: I was afraid of storms and became claustrophobic and agoraphobic. I developed an obsessive fear of illness and drug reactions, meeting Judith

## The exiled child

Herman's observation that chronically traumatised people often "perceive their bodies as having turned against them". The calmer my life, the more anxious I became. My brain was maladapted to "peace time".

Most of my friends considered me delightfully neurotic and eccentric, but my partners struggled to accommodate my relentless array of phobias, distortions, fractures, obsessions, compulsions, internal dislocations, and neediness. Everyone who has loved me has suffered by association. My friends could not have failed to notice my extreme self-absorption, although few had the insight to connect it to anxiety and trauma. Being mistaken for plain self-centred is one of many misreadings. Even if survivors finally see the connection between their past and present symptoms, it doesn't guarantee that others will extend the compassion they crave: if we ignore our past, no one knows; if we discuss it, we risk being seen as malingerers, as people who live in the past – which is, in a sense, exactly what we do, if not consciously.

"Traumatised people feel utterly abandoned, utterly alone, cast out of the human and divine systems of care and protection that sustain life. Thereafter a sense of alienation, of disconnection, pervades every relationship, from the most intimate familial bonds to the most abstract affiliations of religion and community." This passage from Herman's book might sound melodramatic, but it perfectly describes the non-trusting, faith-challenged world of the survivor.

Some time ago I found myself in hospital, a mystery "mass" revealed in a scan. The baffled doctors did not think cancer was likely, but I was not reassured. One night I phoned my father and told him how scared I felt, how certain I was that the news of further tests would be bad. He did what many have tried to do: he reasoned with me. He pointed out other possible explanations and counselled me to be patient, not to jump to conclusions. I was not consoled and he grew exasperated. His voice rose as he demanded to know why I was the way I was, why I always assumed the worst. I shocked myself by breaking down and making, for the first time, a direct connection between my traumatised past and my anxious present. I told him what it felt like never feeling safe, never knowing when the end might come. I told him how, in the wake of violence, a child hopes madly that it will not happen again and when it does, time after time, they learn to expect the worst. The worst feels more reliable than any other possibility. My father listened in stunned silence and his voice, when he spoke, was shaken. It stayed that way for weeks.

After the cancer scare passed, he emailed asking why I had never spoken of the violence. If only you'd told me, he said. I tried to explain the cone of silence that descends on violence and abuse. I can't recall whether anyone ever told me explicitly not to tell, but I knew. There was a teacher once who took a special interest in me. She might have suspected, but she never asked. No one did. If my father had asked the right questions, I am certain I would have told – but it's too much to expect a child who is carrying the weight of her own and her mother's misery and shame to confide in those by whom she feels abandoned. Even after many years of therapy, publicly breaking the silence is uncomfortable. As I write, I wrangle with feelings of disloyalty to my mother's memory and fear of being judged a whinger. But my desire to reach even one other traumatised person so that we both might feel a moment of solace is stronger.

The psychological effects of trauma do have an upside. Survivors often have a remarkable empathetic capacity and many work in the helping professions. Some days I think I'd trade my freakish antennae and super-sensitivity for a non-traumatised childhood and peace of mind in a heartbeat, but we don't get to rewrite the past – only our interpretations of it. When a crisis took me back to therapy a couple of years ago, I focused for the first time on the anxiety and panic disorder and its roots in trauma. Recovery is possible, but it's slow and arduous. Herman describes three stages of recovery: establishing safety and support; remembrance, mourning, reconstructing and telling the trauma story; and reconnection with ordinary life. My therapist thinks I'm in the third stage. Sometimes I think so too, and feel that I'm about to turn a corner into a new life rooted firmly in the present and a solid sense of self. Other days, I'm not so sure.

At the heart of a panic attack is an utterly overwhelmed child, saying: "I can't cope. Help!" Recovery means facing the fact that no one is coming; one must learn to soothe oneself. Medication is sometimes necessary but it is most effective when the survivor makes an active decision to use it as part of a broader recovery process.

Even well into recovery, the chronic trauma survivor remains vulnerable. High levels of stress or fresh trauma can set off a relapse. When my hysterical neighbour was wrestled to the ground and handcuffed in the hall outside my door, my husband did what most people would do: he backed off and watched from a distance, ready to help if called on. Without realising it, the scene triggered a deep cognitive activation in me, and I took my place in the eye of the storm – where I had always been – trying to placate my irrational and frantic mother, begging her to be reasonable and stop "making it worse", imploring her all-powerful assailants who were mismanaging her hysterics to back off and let her go.

When she was dragged off to St Vincent's psychiatric unit for an assessment I called three times to plead her case against committal. And when she was released and taken to the station to be charged with resisting arrest and assaulting a police officer, we were outside at two in the morning, in the cold,

## The exiled child

waiting for her. When she emerged, she said: "I'm broken." She stopped and lit a cigarette with shaking hands before walking off into the night.

I worried frantically about her the next day – ancient neurons were sparking and I was finding it hard to separate my neighbour from my mother and myself. When she knocked on the door and apologised, hiding her face in disgraced tears, I told her I too suffered from panic attacks and that I understood. I suggested she get a letter from a psychiatrist explaining that her behaviour was the result of the fight switch being activated in the "fight or flight response" of a severe panic attack, and told her such a letter might help her defence. I loaned her a book called *Power Over Panic* by Bronwyn Fox (Prentice Hall, 2001). She said wanted to find a therapist and I mentioned gingerly that the majority of people with panic disorder have experienced trauma or profound neglect, and that if this was the case she should look for a trauma therapist. She immediately disclosed that she had grown up with domestic violence. Me too, I said. And there we stood, two survivors, twenty-two years apart.

*Postscript:* The federal government has committed $1.8 billion in new funds for a five-year plan to include more primary health and clinical services for people with mental illness. This means Medicare will now rebate up to twelve sessions with a registered therapist. Australian researchers in 2000 estimated that 20,000 women seek shelter in women's refuges and take out protection orders each year. Clinical studies in emergency departments and antenatal clinics suggest up to a quarter of women will be subjected to domestic violence in their lifetime. Others argue that these numbers dwarf the reality, because they depend on police reports and domestic violence is often not reported.

I look at my neighbour and know she has a long, hard road ahead of her. And while twelve sessions is unlikely to take trauma survivors through all three stages of recovery, it is my hope that this initiative might nevertheless encourage them to seek the help they need to rebuild their minds and lives. ∎

References are available at www.griffith.edu.au/griffithreview

Meera Atkinson is a Sydney-based writer. Among her essays published in Griffith REVIEW are "From a moving car" in *Up North* and "Beauty and the Bêtê Noire" in *Making Perfect Bodies*.
Website: http://meera.atkinson.googlepages.com/

Essay:
**The words to say it**

Author:
**Charlie Stansfield**

*Image: Paul by Paul from the 'Tenant by tenant' series / Source: www.keithsaundersphotography.com*

# The words to say it

The funeral was held in a rural town in New South Wales on the hottest day that year. I nodded at the priest and he nodded at me and then we avoided each other's eyes for the rest of the brief service. A coffin sat in between us unadorned with flowers or symbolic belongings. The silent dry land surrounding the crematorium seemed a fitting backdrop to the event.

There was no eulogy about the great man he was, no generous accounts of the achievements of his forty-six years, no photocopied sheet containing his photo, a prayer and the words of a hymn to be sung. Just thin words that echoed around a room, two sweating professionals waving flies from their faces.

I don't know where he grew up. He was moved to a boarding house when the psychiatric hospital closed down. No historical records accompanied him. I don't know if he had a psychiatric illness, as he couldn't speak, was partially deaf and couldn't be assessed. I know that he had Hepatitis B, as it was written in large red texta on the front of a file with his name on it. He no doubt had a story to tell, but was never taught the words to say it. The boarding house was "for profit", and services from speech pathologists were not provided.

His name was George. I don't know if he had any family. For fifteen years, he lived in this rambling old house with thirty others also discharged from various psychiatric hospitals. They became his people. Sometimes he was "looked after" by other male residents, who occasionally spoke for him. "He needs the toilet," they might say. "He wants his tablets." During these brief relationships, he ran around waving his arms, scratching his legs until they bled, covering his face and hiding in corners. A local GP prescribed Haloperidol to make it easier for him "to be settled". He sometimes spat out the medication and stayed up all night. His end of the bedroom was empty, save for a single bed and mattress; his clothes often went missing. Nobody staffed the place after dark.

I don't know if he liked his tea sweet and white, but that is how it was served to him every morning because that is how it was served to everyone. Large aluminium pots were prepared with no-frills tea bags, powdered milk and sugar. Given the scale of abuse he experienced, it seemed trivial to ask what happened if he wanted his tea black, or in a mug rather than a plastic beaker.

He didn't smoke or drink, he was frightened of dogs, but he seemed to like sitting in the garden, stroking the family of cats who visited. He spent most days waiting at the front gate, his pallid face and distant expression melting into a childlike grin as he rushed to shake hands with the infrequent visitors who came and went. He wore shorts all year round, with his pale distended belly hanging over the top, and grey shoes with zips up the side. His skin was dry and scaly, his hands always cold.

He rarely left the boarding house grounds. Cut off from consumerism, he had neither litter to throw, nor unwanted goods to make landfill. In the pockets of his shorts, he sometimes kept a few smooth round pebbles. His presence was light. Any marks he left treading his small world were fragile, momentary, like footprints in the sand.

George died in hospital just after the boarding house had been closed down when the operator had to shut up shop. Government funding was suddenly made available and residents were moved to smaller community-based houses. He died just after he was given the opportunity to live with paid staff to support him, where perhaps someone would have been able to get to know who he was.

There are many more people buried in George's situation, but no one just like him. Forgotten people, living and dying in a parallel underworld, their voices silenced by neglect, their stories missing from our common history.

Back on that day in the rural west, the coffin creaked its way into the embers, and the priest cleared his throat. We looked at one another, perhaps both aware of a strange fleeting kind of intimacy now hanging in the air between us. The priest had rather kind brown eyes. I said "thank you" for some reason, and I left. I didn't ask what would happen to the ashes. On the drive back, I felt compelled to sing *Amazing Grace* loudly and out of tune to my car windscreen that was dotted with the blood of dead flies.

George's life and death have a bigger picture than the small country town where he and I first met. To look back at the story in a wider context might explain why, forty-six years after his birth, he was buried with only a priest and social worker looking on.

Since the 1980s, there has been at least one report every decade that highlights the failure of government to uphold the basic human rights of people with mental illness. The 2005 *Not for Service – Experiences of Injustice and Despair in Mental Health Care* by the Mental Health Council of Australia and the Human Rights and Equal Opportunity Commission cites New South Wales as one of the worst states in the country for responding to the needs of people with a mental illness. Although this story refers to New South Wales, the patterns are repeated in other states.

The deinstitutionalisation of large psychiatric hospitals from the late 1960s to the 1980s resulted in the discharge of substantial numbers of former patients into "the community". The movement was prompted by a number of factors. Psychotropic medications improved the management of symptoms of mental illness and/or the kind of trauma or pain that is sometimes conveyed in socially unacceptable ways. Although this improvement in treatment often represented a cost to the individual, in terms of side-effects it did also mean that more troubling behaviours were reduced and people no longer needed to be "contained". A philosophical shift promoted the integration of people with mental illness and disability into the community, where it was believed access to more normal lifestyles would be improved.

Unfortunately, the necessary resources did not accompany the movement of people. Even when the process involved the sale of hospital sites on large blocks of waterfront land, funding was not transferred back in any meaningful way to support the people who used to live there. Instead, psychiatric nurses – among other entrepreneurs – bought large buildings in the Blue Mountains, Hunter Valley and Sydney's inner west, then applied for licences and took in busloads of former patients. In short, the care of perhaps the state's most vulnerable people was placed in the hands of those looking for a small business to run.

Of course, standards in boarding houses differ – some provide better care than others – but the motive for all is essentially profit. People affected by mental illness, intellectual disability, brain injury, age-related illness, poverty and all of the above supply this profit by contributing their pensions for board and lodgings. They aren't protected by any of the tenancy rights of other rental situations and many are afraid to make complaints for fear of reprisals. They usually lack family or friends to check on them regularly.

Visit a boarding house in the inner west of Sydney and two things will be immediately conspicuous by their absence. One is light. Houses are characterised by gloomy, damp corridors and windowless rooms. The other is meaningful activity. Residents are often to be found sitting silently in rows of plastic chairs, smoking. They wait for the next cigarette to be handed out, or for the next mealtime to arrive, or they wait for visitors. Mostly, they just wait.

In the early '90s, the Carr Government launched the Department of Ageing and Disability and awarded it the responsibility for licensing boarding houses under the *Youth and Community Services Act* 1973. Initially, the new Licensing Branch was a dynamic. forward-thinking team of professionals determined to improve conditions and enhance people's lives. As a result of its early work, many operators could no longer rely on the profits they had been making, licences were revoked, places closed down. The work of the licensing branch, however, soon began to present the government with a dilemma as places closed; residents still needed somewhere to live. In George's situation, the local community took some interest in residents and there was a well-planned relocation into government-funded community houses. In other situations, places were closed down and people were moved to another boarding house owned by a friend of the first owner. In more than one situation, people who had lived together for twenty years were given a few hours' notice and then sent to live at opposite ends of the state.

While the government was tightening up on conditions, the boarding house operators themselves began to get organised and the Residential Carers' Association was formed. Some members sought legal advice and resisted the imposition of conditions by the licensing branch. As one owner commented: "When I got my licence in 1973 they nearly kissed me. I could go away and do as I liked. No one came near me for twenty years. Now they want to set standards."

In 2002, following complaints from community representatives, the NSW Ombudsman investigated the monitoring of boarding houses by the department, which by then had undergone a costly restructure and changed its name to the Department of Ageing Disability and Homecare (DADHC). The Ombudsman's report cites examples of inadequate investigation, documentation and resolution of allegations of neglect, sexual assault, abuse and financial mismanagement. In response, the department refers to 1999 legal opinion that advised it was beyond its power to legally enforce conditions other than the number of residents, the physical and structural requirements of the premises and certain record-keeping responsibilities. This Crown advice was received after seven successful prosecutions under this Act up until 1998.

A second Ombudsman's report released in 2006 raised concerns that the department was "still progressing" the integral issue of legislative review. Seven years after the gaps had been identified by several expensive consultants' reports, the inadequate legislation had still not been addressed because of what the department described as "competing priorities".

The tightly knit centralised licensing team has now long been disbanded. Instead, positions are regionalised and a more conciliatory approach to the monitoring of licences has been adopted. This is partly because the legislation doesn't support more uncompromising approaches and partly because the government does not want to deal with the problem of what to do with residents if sub-standard places close.

The department cannot insist that the criminal records of staff employed in boarding houses are checked. Nor can it ensure that residents are adequately nourished, or have medication dispensed properly. Although in some situations the act of monitoring and reviewing boarding houses has lifted standards, there is no legal weight behind department officers if they insist that an operator does something differently. The limitations of the legislation mean the department charged with responsibility for ensuring their care lacks the legislative power to protect residents. In one establishment, two women paying full board and lodgings with three-quarters of their pensions were also doing the cleaning and laundry for all other residents with no pay. In another, where there was allegedly no continuous staff presence and a front door that didn't lock, three women reported that they had been raped.

In a service model for vulnerable people that relies on "for profit" accommodation, monitoring of conditions and insistence on standards is vital to safeguard their wellbeing. While DADHC attended to its other more competing priorities, the people it can't legally protect have continued to wait and a new issue has begun to emerge.

A mysterious dwindling of the number of people reportedly living in licensed boarding houses has occurred since the early 1990s. In 1993 there were 179 licensed facilities across New South Wales, providing 3,900 beds. Currently there are fifty-five licensed facilities providing nine hundred beds across the state. Even allowing for the relocation of a group of five hundred very high-support needs people in the late 1990s, coupled with referrals to aged care and deaths, nobody officially knows exactly where the other thousand people have gone.

The department recently advised that there is now a closure process in place that incorporates an inter-departmental approach to assisting residents who might need relocation from a boarding house. It advised that "the majority of residents are able to choose their own accommodation in the event of relocation and the Department does not maintain records on their choices".

This policy decision makes it very difficult for long-lost family or friends who might want to regain contact to find a resident. "Choice" of alternative accommodation is often illusory. As the numbers of available beds in licensed facilities have decreased, there has been an increase in the number of operators who simply set up shop without applying for a licence. In the inner west of Sydney, there are an estimated ninety unlicensed boarding houses. Across the state, there are many more. Although a government licence does not guarantee a standard of care, it is almost impossible to monitor the unlicensed sector. In the same square of the city famous for its "baby chinos" and home renovations, there are reports of rooms in unlicensed boarding houses infested with cockroaches and other vermin, as well as unsafe structures – a ceiling fell in on a bed – which come from the non-government service providers who walk a fine line between supporting residents and not upsetting owners. It is hard to know how many people with disabilities or mental illness wait out their lives in these places. Since premises are not licensed, officially they do not exist. The residents remain something like patients of the old state asylums, confined to a parallel underworld – unseen, unheard and unknown.

Self-advocacy is a vital skill when your human rights clearly can't be upheld by legislation. For those who can choose, who perhaps have family support, life in a profit-making facility where conditions are reasonable might be preferable to living alone in a towering Department of Housing block. Most boarding house residents have, however, had years of disempowerment and little family contact. Those who cannot speak for themselves should be covered under the various treaties and international declaration of principles that Australia has been involved in developing, such as the Principles for the Protection of Persons with Mental Illness and for the improvement of Mental Health Care (United Nations General Assembly, 1991) for example. However, it is one thing to subscribe to human rights treaties, and quite another to implement them.

Sister Myree Harris of the Gethsemane Community has been an advocate on behalf of people living in boarding houses who cannot negotiate the system for themselves for over a decade. As part of the Coalition for Appropriate Supported Accommodation for People with Disabilities, she lobbies government departments and acts as a watchdog of the industry. She writes a lot of letters. Recently, she sent off another round to try to figure out why the 2006 year's funding for allied health was not transferred from DADHC to local health services. The lack of money meant that some boarding house residents who had been funded to receive essential podiatry services "to enable one woman to stand up" or dental care had to pay for it. One man had all his teeth removed and then had to wait twelve months for dentures. When he was finally eligible, his gums had shrunk and he could no longer wear them. Sister Myree painstakingly documents the human costs of bureaucratic slip-ups in her letters to various ministers and departmental heads. She tries to effect change, and freely admits to the frustrations inherent in her work. "It's the *absolute* poverty that gets you down," she says.

For the past two years, she has received a grant from the Paul Newman Charitable Trust. She uses the money to buy shoes for those who might otherwise manage through all seasons in a worn out pair of rubber thongs.

"Someone will go out with a volunteer, might have a coffee and buy a pair of shoes – have the sort of day at least once a year the rest of us take totally for granted," she said.

It's not enough money for all residents who might need shoes, but it is enough to help some. It's tempting to wonder where priorities might lie if our politicians and business leaders were to walk a mile in the old shoes of a boarding house resident.

It is easy to demonise the proprietors of licensed boarding houses for wanting to make money by cutting costs when providing care. However, some are people of goodwill who represent both the market's response to a shortage of low-cost affordable housing and the state's opting out of the responsibility for its most vulnerable. There is a lack of affordable housing in major cities across Australia – the kind of accommodation that can be secured by someone without rental references and a credit card to put the bond on.

In the sector generally, and certainly within DADHC, there has been a gradual tacit acceptance of conditions that the community and licensing teams once lobbied to change. Long-time workers in the field now find themselves saying that "some places aren't too bad" and others are "good enough". The yardstick "good enough" has plummeted since the deinstitutionalisation promises of community living. What we mean by "good enough" seems to progressively drop, year after year, as house prices rise.

Sister Myree fears that a crisis – a large-scale disaster – is what is needed before anyone will take this matter seriously.

"What kind of crisis?" I wonder out loud. "A resident being killed?"

"Nobody will care about that!" she snorts.

Martin Place is in Sydney's CBD. During weekdays at lunchtime, men and women in suits form impatient pin-striped traffic jams in a food hall that boasts cuisine from across the globe. One night I walked through this enclave where the banks and office towers rub shoulders like marble giants. An unusual stillness surrounded the place. Underneath security lights, a couple of men in a lone white van handed out plates of steaming food to a crooked queue of more than two dozen people. A young woman in a filthy tracksuit ate hers propped against a Harvey Norman store sign. Above her head, desktop devices to display digital photographs were advertised. From out of the shadows, a wild-haired man shuffled forward conducting a florid argument with an unseen entity, his feet pink with cold and black with city grime.

It's not really a mystery where the missing boarding house residents might have ended up, on a journey from state hospitals to licensed boarding house, and from unlicensed boarding house to the street. They're not even missing, really, but hidden. To be missing, someone has to officially notice that you're gone.

If we accept that the market can take care of impoverished people who have no choice, or that funding to mental health services in Australia at half the rate per capita than in the United Kingdom, the United States and New Zealand is satisfactory, are we not also supporting a view that people with mental illness, complex needs or disability do not deserve the lifestyles and conditions enjoyed by the rest? As many of us work long hours and struggle with our mortgages, other people's neediness seems to become another demand we don't want to think about. Meanwhile, we allow our elected representatives – who three decades ago had responsibility to support people with complex needs – concern themselves with more pressing vote-catching issues. ∎

---

Charlie Stansfield is a writer and social worker living in the inner west of Sydney. She thanks Sister Myree Harris from the Gethsemane Community, Leigh Connell from the Newtown Boarding House Program for statistics and stories and for discussing the issues, Katie Perry for the Martin Place anecdote and those who cannot be named.

# Tenant by Tenant

*Ann by John*

'Tenant by tenant' is an ongoing project, part of BighART's 'Northcott Narratives'. I work with tenants of the Northcott housing estate, in Sydney's Surry Hills, to make portraits of neighbours and friends on the site. Tenants are given the opportunity to find and invite a subject to be photographed, the only rules being those people must live at Northcott and the photograph must be taken at Northcott.

I don't teach the participants about the technical side of photography, though they learn about this during the process, but rather I am interested in the relationship that forms as a result of the portrait session.

These portraits have been instrumental in creating strong relationships between individuals, groups and communities on the Northcott Estate.

— KEITH SAUNDERS

*Other images from this series can be found featured throughout this edition and at www.keithsaundersphotography.com*

Essay:
# Boom! Excursions in fantasy land
Author:
# Julienne van Loon

Image: Margaret, Stickybricks dance night from the 'Tenant by tenant' series /
Source: www.keithsaundersphotography.com

Divided Nation

# Boom! Excursions in fantasy land

Midland: Recently I watched a small group of drunks on the pavement across from the Midland library swinging punches at each other. There were four of them standing in a circle, each giving voice to slurred phrases that I understood to be insults only because of the gruff musicality with which they flew from the mouth. One, a fellow in his sixties and too well-dressed to be a street-dweller, drew my attention. He had a certain dignity about him. I admired him as he stood tall, tilted his chin and challenged the man opposite. But then he swung his fist in a fast, wide arc, and the passionate force of it was all too much for him. He lost his balance and landed with a loud slap, flat on the grey cement pavement. The punch hadn't come within an inch of the other man, who stood tottering and looking as if he might fall over of his own accord at any moment. I wanted to laugh at this impromptu, weekday-afternoon slapstick: the grand, proud swing of the empty punch, the comical self-inflicted damage done by the fall. Part of me wanted to stay and watch the rest of the show, but my initial smile passed quickly.

There was suddenly something about the scene that was not at all funny. I bowed my head to climb into the car. As I started the engine, I took one last look at my man, still spreadeagled on the ground and moaning. No doubt he'd hurt himself. All that pride and energy in the swing, I thought, and for what? The street rang out with the futility of it.

In the recent Australian feature film *Last Train to Freo*, adapted from a play by Reg Cribb, two thugs get on a train at Midland, Perth's easternmost suburban rail terminus, and travel the full length of the line to Fremantle. As they do so, they leave their own welfare-class people behind and travel towards the city, and then beyond it, into the elite western suburbs where they plan to run amok.

"Not much dog shit around Midland anymore," says Trev, the tall thug, at the beginning of the film.

"No," replies his buddy Steve.

"The locals are pretty good at pickin' up after their dogs now."

"Yeah."

"Not much dog shit around Perth anymore really."

"No, not like the old days."

As a resident of Western Australia for the last ten years, I have dwelt mainly in the far eastern urban fringes of the state's sprawling capital – hence my local commercial centre is Midland. If you know Sydney, you know the term "Westie" and you are familiar with the idea that the city spreads from rich to poor, roughly speaking, along a route more or less east to west, from coastal plain to foothills. Here in Perth it's the same, though the compass points are reversed. The rich have water views along the western coastline, while the poor peg out land further inland, where the heat intensifies and the Fremantle Doctor fails to reach.

Midland interests me in part because of its huge number of welfare-class residents – Steve and Trev are recognisable types – but also because of the astronomical rate of development that has hit the area during the last few years. I didn't live here during "the old days", but one doesn't need to have been around for long to have witnessed radical change. Trev is right about the dog shit disappearing. At the moment, the whole commercial centre of the town is one vast construction site. The state government set up the Midland Redevelopment Authority (MRA) several years ago to steer in the changes and to excite investors. "Be a part of the New Midland," advise huge MRA billboards all over town. The place is being reimagined, reinvigorated. In commercial and residential real estate terms, it is positively booming. And yet a huge number of people you pass on the streets and in the shopping centres are recognisably poor, uneducated, many of them drug-fucked, unwell, aimless.

"I know, in this boom-time Perth," says Reg Cribb when I meet him for coffee in a neighbouring suburb, "in this boom-time stupor that we're in – our football team has won and our house prices have gone up, doubled – that there are real problems under that, which people in Perth are not interested in looking at."

Cribb's script takes a ruthlessly realist approach to representing the "white trash" element of Midland through the two main characters, Trev and Steve – one an ex-con and the other his young sidekick. The film makes obvious the growing divide between one class and another, and focuses pointedly on the ongoing problem of violence on Perth trains. While *Last Train to Freo* has been well received on the east coast and overseas, reviews published in Western Australia have been cold, even scathing. It seems reviewers in the West are offended that the City of Light might be represented in this way.

"People are not interested in seeing anything that challenges them at the moment, socially, politically," says Cribb. "One of the reasons I wanted to write [the script] was [because] I thought why, in the luckiest city in the world, are there so many unhappy people? I feel it. Steve says, in his monologue, he says everyone's richer, everyone's more beautiful, and you read the magazines and the paper and you think, I'm not feeling that way. I'm supposed to be, everyone's telling me I should be, but I'm not feeling that way. So, there's a lot of discontent around, you know, in the boom period. That interests me. And as soon as you say, in the paper, money doesn't make you happy, everyone goes 'Oh, come on, what do you know?' Or, 'Don't tell me that. Don't tell me I can't go to Morley Shopping Centre and be happy. I got nowhere else to go.'"

Julienne van Loon

A few blocks from the Midland library, my stepson lives with his girlfriend in a rented red-brick 3x1. They've just had a baby, my first grandchild – well, my de facto step-grandchild, to be precise.

"People use the term *non-biological*," these days, says a friend of mine. "It's just easier."

As I pull up in Leon's driveway to see baby Anna for the first time, I'm thinking about John Howard's $3,000 baby bonus, and what it means for a young couple like Leon and Sam, living entirely on welfare. As it turns out, their eyes are wide with the possibilities. Three thousand dollars is a great deal of money to a family of four living off six hundred dollars a week in outer suburban boomtime Perth. They mention digital cameras and MP3 players and possibly a second-hand car. I think about the cost of running a car – petrol, registration, maintenance – but say nothing, not wanting to rain on the parade.

Anna is sleepy, slightly jaundiced, only three days old. She is the perfect newborn, utterly awe-inspiring, even to a non-biological grandmother. Her eyes are closed, but her tiny face is expressive, attuned to every small noise or bodily sensation. She seems completely content in my arms. In the weeks leading up to Anna's birth, I have been worried for her. Her father, twenty-six, is a recovering addict. He was bright once. As we sit in the toy-strewn lounge room on a hand-me-down sofa, the television delivers brightly coloured light and noise to an otherwise dark room.

Sam seems remarkably confident and happy, even just a few days after the birth of her second child. She tells me she arrived at Swan Districts Hospital at nine on Friday morning, gave birth to the baby at midday, and was home again by five o'clock. She's very young. I wonder how many more babies are to come, and whether Leon can straighten himself out for them. If not …?

The newborn's face flinches slightly as her toddler half-brother slams a toy truck down sharply on the coffee table.

"She can hear you," I say to Jess, the toddler.

Anna's tiny lips purse and she screws up her face, as if to begin to cry for her mother, but then the idea is gone, quickly as it came, the face dreamily blank once more.

As I prepare to leave, the community nurse arrives, her bag bulging with the tools of her trade. She set up her scales in the middle of the coffee table and proceeds to place the naked Anna on the metal plate atop some light fabric.

"She's lost 600 grams," the nurse announces to two new parents whose faces seem suddenly stern and serious.

"Why's that?" says Leon.

"No, it's fine," says the nurse, reassuringly. "It's good. She's doing really well."

## Boom! Excursions in fantasy land

I wave goodbye, smiling at Leon who is still looking at the baby. There's hope for Leon in my heart, for the first time in a long time.

Port Hedland: I'm sitting in a hire car overlooking the coast at Port Hedland, some 1,800 kilometres north of Perth. This is the Pilbara, the so-called economic heart of Australia. Some years ago, I lived in this area and the place still captures my imagination. My second novel is set here, hence the reconnaissance mission. I am seeking details.

It is particularly obvious to me in a mining town like this, however, just how odd the pursuit of the arts can seem in the face of other, more immediately prosperous ambitions. Here I am, driving around in a hired Toyota, pulling up at the scene of a fictional murder and noting the colour of the dirt, the direction of the breeze, the scent of the wind. Or I'm trailing a character who seems to literally materialise as I traipse on foot along the Spinifex tracks past the edge of town at dawn or at dusk, trying to commit to memory the way the sky changes colour, how the light floods in, while dusty work vehicles, their tyres purring on the hot black streets, carry tired workers to and from their latest shift.

I visit the tourist information centre at least every second day, mainly to look up the common and botanical names of local flora and fauna in a glossy picture book I don't want to have to carry back with me on the plane. It is July, and peak season for the grey nomads – relaxed couples who travel with camping trailers, caravans or Winnebagoes that crowd the parking bays in the main street. Their conversation with the tourism officer is always the same: they are looking for accommodation, and the woman at the desk is phoning one place after another on their behalf. The answer is always in the negative. She relays this with a shake of the head during her mostly monosyllabic dialogue with the person at the other end of the phone line.

"What are we going to have to do?" says a man in long socks and sandals, his shorts hitched high on his bulging belly. "Camp in the gutter?"

"I'm sorry, sir, there's just nothing."

"The only thing I can suggest is to keep driving. Are you heading south?"

"Yes."

"You could try the caravan park at Karratha."

I feel sorry for the nomads. Everybody knows the caravan parks in Karratha are overflowing. There are whole families camped there for months on end. Last week's paper had a photograph of a boilermaker and his wife with two kids under five. They'd been living in a tent for more than a year. As a sub-contractor, there was no employer-sponsored accommodation for them in the town, and they couldn't afford to pay the going rate of six hundred dollars a week to rent a house. The couple were talking of moving back down to Perth.

"How far is Karratha?" the retiree at the counter wants to know.

Julienne van Loon

"Two hundred kilometres."

Theirs is a variation of the same conversation I hear each afternoon as I sit in the foyer at my motel and check my email, while the receptionist answers one phone call after another.

"No, I'm sorry, we've got nothing."

"Have you tried Best Western? Nothing there?"

"No, I'm sorry. We're fully booked."

In the early evening, I sit gratefully in my lack-lustre motel room, filling in the details of a scene for the new novel. The scene is set on the edge of the coast a little north of town, where two lovers get to know each other better amidst a broad, unfamiliar landscape. I have one or two paragraphs still to develop, but my concentration is waning. I am distracted by the booming voice of a contractor who has arrived to take up residency in the room next door. He's just flown in from Darwin and, for the last forty minutes, he's been walking up and down in his room, and sometimes out along the landing, bellowing instructions into the mouthpiece of his mobile phone.

"If my voice is funny tomorrow morning, you'll know it's because I've got me nuts in a vice," he'd confided to the couple of workers who'd dropped him off earlier.

"Ah, you'll be right, mate. It'll be fine," said one of the men.

"I hope so, mate."

Since then, the man from Darwin has been spending money like it's going out of fashion. He's just ordered at least half a dozen big pieces of machinery over the phone – dozers and excavators and trucks – spending tens of thousands of dollars at a time.

"Listen," he is saying into the mobile, "I think what we're going to have to do is send someone out to the site to service them every coupla months. I think that might be the best way to do it. Save us fart-arsing around with having to bring 'em back into town."

I feel suddenly inadequate. It is as if my project is worthless, as if my reason for being – a writer of fiction *for chrissake* – is just a mere speck of fly shit on the exhaust pipe of one of these great yellow Tonka toys the mining boys bash about up here. But then, I wonder, whose fantasy is this? It strikes me that the boys themselves are living in one great big imaginary sandpit. Sure, there's money to be made, but when the bubble bursts, there'll be one hell of an empty landscape – far emptier than it was when *wadjilas* first arrived.

On the plane home, I sit next to a mine worker a few years younger than me. He's fine looking, in a boyish way, and shares a joke periodically with one of his workmates, who sits in the row in front of us. He and I smile at each other, but stop short of conversation. Once the plane reaches full height, we both lean back in our chairs and sleep. When I open my eyes, half an hour from Perth, the young miner is looking at me.

"How'd you sleep?" he asks.

We get to talking and I discover he works at a remote mine several hundred kilometres north-east of Hedland, eight days out of fourteen. He does rolling ten-hour shifts. And now he has six days off and he's flying all the way to Melbourne just to go to a party, his younger brother's twenty-first. The young mechanic has worked at various mine sites in the north-west and in the territory as well, he says, but he hasn't stayed anywhere longer than eighteen months.

"It's pretty rough and ready out at the mine," he says. "No telephones, no television."

No women, I think, but keep that to myself.

"I don't know how you can stand it."

"It's good money."

This is true. When he'd first asked me about my work, I told him I was a lecturer at the university. He'd looked embarrassed when I returned the question.

"Oh," he'd muttered, "I'm just a mechanic."

But the fact is that as a mechanic he earns something like $85,000 a year, which is more than I earn, and more than most Australians earn.

"What do you do with it all?" I ask him.

"Hey?"

"What do you spend all your money on? All that time out at the mine with nothing to do …"

"Just …" he falters, "well, just party, really. On my days off, I come into town, and live it up a bit with me mates."

Fly-in, fly-out: My sister's house in McMasters Street, Victoria Park is a two-bedroom double-brick place built almost a hundred years ago on a massive block. "The plan is to put two or three townhouses at the back," Lola explained when she and the family first moved in a year ago, "and then we'll fix up the main house for ourselves with a little courtyard garden at the front." At the moment, though, the backyard is an expansive dustbowl, good bathing for the family's fifteen-year-old dog, who looks decidedly miserable most of the time. The townhouse plan has not yet got to paper, mainly because a huge amount of money is tied up in a second investment property fully mortgaged up in Broome.

In the meantime, Lola makes me tea in the tiny crumbling kitchen, tacked on to the back of the house some decades ago and untouched since, bar a paint job or three.

"Do you want to go halves in a muffin?"

Julienne van Loon

This is inner-suburban living, Perth style. Victoria Park is walking distance across the causeway bridge to the CBD and the home of the former premier, Geoff Gallup. According to the City of Perth website, the city is officially "Boom Capital of Australia". The council boasts that "Western Australia's domestic economy grew at 14 per cent in the June quarter 2006, higher than China's growth rate of 11.3 per cent and higher than Australia's GDP growth of 2.3 per cent". Indeed, Perth has become one of the major centres for the energy and resources industry in the Asia Pacific region. But it is also the capital of a kind of single-parent household difficult to measure using official figures.

Lola's house is one such example: it is a house run almost entirely by women. My brother-in-law works several thousand kilometres to the north and flies home for the weekend once every three or four weeks. Lola's son, aged twenty, also works away, in his case via a fly-in, fly-out arrangement at a mine north of Kalgoorlie. Lola and her teenage daughter have the house to themselves most of the time, which also means that they have more than the lion's share of the household chores and responsibilities.

Men involved in the mining industry – particularly those employed using a fly-in, fly-out rostering practice – are earning huge money, working long shifts. Out at the mines, the men are fully catered for with three meals a day and serviced accommodation. Most of the time, however, their accommodation is a single bed in a donga the size of a wardrobe. According to the latest figures, West Australian men now earn an average of $1,168 a week, which is $63 above the national average. Meanwhile, women in this state have a full-time wage which is $56 below the national average, and those with husbands working away carry the added burden of living day to day as a virtual single parent.

What interests me about the households of these long-distance commuters, however, is not so much the economics of their situation, but the emotional and psychological effects of these strange living arrangements. The dynamics of such households vary enormously, depending on whether the patriarch is present, absent, expected any moment, or just on his way out the door. Children demonstrate a kind of Jekyll and Hyde behaviour accordingly. But it is not just the women and children who are affected in the long term. Nicholas Keown, a researcher at the University of Western Australia's Rural Clinical School, conducted a study on the health of male workers in the goldfields region and is quoted in *Australian Mining* in August 2006 as being particularly alarmed about psychological problems among male mine workers. According to Keown, more than one in three long-distance-commute workers show symptoms of minor psychiatric problems such as anxiety, depression, substance abuse-related disorders or chronic fatigue. And who wouldn't? These are people working ten or twelve-hour revolving shifts, living in austere accommodation amongst an almost purely male population, and so far away from family and friends that their mobile phone goes completely out of range. It sounds like a kind of Siberian hard-labour camp.

# Boom! Excursions in fantasy land

I am not trying to suggest that anybody is being subjected to such situations against their will – there are, after all, vast quantities of money to be made. Last week, at my local supermarket, I listened to two mothers of young children in the line in front of me comparing notes about having their husbands working up north.

"Well, it's just the way it is, I suppose," one of them concluded. "We just have to get used to it."

"Yeah, that's it," said the other.

"Everybody knows somebody in exactly the same situation."

"Absolutely."

I heard a story recently from a working mother who lives in one of Perth's new housing estates. Sue was running late to pick up her kids from school and, as she reversed out of her driveway, she noticed a little boy of around three standing alone on the neighbour's verge. The boy looked lost and confused. Sue stopped the car and got out to ask the child if he was okay. The boy was too shy to speak. Sue didn't know what to do. She didn't recognise the boy's face as a local to the area and she was conscious that she was already running late, but it didn't feel right to leave the child. After a few minutes of one-way conversation, she coaxed the boy into her car, and drove on up the street. She thought perhaps he belonged to a neighbour she didn't know, a little further along, and that if she drove slowly he might recognise a house. Hers is a long, winding street, house after brand new house – all neat as pins – and as Sue drove along, she realised that she didn't really know any of the people in her own street.

The front yards were uniformly devoid of life. Everybody, including herself, was usually so busy with being at work, or getting on with day-to-day commitments, ferrying kids here and there, that they didn't have time to recognise each other, never mind stop and speak. The little boy sat beside her in the front passenger seat looking puzzled. She drove on, and wondered what people might think of her, having just put this child in her car and driven off with him. Suddenly the child's eyes widened, and Sue thought perhaps he recognised where he was. There was a particular house. She pulled up the car, and followed as the boy sped around the side through an open gate, and into a backyard where a woman was crouching down, her back curved over her gardening. The boy's mother said: "Oh, he was just here with me a minute ago," and Sue said: "Well, actually, that can't be right, because he's been with me for more than twenty minutes and it must have taken him quite some time to walk all the way up to my house."

Afterwards, it was not the boy having wandered off or the mother's negligence that bothered Sue. Rather, it was the sense of isolation – the terrible knowledge that she lived in a community of strangers. Here they all were, working madly to pay off new mortgages, and feeling safe in the knowledge that the price of real estate was increasing, they were investing in their future, and yet ... this is the street where she lives. Every house harbours a hard-working couple, and she doesn't know any of them. They don't know her. Where is the security in that? And what are they worth to any of us, really, she thought – these sparkling, half-million-dollar houses? What do they actually cost?

Coda – Midland: It's a weekday morning and I am back at my local shire library in Midland. The building is a double-storey affair with a modest fiction collection and a predictably motley set of regulars who the librarians know by name and who spend long periods reading newspapers, or conducting loud nonsensical conversations with themselves as they circle the stacks, passing the time, passing the time. Public libraries suit me well, and I have done some of my best writing in them, the background muttering of slightly lost souls, coupled with the occasional high-pitched squeal of a toddler letting loose a tantrum in the children's section, permits me to observe and eavesdrop in between productive periods of hush. Today, however, I am not here to write, or even to research, so much as to get out of the house.

Writing fiction is rarely a full-time job for me. In a good week, I can manage to spend three solid half-days on my latest work-in-progress and occasionally, thanks to a break in the university calendar or an official writer's residency, I manage a stretch of a few intense weeks at a time. But lately, I have been making use of a grant from the Australia Council, and have the rare gift of a three-month stretch with which to make good headway on a new book. Yet I find myself edgy, distracted, even distraught. After a month, I am wishing for any other kind of job – any other occupation at all. I am too much inside my own head.

This morning in the library, I am caught up – as usual – in daydreams. I am like a ghost, living half inside an unwritten draft of something only half-imagined. The other half is lodged here, in the real physical world of the fluorescent air-conditioned library building with its gaudy colour-coded stickers on the spines of every book. I am on the second floor and I can't find what I'm looking for in the non-fiction section; I'm not sure the thing I am looking for even exists. As I return to the stairs to make my way back to the ground floor, I pass a man in a creased blue rayon suit seated at one of the desks. I had seen him out on the street a little earlier, and something about the way he walked with his arms hanging stiffly at his sides and his gaze glued to the pavement made his destitution obvious, even at some distance. Now, in the library, I trace a path around him as if to give him a wide berth. But then I notice that he is busily writing something with a blunt pencil on the back of a recycled sheet of A4 paper. I change direction, walk a little closer and glance over his shoulder at the untidy scrawl.

It begins: "In London, the ...

I am strangely reassured to find that there is some kind of narrative going on inside his head, as there is so frequently in mine, something calling out to be extracted, expressed, something not completely obvious to the outside world. But then there is the man's body language, the way he hunches forward over the page, one hand fingering, obsessively, the fabric of his blue rayon pocket. Perhaps I have been too quick to romanticise. Perhaps his scrawl is the merely the product of a serious delusion. He probably thinks he actually is in London. "Yes," I think, "that's right; he's in fantasy land, whereas the rest of us are … what?"

We all have the need to invest in some kind of narrative, some kind of future scenario, collective or solitary. How else could we get out of bed in the morning?

Later I pass the man in the blue suit again, as I drive home. I wonder what he is thinking. He is in the thick of The New Midland, heading for a small public park opposite the old Midland primary school (now fully renovated and home to the Australian Opera Studio). Perhaps "park" is not the appropriate term for this small square – "green space" might be better. The word "park" implies somewhere people might want to play, or sit, or meet. But this new zone, the centrepiece of which is a bright new metal sculpture – an abstract human body with an expressionless face – has no seats for passers-by, and the trees have been planted in raised beds full of ground cover and wood-chip so that the grassed area in the centre harbours no shade. This is a space designed to be looked at, not used. The drunks, the homeless, the drug-fucked are not welcome here. Which begs the question: if those left behind by the resources boom cannot dwell here, where can they dwell? After all, this particular suburb – as it is so clearly represented in Reg Cribb's *Last Train to Freo* – is already the end of the line.

Notes: For the sake of privacy, the names of several of the people mentioned in this essay have been changed. Donga is a colloquial West Australian term for the transportable accommodation frequently used as single men's quarters at remote mining sites. Most dongas fit the dimensions of a sea-container to be transported easily by truck. For more information on wages, see David Uren and Alana Buckley-Carr's article, "WA wages boom", *The Australian*, 19 May 2006. Nicholas Keown's research is quoted in "Health Crisis in Goldfields", www.ferret.com.au, 15 August 2006. ■

Julienne van Loon is the author of the Vogel Award-winning novel *Road Story* (Allen & Unwin, 2005). Her new novel, *Backtracking* will be published later this year. Her essay "Everyday violence" was published in *Griffith REVIEW 13: The Next Big Thing*.

Divided Nation

# Memoir: Stranger in a strange land
## Author: Phil Brown

"You don't look Chinese," said one of a small group of boys who had encircled me.

"I'm not," I said, stating the obvious.

"But ya come from Hong Kong?"

"Yes," I agreed.

"What language do they speak there?" asked one of the others.

"Cantonese."

"Well can you say something in Camponese," said the one who appeared to be the ringleader. "Go on … Chink."

I obliged, feeling like an act in a cruel circus sideshow. It was my first day at Miami State High School on Queensland's Gold Coast in late 1969 and I may as well have come from the moon. Nowadays, immigrants from the southern states stream into the Sunshine State (or Smart State, as the Premier would have it) at the rate of around a thousand a week, heading for the booming southeast. Queensland has had the largest net migration of any state since 1971, when about 250 more people arrived than left the state each week.

So, even when I arrived, there were other newcomers – but few from Hong Kong. Nowadays the hordes that flood across the Tweed River have a pretty good idea about the place they are moving to. I came completely unprepared. I felt like Billy Bunter might had he been lowered on to the set of *Lord of the Flies*.

Pallid, bespectacled and with an international accent that was not quite British – but British enough – I was a stranger in a strange land where I should have belonged. We were, after all, Australian. I had lived in Hong Kong for all my primary schooling and two years of high school. I had been tutored in British history by British teachers, discovered literacy with a little help from Enid Blyton and A.A. Milne and comics like The Beano and Dandy. We were members of the exclusive and rather colonial

## Stranger in a strange land

Kowloon Cricket Club, had servants at home, and at night my transistor would lull me to sleep with the sounds of the BBC.

Our migration back to Australia and to the Gold Coast – our promised land (we had holidayed there and my parents fell in love with the place) – was a jolt. It gave me an enduring window of understanding into what it is like to be displaced and divided from the dominant culture and people of a place – a place you hope to call home. At least I looked vaguely the same, despite minor anomalies – thickish spectacles, hair too short and a refined accent that had to be expunged as soon as possible.

I was appreciated as an oddity, though my ability to curse in Cantonese did give me some cachet. But I was different.

For a start, I was actually from New South Wales, although I recalled little about the place that I now know is a reviled state where the people are riven with envy of their cousins in the land of the cane toad. Decades later I find the clarion call "Queenslander" rising in my throat around State of Origin time and, though I have never joined the boo-a-blue campaign, I understand the urge to do so.

But not back then, on the cusp of my teens. I was marooned in the dusty surfside schoolyard with no cultural terms of reference and little understanding of the lingo. Colloquialisms left me dumbfounded. I didn't know how to respond to even the simplest "G'day" and the surfing sub-culture to which most boys were hip was entirely foreign to me.

Gingerly, I felt my way, – mastering phrases like "fair dinkum" and beginning to understand what "board shorts" were and what "stoked" meant. I began to lose the smooth tones with which I had come equipped from King George V School in Kowloon.

I realised I was totally cut off from my fellows by my inability to surf. Riding a surfboard at Miami – where good waves meant mass truancy and surfing ability established your status – was a vital ingredient for belonging.

I talked my father into buying me a surfboard and spent difficult months humiliating myself in the shore breaks south of Surfers Paradise, away from the crowds, trying to gain some mastery of the sport. Blond hair was de rigueur and, after long enough in the sun, the top layer of my hair lightened and the constant exposure to the sun turned my skin a deeper brown than it had been. I started to look like I belonged.

But a feeling of being an outsider lingered, even as I climbed the ranks of the surfing subculture. In the final years at high school, I was accepted into a fraternity of local surfers around Broadbeach –

by invitation only – but still felt like an outsider looking in, even though I had mastered the equipment and the language of my chosen milieu.

Once experienced, that feeling of displacement, of otherness, remains. It has been rekindled in country towns and cities in the decades since my initial displacement.

It resurfaced when my wife and I moved to Melbourne in the early 1990s. I felt that same sense of isolation I had experienced when I arrived on the Gold Coast for that dusty school year. We landed in Melbourne the month Jeff Kennett was elected premier in 1992. At the time, Victoria was bleeding northwards as the climate migrants were joined by the economic migrants on the road north.

Driving into the city, past Pentridge Prison, down Sydney Road, through Coburg, we were amazed to find ourselves jockeying with trams for space on the narrow road. We sensed that we were going in the wrong direction. A Queenslander in Victoria felt like being a boy from Hong Kong on the Gold Coast.

During those first months in Melbourne – months when it barely stopped raining – I worked casual reporting shifts at *The Sunday Age*, where my co-workers seemed amazed that I could use a computer and that I wasn't still scratching my name in the ground with a stick. To those Victorians who didn't aspire to become Queenslanders, we banana benders (I counted myself as one by then) seemed a near-Simian species, relics of a pre-Neanderthal world, heathens who didn't worship the Gods of aerial ping pong – a crude people ruled over by an inarticulate dictator who grew peanuts when he wasn't lording it over the populace.

Back in Brisbane several years later, I found that I actually felt at home. I had only moved to Brisbane in 1986, but had been living in Queensland – despite a couple of forays to Sydney and that three-year stretch (I sometimes find myself describing it as a "sentence") in Melbourne – since 1970. But I still felt like a foreigner at times.

As welcoming as Brisbane has always seemed to me, I am aware that I am not a native. However much I feel like one at times, I know I am not, and this divides me – in fact, us – from our neighbours. My wife is from Townsville – a place even Brisbane folk feel they can look down on – and she feels the same.

Not having grown up and been schooled in the place where you live is one way you are always separated from those who have that experience. It becomes obvious when people talk of local loyalties. The private school old boys' and girls' network is the most obvious example, and demonstrates how a certain foreignness can never be overcome. Our son Hamish, born in Brisbane's Mater Mothers Hospital and a true native of this subtropical city, goes to a small Catholic school in Brisbane's inner north. Many of the parents who have kids at this school went to school together in the surrounding suburbs. Their networks, based on this shared history, seem impenetrable to us. Through shared experience, they have strong bonds of locality and fraternity, and outsiders like us can never quite get inside.

The private school network is strong in Brisbane, and separates an echelon of society from the rest of the populace. I went to a rugby game at Ballymore once and felt isolated in a sea of people, most of whom had the private school system in common. The men who surrounded me – doctors, lawyers, dentists, bankers – all shared school and sporting bonds that had lasted through university and on into their business and family lives.

One cannot under-estimate the importance and power of the ties – literally, the old school ties – that bind these people.

As an outsider, you clutch at straws to try to establish credibility as a sort of local. I'm lucky: my mother is a Queenslander – born in Bundaberg, the second daughter of an Ipswich-bred bank manager from an established family. The family's roots go back to the early colony when an ancestor, John Scott, arrived in Brisbane from Scotland. He started a school in the fledgling city and later another in Ipswich, and is noted as a man of achievement in the book *Moreton Bay Scots*. I quote this regularly in attempt to establish my bona fides as a member of a founding family. My mother went to Brisbane Girls' Grammar as a boarder, which is also helpful in establishing a line of credibility in the social strata of Brisbane. Still, deep down, there is unease and a feeling that, despite her pedigree, I will never truly belong in the way others do.

Mind you some of those who really belong also feel they don't. If anyone has earned the right to belong, it is David Malouf, who is lauded as the quintessential Brisbane author, even though he hasn't lived here since he was a young man. His *Johnno* is still recognised as the great Brisbane novel and was recently dramatised. His Queensland roots resurfaced in his last two superb collections of short fiction, the brooding *Dream Stuff* and *Every Move You Make*.

But Malouf is an insider who always seems to have felt like an outsider, and this underpins the consciousness of Dante, the protagonist in *Johnno*. Perhaps there is some value in this. Certainly the feeling of otherness provides perspective that is valuable for a writer. Being relaxed and comfortable, feeling part of a place and happy, connected and at home probably don't help engender the creative tension a writer needs – which makes one look and question, rather than accepting the status quo.

Being an outsider can be uncomfortable, even painful. In a city, you can be invisible. But there are plenty of others in the same boat.

In a small country town, an outsider stands out. When I lived in the Central Queensland town of Monto for a year in my early twenties, I felt this intensely. I had long hair, an earring and John Lennon glasses, and was a distinct oddity on the local scene. In my first weeks, I was an object of interest and ridicule. What passed for the town bikie gang leader challenged me for being in "his town" on one occasion, and I narrowly escaped a beating thanks to the intervention of a larger, friendly local.

I joined another small group of outsiders – bank Johnnies, teachers and the local dentist – as a bulwark against the alienation. Luckily, a close friend from uni days lived in the town, and this gave me an entrée.

In Brisbane, things are different. I have now been here long enough to feel like a real resident. I have spoken to other immigrants – I know I will always be one – and they suggest that after a decade or so they too felt they began to belong. This expresses itself as a change of loyalties: I should probably support the Newcastle Knights (as I was born in the Hunter Valley) and the Blues, but some time in the early '90s I noticed I had become a rabid Maroons fan. As an outsider, you tend to cling to things that connect you to the culture. Sport is a good shortcut.

One of the reasons we felt alien in Melbourne was disinterest in the local sporting religion – AFL. When challenged about which team we supported, we looked blank and said "none". This was usually met with utter disbelief, sometimes anger, followed by abuse. We knew we were undesirable aliens.

There is a lesson to be learnt from this. When I'm at lunch and I hear someone talking about the ripping try they scored in a GPS rugby match between Nudgee and Terrace in 1974, perhaps I should nod knowingly. But I would probably give myself away sooner or later. Those who truly belong have a shared language that connects them to their common past. Only the initiates speak this language; it is the verbal equivalent of a secret handshake.

In a different way, many of those who come to Queensland from Victoria have developed their own sense of belonging by continuing to act as if they still live in Victoria. When you move to Victoria, you are supposed to convert to AFL football, for example, and blend in with the culture; when the Victorians came here they brought their own football. They flock to support the Brisbane Lions and, at The Gabba, imagine they are still at the MCG shouting "c'arn, c'arn" until hoarse. Some hang on to their traditional teams as well, and still live in a virtual Victoria, oblivious to local customs and culture. The Brisbane Broncos or the Queensland Reds are, to them, proponents of "cross-country wrestling". They will never understand why Queenslanders bother with such foolish games.

I have even heard Victorians claiming to have invented Queensland, as a place to escape to when the grey days of winter become intolerable. Noosa, a Victorian newspaper once posited, is a Victorian invention – an enclave in a foreign state set up largely for and by them, a place to share their culture with the inferior long-term locals.

A superiority complex is a novel way of overcoming the problems of being a stranger in a strange land. ■

---

Phil Brown is a Brisbane-based journalist and author. His most recent book is *Any Guru will do* (UQP 2006). His memoirs have been published in *Griffith REVIEW 10: Up North* and *Griffith REVIEW 12: Hot Air - how nigh's the end?*

Fiction:
# I'm not here
Author:
**Dominique Wilson**

*Image: Ling Zhang by Peter from the 'Tenant by tenant' series / Source: www.keithsundersphotography.com*

# I'm not here

If she hurries she may still eat today. She shuffles down the empty street, a small Vietnamese woman dressed in a floral polyester dress and a man's grey cardigan with a long ladder up one arm where the wool has unravelled, held closed by a piece of rope at the waist. On her legs a sagging pair of football socks hand-knitted in bright red and white stripes, on her feet a pair of men's black lace-up shoes without laces. A burn scar, brown and wrinkled and tight, runs on the left side of her face from her lip to her ear and down her neck, pulling the skin downwards so that little white puffs of moisture punctuate each of her breaths as air escapes the permanent gap that exposes broken and rotting teeth. She clings to two white supermarket bags that bulge with her treasures, and as she shuffles she mutters: "I'm not here. I'm not here. I'm not here."

She hurries, crossing Queen Street diagonally, anxious to get to the market. She's late. The sky is just beginning to lighten and she knows the market-gardeners' trucks have started to arrive, their drivers loud and boisterous, cheerfully unloading their crates of produce in readiness for the day ahead. As she crosses the car park, the lights of Melbourne's Queen Victoria Market come on. She's too late. For a moment, she stands still in the dark, watching. She hears a truck coming up behind her and turns, blinded by its headlights. The truck swerves and she hears the driver's curse but doesn't understand his words. She watches it enter the market. There is still a chance.

Bent at the waist so as to better see under the empty stalls she zigzags across the market, occasionally picking up a wilted cabbage leaf, a half-rotten apple. Under one stall she finds an onion, whole and glossy and fresh, and she holds it in both hands for a moment, gently stroking its brown papery skin before placing it carefully at the bottom of one of her bags.

"Hey Tony, get a load of this!"

"Leave 'er, mate. She comes here sometimes. Doesn't do any harm."

She looks at the men, alarmed. She hadn't heard them arrive. *I'm not here. I'm not here.*

"Shit! What happened to her face?"

"Don't know, mate. Reckon she's been in an accident or something." He turns, takes an orange from his truck and holds it out, but she dares not approach. "It's okay love, you can have it …" and he gently rolls it towards her. She watches it until it stops at her feet, picks it up and scurries out of the market into the dawn.

I'm not here

A fine drizzle falls as she uses side streets and laneways to avoid roaming patrol cars, but today she doesn't mind the rain. She has food. And she has the onion and the orange. She will keep the onion for a day when she has nothing else but the orange she will share tonight with Ted. She sidesteps a drunk curled up in a doorway, watched by a black and white cat. The city is beginning to awaken. Cars swoosh across tram tracks. Eager office workers, their grey suits echoing the grey buildings they hurry towards, pass her by, oblivious to her presence. A young woman runs toward her, umbrella held high, the tight skirt of her business suit hindering her steps, high heels click-clicking on the footpath.

"Michael! Michael, wait!"

*Michael? Is Michael here?* She turns, her gaze following the young woman. *Michael?* She watches the woman rise on tiptoes to kiss the man, watches them link arms and walk away, umbrella shielding both. *Michael?*

Thuy stirred rice noodles into the pot of *pho*, breathing in the fragrance of ginger and onions. Soon Father and Younger Brother Quan would return with their catch, and would expect their breakfast while she helped her mother sort the fish. She removed the pot from the fire and looked out over the rice paddies that spread out to the hills. The rains had come early to Phuoc Tuy Province and the rice crop promised to be abundant – if it was given a chance to grow, and was not destroyed by Nature or Man.

She thought of the soldiers who had come through her village since she was a little girl – the Viet Cong mostly at night, the South Vietnamese during the day. Then, when she was about eleven, a new type of soldier had come from a country for which they had no name, and so they had called them *Uc-da-loi*, which meant "Men from the South". More and more had come each day, and they had frightened her with their uniforms and guns and helicopters that swept low over her village. But her father had comforted her and said he would not let them hurt her, because although she was only a girl she was his treasure and he would always protect her. More than four years had passed and now she had grown used to them, as had everyone in the village. They knew their country was at war, but their lives and thoughts centred on growing enough food and catching enough fish to feed the village, and the constant stream of hungry soldiers.

The morning was already hot and the air smelt of wet earth, smoke and spices. Thuy could hear gunfire in the distant hills, but this too had become normal. She saw a jeep speeding towards her village, the soldiers shouting and shooting into the air, and she ran behind the woodpile, ready to slip into the tunnel it hid. The jeep skidded to a stop. A Viet Cong jumped out, still yelling and shooting, and Thuy knew this visit would be different. She saw Father and Younger Brother enter the village carrying a basket of fish between them, and she wanted to call to them to stay away. The soldier saw them and ordered Father to him, made him kneel and kicked him in the groin, demanding to know where the *Uc-da-loi* were hidden. Her father shook his head, mumbling that there were none in this village, but the soldier did not believe him. Thuy saw him place the muzzle of his gun against her father's temple and she knew she could not let him die. She ran from her hiding place, pointing down the road and yelling: "That way! That way!" The soldier pulled back the hammer of the gun but another called out something from the jeep, so he pistol-whipped her father instead, the crunch of metal against bone punctuating the seconds until at last the soldier climbed back into his jeep and drove away. She watched the jeep until it disappeared, only then becoming aware of the total silence behind her. She turned and saw her mother and Younger Brother Quan helping her father. She ran to him, but he pushed her away, the blood on his hand staining her *ouida*.

"Father?" But her father would not meet her gaze – would not answer. "Father?" she asked again, and this time it was her mother who pushed her away. "But what have I done?"

Her mother signalled Younger Brother Quan to help her father, then turned to face Thuy. "You have shamed him," she said.

"I saved him!"

"No! You have shamed him, and this village. You did not allow him to die like a man." Her mother turned and walked away.

Thuy looked at the villagers as each turned away without a word. Even the children refused to meet her gaze, and Thuy realised she could no longer stay in this village.

Thuy walked towards the hills, the rim of her *non-bai-tho* pulled forward to hide her shame. She had been told there was a town on the other side of the hills, but had never been there, had never left her village. The sun was now high in the sky, the gunfire she had heard all morning had stopped. On either side of the dirt road, rice paddies surrounded by low earth dikes spread like green patchwork quilts, and for the moment all seemed peaceful. Then, softly at first, the throb of helicopter motors and the whooshing of their rotor blades. Thuy saw them coming, flying low like monstrous dung-coloured birds seeking small prey, their soft throb becoming louder and louder. She ran to crouch in a rice paddy, covering her ears to block their shriek. She could feel the air pulsate in a continuous assault that threatened to crush her small body into the mud. Dust and small rocks tattooed her face and hands, and she prayed to Buddha to make these great birds go away. They flew on, and the air became still and moisture laden once more.

Thuy climbed back on to the road, her clothes clinging to her body, dripping mud, the stain of her father's blood washed away. She saw jeeps come slowly down the road and soldiers on foot, their packs heavy on their backs. She stood there as they passed, as frightened as when she was a very little girl, but these soldiers looked tired and dirty and paid her no attention. Some were wounded, their bandages oozing blood. She looked into their eyes and saw nothing there. No fear, no sadness, no anger. Just emptiness. Thuy walked on.

She reached the foothills that afternoon. The road was dappled from the shade of trees, the air cooler here but thick with the stench of death. She walked cautiously now, aware of the stench but not of where it came from. A bird trilled. Insects buzzed and creaked and scurried. A butterfly fluttered before her as if guiding her way. It circled and dipped just ahead and she followed it around a bend in the road. The butterfly rose higher into the air, looped the loop, and Thuy's gaze followed it as it came to rest on the disembowelled body of a child.

There were fifteen of them, from a neighbouring village perhaps, their trousers and *ouidas* stained with blood and urine and faeces and sweat, the ground under them a dark brown shadow of absorbed blood. At the side of the road, women, old men and children lay across each other, arms and legs entwined in a jigsaw of destruction. An old couple still holding hands, the woman staring lifelessly at the man. His eyes rolled back as if trying to see the bullet hole in the centre of his forehead from which a steady wave of small green ants ebbed and flowed. A young boy lay face down along the road, arms above his head, stopped at that moment when courage left him, a piece of shrapnel embedded in his spine. Geckos exploited this macabre cornucopia. A baby lying on top of his mother, his lips still surrounding the nipple of her now-dry breast, apparently unhurt except for a missing foot. Bellies swollen with methane and sulphur gas. Flesh decomposing, liquefying.

Thuy held her hands over her nose, trying in vain to stop the smell, the spasms of her stomach. She had seen death before but not like this – days later. Bile filled her mouth and she vomited, the muscles of her belly squeezing reason and beauty and logic from her body until she had no more to vomit but still she retched. A movement caught her gaze and she stared at the butterfly as it gently looped the loop once more in front of her, then disappeared into the treetops.

Tradition nudged the corners of her mind as she looked at the cadavers, their mouths open as if awaiting the grains of rice and gold coins that were their due. The sky darkened, rumbled as if angry at her inadequacy. She knew the afternoon rains were near and wanted to find shelter, but she couldn't just walk away. *I don't want to be here*, she thought. Holding her breath she went to the old man and lifted his head. Ants covered her arms and bit her flesh as she pulled his *non-bai-tho* around to cover his face. She did the same to the old woman. *I'm really not here, it's just a dream.* One by one she moved amongst them, covering faces, pulling down clothing. Only the boy with shrapnel and the mother and baby had nothing with which to cover their faces. Taking her own *non-bai-tho* from her head, she placed it over the mother so its rim just covered the babe as well. Then, as the first great drops of rain fell, she put her hands together in prayer and bowed low, apologising to their souls for not giving them a proper burial.

"Hello *Uc-da-loi*! You buy me Saigon Tea?" Thuy smiled at the tall Australian. Of all the men who came here to forget the horrors of their day, he was her favourite.

She had been working as a bar girl for six months now. Had become tougher, less naïve – Mamma-san had seen to that. Starving, living on the streets where each week someone was killed or raped or mutilated, she had been happy to work as a hostess to these men whose language she'd barely understood, and whose ways she found strange. She had been shy at first, frightened of them, but she would smile and nod while thinking of her village and her family, knowing she would never go back, worried these men would realise the "whisky and coke" she made them buy for her contained no whisky. The woman on the radio sang the song she heard many times a day and Thuy smiled now, understanding the words:

Uc-da-loi, Cheap Charlie,
He no buy me Saigon tea,
Saigon tea costs many many P,
Uc-da-loi he Cheap Charlie.

Uc-da-loi, Cheap Charlie,
He no give me MPC,
MPC cost many many P,
Uc-da-loi he cheap Charlie.

## I'm not here

How she hated these MPCs. She'd thought it so valuable at first, this military money, and had hoarded it until one day she'd gone to pay her rent and the landlord had refused it, saying it was now worthless. That was when Mamma-san had seen an opportunity and convinced her that she could earn twice as much by being more than just a hostess. She'd had no choice really – she had to live. But now she knew how it all worked, and she could sleep with these men, pretending she wasn't really there, feeling little emotion.

Uc-da-loi, Cheap Charlie,

He no go to bed with me,

Bed with me cost many many P,

Uc-da-loi he cheap Charlie.

Then one night she had noticed this quiet young soldier. She noticed he alone bowed to the Buddha shrine when he came in, treated the girls with respect, and never drank as much as the others. So she had made sure he sat with her, and he'd spent the evening telling her about his country. She hadn't understood many of his words but learnt his name was Michael and that his family were farmers, and that he didn't want to be here but his government had forced him. The next evening he had come again, then again the next and the next. He never asked to sleep with her and Mamma-san became angry and told him he would have to pay more, but he didn't object and so she was still his hostess each evening.

"You want more Ba Moi Ba, Michael-san?" Thuy asked and he nodded, ordering another Saigon Tea for her as well – he too knew how it all worked. She looked at the little brown bottles of beer on the table – more than usual.

"You okay, *Uc-da-loi*?"

"Sure I'm okay. I'm okay, you're okay, everyone in fucking Vietnam is fucking A-okay!" He drank the bottle in one go then ordered another. Thuy frowned. She had never seen him like this. He ordered still another beer, then another. He didn't talk to her, just raised his beer to her each time he started another, and she just sat, nodding, smiling. She heard a commotion outside the bar, heard the police whistle.

"Bloody White Mice!" he said, easing himself out of the booth, unsteady on his feet. "Bloody White Mice and their bloody whistles."

"Michael-san, where you go?"

"I'm going to shove his bloody whistle …"

"No, Michael-san! He shoot you! You stay here."

But Michael stumbled down the bar. Thuy ran to him, not knowing how to stop a man so much bigger than her, and so she reached up and pulled his face down to hers and kissed him as she'd had men kiss her. He tried to pull away so she jumped up, wrapping her legs around his waist. His arms encircled her.

"Okay, Little Thuy, I stay …" he said at last, and he walked back to the booth still holding her to him, her legs still around him. He ordered another beer and Saigon Tea.

Thuy looked at Michael slumped back in the booth, asleep. Soon Mamma-san would close the bar and kick them out into the street.

"Wake up, *Uc-da-loi*," she said softly. "Wake up!" and she shook him, none too gently. With a start he woke, his hands around her throat pushing her down on the seat squeezing her throat. "Michael-san!" she managed to gasp, and for an infinity he looked down at her, confused, his hands still around her throat. Then, horrified, he jerked back.

"Oh my God! I'm sorry! I'm sorry, Thuy!" and he pushed his hands through his hair, head back, eyes clenched closed. "I'm sorry."

She sat up, coughing. Gingerly felt her throat. Noticed Mamma-san staring their way. "You buy Ba Moi Ba."

"What?"

"Buy Ba Moi Ba. Mamma-san, she look at you." He ordered another beer, downed it in one go. "We go now," she said then.

Together they walked down the length of the bar, past the Buddha shrine, out the doors. The evening rains had stopped, the soldiers gone back to camp to meet curfew. She saw Michael leaning against a wall, slowly sliding down to the footpath.

"You come," she said, pulling his arm around her shoulder.

Together they walked, stumbled, walked past shops and bars. Through open doorways the voice of Hanoi Hannah was listing the names of American GIs whose girlfriends were sleeping with someone else back home, and Connie Francis sang about losing her mind. Thuy thought she must be losing *her* mind, taking this man back to her flat. It was her second most important rule: never let them know where you live. She unlocked the door, walked him to her bed, pushed him on to it. He giggled.

"Sweet little Thuy," he mumbled, trying to focus. "Sweet gentle little Thuy, helping the Aussie soldiers."

I'm not here

"You sleep." She untied his boots, pulled them off his feet. Pulled off his damp socks.

"You going to help the boys in the minefields too, Thuy-thu?"

She undid his belt, pulled it off. "You sleep now."

"Whatch'a going to do with his arm, Thuy-thu? He's still holding his rifle, you know …"

"I make tea."

"Still holding his rifle … isn't that funny?" He giggled, and the giggles grew and grew, filling the room. "Holding his fucking rifle but his arm ain't got no fucking body on it!" and the giggles subsided, to be replaced by sobs. Great body-convulsing sobs that frightened her, not understanding all he had said but aware of his pain and his anger. So she lay next to him and he clung to her as if she could save him, still sobbing but quietly now, until the beer and exhaustion finally worked and he slept.

He woke confused by the light globe shining in his eyes and the unfamiliar room. Thuy was curled towards him, asleep. She seemed so tiny, so innocent, and he wished he could bury himself in her and forget where he was and what he did every day. He wished he were back home where he could make love to a woman without fear, without condoms and penicillin parades, without thinking this may be the last time. He saw the red marks on her neck and felt guilty. Gently kissed each one, then unbuttoned her blouse and kissed her small breasts, burying himself in the smell of her. She half woke, sensed his need, and allowed him that night to break her number one most important rule.

Thuy rubbed her tight swollen belly, wishing Michael were here. She was bored. At first she had enjoyed playing house, going with him to the markets to buy food, spending evenings making love. But the novelty had worn off and she'd gone back to the bar sometimes when she knew he'd be out on patrol, until her belly began to swell and Mamma-san had told her to stay away – pregnant bar girls were no good for business.

Now she was so big she didn't go out much. She looked out the open doorway but there was no sign of Michael. Drops of sweat wriggled down her back like fat, lazy tadpoles. She carefully lowered herself on to her bed. The sky rumbled, the rains fell, she slept.

When she woke, it was dark and she was still alone. She waited, all the next day and the next. After a week she hung around outside the bar at night hoping to see someone who might give her news of Michael, until Mamma-san yelled at her to go. She went back home and counted the money she had left. If she were very careful, she would have enough to stay here until the baby was born.

The child came before dawn after two days of labour. Eager to leave her too-small body, he had pushed and ripped his way down but still would not be born, and she had screamed and panicked and lost her reason until the woman next door had heard her and come. She had understood the problem and cut Thuy with a kitchen knife, and when she placed the naked child still attached to Thuy's body into her arms, Thuy had smelled the blood and seen her father and the bodies once more and she had pushed the child away thinking This is not real, it's not happening, no I'm not here, I'm not here. But the woman was wise and she'd wrapped the child and placed him on the bed next to Thuy and cleaned her up, then left. Thuy slept then and when she woke it was morning and she could hear Country Joe and The Fish on someone's radio telling American mothers and fathers not to hesitate to pack their boys off to Vietnam:

Send 'em off before it's too late

Be the first on your block

To have your boy come home in a box

And slowly her reason was called back by the child's whimpers, and she saw she had a son and that he looked like Michael. She named him Tan.

Tan was three months old and wanted to sleep, but Thuy shook him every time he dozed. She wanted him awake now so he would sleep deeply when she went begging – a floppy, sleepy child always extracted more money than a cheerful one. A plane flew overhead. A shower of white paper fluttered from the sky but no one reacted – just more propaganda butterflies. This was the first day of the Vietnamese New Year and tonight there would be celebrations in the streets and more begging opportunities. A flash of light. A building exploded. People screamed. More explosions. Gunfire. Thuy ran. She tripped. Tan screamed.

"Thuy!"

She felt a hand grab her and pull her back into a doorway. "Michael?" She looked up. "Quan! Younger Brother!"

"Thuy! You're in Saigon?" Another explosion. More screams. "We can't stay here. Come."

Together they ran. Quan led them to a part of town where there was less fighting, less destruction. He unlocked a door and pushed them in. Thuy looked around. Modest, but better than anything she'd known.

I'm not here

"You live here?" she asked. Quan nodded, pride in his gaze. "Father? Mother?"

Quan shook his head. "They bombed our village. When they finished, nothing was left. I was fishing so I escaped. But Father, Mother, most of the village, they all died. I came here. Found work."

Thuy nodded.

"So who's this?" he asked, indicating the baby.

"Tan. My son."

Quan looked at the infant, at his blue eyes and fair hair. "Ah! Bui Doi!"

Thuy flinched. Bui Doi – dust of life – the value of a child born to Vietnamese girls from American or Australian soldiers was worthless.

"No. His name is Tan." Thuy stared at her brother, and he saw in her something that warned him not to argue. "Quan, can we stay here with you?"

"No. Yes. Look, you could, but *I'm* not staying. I'm leaving Vietnam. It's supposed to be tonight, but now, with all this …"

"Take us with you."

"Thuy, it costs a lot of money …"

"Take us with you."

Quan sighed. He looked at Thuy, so skinny, so ragged. She had shamed Father and the village. But Father was dead. The village no longer existed. And she was his Elder Sister. The Bui Doi was his nephew. He, Quan, was the man of the family now – the only man.

"Maybe. I'll see what I can do. You stay here. I'll be back when I can."

For three days the battle raged. Fires burned, planes flew overhead and a layer of smoke dulled the sun. Quan returned and said the American Embassy had been broken into. Thuy didn't care. All she wanted was to leave Vietnam.

She awoke on the fourth day to silence. Out in the street the town seemed deserted. Only the chirping of birds. Quan left early. Was back by midday with news – they would leave that night.

They made their way via back streets to the riverbanks and hid amongst the grass. They waited. Half an hour. An hour. A light quickly flicked on and off on the river and Quan responded with a torch. Thuy heard the whisper of oars in water and a small fishing boat glided up.

Thirteen other adults plus infants were already on board. Thuy and Quan found a spot to sit on the crowded deck, their backs against the engine compartment. The engine started, its sound muffled with rags and canvas. No one spoke as they passed various checkpoints. As they made their way slowly down the river Thuy saw that many towns and villages had been attacked. It seemed the whole of South Vietnam was destroyed.

The boat continued slowly through the night. The drone of the engine lulled Thuy, and when she woke they had made it out to sea and it was day but no one was celebrating. All were aware of the dangers ahead, and all they had left behind. Tan woke and Thuy fed him then cooked a bowl of rice for Quan with slivers of dried pork from their provisions. They had brought enough food for five days. More than enough for the three-day trip to Malaysia.

For the first two days, the weather was perfect, the sea calm. The men kept watch for patrol boats. There were rumours of pirates from Thailand. Sometimes dolphins would play close to the boat as it made its way slowly towards land.

On the evening of the second day, the sky darkened with great rolling clouds and lightening forked down to meet the sea. A wind sprung up. Great waves tossed the small wooden boat. People vomited and a woman cried that they would all drown. Rain fell and the boat rose and plunged down columns of waves. The engine stalled. The boat filled with water but the small pump would not work and the men bailed by hand. All night the boat tossed and creaked and Thuy was sure they would drown.

Daylight came and the storm abated. The boat smelled of vomit and fear and engine fuel. They spotted a ship and everyone cheered and waved clothing to attract attention, but it just sailed past. The engine could not be started. The captain ordered a stocktake of all food and water, and it was then they all realised much of it had been lost in the storm. They cleaned themselves and the boat as well as they could and settled down to wait.

They drifted for three more days. Occasionally they would see a ship and burn clothes to signal, but no ship signalled back. They knew now that they were being ignored. The sun burned down and the smell of fuel grew stronger each day. Quan spent his time with the men, while Thuy tended Tan and was ignored by the women who would look at Tan then turn away. Bui Doi – the dust of life.

On the afternoon of the eighth day, a boat came towards them at high speed. It pulled smoothly beside them and five men with machetes jumped

I'm not here

aboard. One produced a large automatic pistol that he waved about as he shouted orders and another busied himself securing the two vessels together. They held knives to everyone's throats, demanding money and jewellery, then announced this bounty was not enough and went from person to person looking into mouths until they found an old man with gold teeth. They twisted a rope around his ankles and wrists and up around his neck then used a hammer to try to dislodge the teeth. Thuy watched in horror and the old man screamed and bled, but still the teeth would not come out until one of the pirates found a pair of pincers and successfully harvested the teeth.

Once more the pirates walked along the line, pulling out the youngest women, Thuy included. They tore at the women's clothes, the material weak from seawater and sun. Thuy still held on to Tan, and one of the pirates ripped him out of her arms and threw him on to the deck then, with one sweep of the machete, beheaded him, the momentum of his swing sending the small head skidding across the deck into the ocean. People cried out and the small body twitched for an instant as a fountain of blood gushed from his body spraying those on deck in gruesome, ever-reducing arcs until the small heart had no more to pump. Thuy felt her sanity escape this surreal hell and she was transported back to the corpse-filled hills, but only for an instant and then she was back staring at the small lifeless body of her child. Time unravelled in slow motion. She watched in horror as the pirate picked the small body up by a foot and tossed it overboard. She welcomed the oblivion that enveloped her consciousness, her knees giving way under her, but a pirate grabbed a handful of her hair and pulled her up again. *I'm not here*, she screamed silently. *I'm not here I'm not here I'm not here I'm not here!* Her gaze frantically swept the faces on deck and she saw Quan slowly withdraw the small fishing knife he kept strapped to his leg. But a pirate saw him too and without warning put his gun to Quan's temple and pulled the trigger. Blood and fragments of bone and brain tissue splattered onto the men near him and on to the naked bodies of the women. Thuy's moan was silenced by a fist.

Then the pirates threw the women on to the deck – now a mixture of blood and vomit and urine and bone – and raped them while the boat rocked gently with the movement of the sea, and beside the boat dolphins dived and played and whistled. Thuy's tormented gaze sought that of the men, begging for their help, but the only help they could give was to avert their gaze so as not to witness her shame.

Once more they drifted. They had been robbed of food and water, all except one small container in the engine room that had been overlooked, and this was restricted to just a small sip a day. One morning they found a couple missing – they had preferred drowning to this hell. The sun blistered their skins, the glare of the ocean blinded them, and at night they shivered from cold and shock. They woke one day to see land on the horizon, but the current was pulling them away. A man ran to the engine room and tried to start the engine. An explosion. A flash of flames and Thuy screamed as her hair caught fire. Another explosion.

"Can't tell if it's alive or dead. Bring 'er around a bit more."
"Must be dead, Sir. Badly burned. Hang on, I've got it. Bloody hell, it's a woman … Oh God! Her skin's come off in my hand!"

Thuy did not regain consciousness when they lifted her on to the Australian ship out on manoeuvres, when they inserted a drip and pumped her full of antibiotics. Nor did she regain consciousness when they transferred her to a helicopter and flew her to Darwin. She came to in a strange bed. Tubes entered her body, some attached to bottles, others to machines. Her gaze darted around the room, taking in other beds, other machines, other tubes, and she became frightened by the strangeness of it. Two men in white stood by her bed and she knew that white was for funerals and therefore she must be dying. Once more she lost consciousness.

When she came to again, the sun shone outside her window and a young woman stood beside her bed, holding Thuy's wrist and looking at a watch.

"Hello, you're with us then?" And Thuy recognised the language of the *Uc-da-loi*. The woman took a glass of water from the locker beside the bed and gently put the straw to Thuy's lips. "Just a sip, or you'll throw up." Thuy sipped the water. It tasted fresh and sweet on her swollen tongue. She kept her gaze on the woman. "I'll just get the doctor," she said, and left Thuy's side.

Thuy knew the word "doctor". She was in hospital, then. She raised her hand to her face and felt a bandage. There were bandages on her body as well. A man in a white coat came and she thought he was Michael, but when he sat on the edge of her bed she saw it was a stranger and she cowered back into her pillow.

"It's all right. I'm Doctor Nelson. You're in Australia. Darwin. Do you understand? Australia." Thuy stared at him expressionless. "Australia. Yes?" He sighed. "You don't understand a word I'm saying, do you?" He rose and left the room. Thuy had understood him but her instincts warned of unknown dangers, and that it was wiser to pretend not to understand. Her head pounded and her tongue felt dry and tasted foul and she wished she

## I'm not here

could have more of the sweet water, but thinking tired her out and she slept.

When she woke again, the woman was beside her with men in a uniform she didn't recognise and she panicked at the sight of them, begging the woman not to let them take her, in a mixture of English and Vietnamese, and the woman understood her fear and reassured her.

"You're been transferred, dear. To Melbourne. They're really good with burns there. They'll be able to fix your face up." They lifted Thuy on to a barouche and she struggled, but the woman patted her hand, saying: "It's okay, it's okay", and those words Thuy understood so she laid back and let them move her into an ambulance. But when they drove up to a military aircraft, Thuy panicked, because planes meant war and soldiers and bombs and were not for girls like her, and she screamed "No! No! I'm not here! Please, I'm not here!" until she felt a pinprick in her leg and lost consciousness.

Thuy opened her eyes, rising from a nightmare of bodiless babies sucking her breast and soldiers drowning in a sea of blood. Rain beat a tattoo on the window. She tried to sit up, but quickly lay back feeling faint. She was in hospital once more. But hospitals cost money ... lots of money. And she had none. Only the rich and the foreigners could afford them. Once more she tried to sit but she was so weak. She closed her eyes and slept some more.

It took five weeks before Thuy was strong enough to walk around the ward. The staff were kind to her and she could understand what they said, although she pretended not to, preferring to find sanctuary behind a facade of incomprehension. They brought in an interpreter and Thuy noticed the young woman constantly glancing at her watch, so she answered a few questions then pretended to sleep and the woman left.

Several times in her wanderings, she would see a man in the distance she thought was Michael, but it never was. And as each day passed she worried more and more about what she would do when they asked her to pay for her hospital stay. Then one day during visiting hours she found a room temporarily without its patient and she stole the dressing gown left on a bed and walked out of the hospital and into the cold.

She spent her first night shivering in a doorway surrounded by others without homes. In the morning, one of the men looked her over, taking in her damp clothing and bare feet, her features bluish with cold, her scars, and told her his name was Ted and that he had fought in Vietnam. She looked into his eyes and saw there the same hurt she had seen in Michael's eyes, and an instant bond developed between them. He took her to a place where they were given porridge and tea with milk and sugar, which made

Dominique Wilson

her gag but warmed her inside. When shops and offices opened, Ted took her to a place where he spoke to a man who took them to a room filled with second-hand clothes. Ted told her she could pick out some clothes for herself and so she chose a dress with a floral pattern and a grey cardigan. Then, out of a basket, Ted pulled a pair of woollen red and white striped socks, and she smiled for the first time in months. But Ted insisted they were just the thing for Melbourne and so she put them on, and they were so thick her feet could only fit in the black shoes with no laces.

From Ted she learned where it was safe to go and where to stay away from. She learned not to go to the same soup kitchen too often or the people there would ask too many questions, and to look out for patrol cars and how to avoid them. Once she found herself amongst a mob of people with placards and signs marching and shouting and she had run to her alley and cowered until Ted told her they were fighting for peace and would not harm her.

Then one day Ted said he knew of a place looking for workers, so she had gone there and found a room full of women like herself, who would not look anyone in the eye and spent their days sewing sheepskin souvenirs on big industrial machines. The man in charge would yell and swear at them, but Thuy was glad of the money. She rented a room in a building Ted called a "people's palace", which had cockroaches and bedbugs, but at least it was indoors. Sometimes she would sneak Ted in and they would both curl up on the floor to avoid the bedbugs, and Ted would make jokes about the man in the next room who urinated into bottles each night, lining them up on the window sill till morning, and they would sleep till daylight, warm and safe. But one day at work Thuy was thinking of Michael and lost her concentration until she felt the needle of the machine pierce the flesh of her finger and break against the bone. The pain and the blood oozing on to the sheepskin flashed her mind back to the bodies of her son and brother, and she curled on her chair trembling and mewing until the man in charge screamed at her and pushed her out the door, telling her not to come back and refusing to pay her because she had spoiled the sheepskin with her blood and sheepskins cost money.

She shuffles down the empty street, a small Vietnamese woman dressed in a floral polyester dress and a man's grey cardigan held closed by a piece of rope at the waist. On her legs a sagging pair of football socks, on her feet a pair of man's black lace-up shoes without laces. A burn scar, brown and wrinkled and tight, runs on the left side of her face, pulling the skin down-

I'm not here

wards so that little white puffs of moisture punctuate each of her breaths. She clings to two white supermarket bags that bulge with her treasures, and as she shuffles she mutters: "I'm not here. I'm not here. I'm not here." ■

*I-Feel-Like-I'm-Fixing-To-Die* by Country Joe & The Fish, was originally released by Vanguard in November 1967; *Uc-da-loi Cheap Charlie* was a song popular during the Vietnam War, author unknown sung to the tune of *Nick, Nack, Paddywack, Give a Dog a Bone*.

Dominique Wilson is founding Co-Managing Editor of *Wet Ink: the magazine of new writing*, and a PhD student at Adelaide University.

# VIETNAM VETERANS

## by DAVID NIELSEN

**David Nielsen** recently graduated from Griffith University's Queensland College of Art with a Bachelor of Photography and a major in Photojournalism. He has devoted much of the past three years towards the documentation of Australia's war veterans.

Neil Antony 'Bomber' Bower-Miles

*I remember sitting in my parent's kitchen, and everyone had gone to work, and I'm sitting there thinking what the fuck am I doing here? I wanted to be back in Vietnam again. I was worried about my mates because we engineers got replaced, one for one. I've seen it when blokes come out of jail, it's the same thing, you feel like a stranger in your own fuckin' home town.*

◂

Zev Ben-Avi

Guy M. Robinson & Gillian Jean Robinson

Jim Kjellgren

Robert 'Padre' May

*So while it was only one year of my life, now it basically rules my life. It changed my life completely.*

Brian Normand Purser & Elizabeth (Mary) Purser

*I know when I came back from Vietnam, no-one was really interested in hearing what I had to say, and that goes for pretty well everybody, nursing college's, army colleges; the idea was you were telling 'Waries', which was 'War' 'Stories' and no-one was really interested in them. – Elizabeth*

Gary J. Street

*That's why most blokes didn't start marching for years; because of the public resentment, especially while the Vietnam War was going on anyway. For the first eight years I didn't go near an ANZAC day parade.*

Stefan 'Animal' Rojek

*Like the majority of veterans, irregardless of what conflict, you have nightmares. It's reliving the things when it happens. My wife and I have to sleep in separate bedrooms because I'm a very restless sleeper, otherwise I end up swinging my arms around and she wears it.*

Essay:
## The gap between work and choices

Author:
**David Peetz**

*Image: Workplace Rally Melbourne. Thousands of workers rally against the new federal Workchoices legislation. / Photographer: Jason South / Source: Fairfaxphotos.com*

Divided Nation

# The gap between work and choices

On the grass outside an abattoir on the Western Plains of New South Wales, in the dark, cool air, a few workers are forming the late-night shift of a picket. Some journalists are hanging around, talking to them.

It is less than a week after the federal government's new industrial relations legislation, known as "WorkChoices", has taken effect. The men are outside the Cowra abattoir, not inside, because they have received termination notices. Twenty-nine have been sacked from their jobs – for "operational reasons". And they have been offered re-employment. To be precise, an unidentified twenty of them will be offered re-employment – if they go back to work for substantially less than what they had been earning before the new law came into force. The drop in pay is typically around $180 a week, nearly a quarter of their wage. For some shift workers, it is as much as $300 a week. The men are angry. Some do not know how they will meet their mortgage repayments on the lower rate of pay.

What is happening at Cowra on this April night in Cowra tells us much about the WorkChoices legislation. For one thing, it shows us how much easier it is for employers to dismiss employees.

I met Brad at a local meeting that had been organised by a Brisbane community group to talk about WorkChoices. He was an EFTPOS technician – well-dressed, tall and quietly spoken. He told how his workplace life had been getting harder. He had been harassed, mainly by his supervisor. Eventually he lodged a complaint. A top manager came to Brisbane, met with Brad, his supervisor and others, sorted it out and went away. Mission accomplished. Except it wasn't. The harassment started again. And it got worse. So Brad lodged another complaint, to someone else at the top. On his first day of holidays, Brad got an SMS from his general manager, asking for his home address; he was told they had some important "confidential documents" to send him. When he got back, there was a registered letter waiting for him. It said that he had been made redundant with the offer of a few weeks' redundancy pay.

His firm had more than a hundred employees. But Brad had been dismissed for "operational reasons" – just like the Cowra workers. And under this provision, even if you have been unfairly and capriciously targeted for dismissal – whether you have been singled out because you ask too many questions or do not share the corporate culture – the reason you were selected for redundancy is "irrelevant". An operational reason – that is, something of a technical, economic or structural nature – does not have to be the main reason why you lost your job. It just has to be *part* of the reason.

Cowra also illustrates how WorkChoices can be used to cut pay and conditions. I do not wish to overstate the problems with WorkChoices. Whatever the negatives WorkChoices holds for Australian workers, exaggerating them only serves to disempower the already weakened, making it harder to move forward. That said, there are many examples of cuts in pay and conditions – particularly through the use of AWAs – that have become widely known.

In Sydney, within days of WorkChoices taking effect, Amber Oswald, a sixteen-year-old casual working in a juice bar, was put on to an AWA that cut her weekly pay from $97 to $65. Her boss told the media: "If they don't want to sign, they can leave … It's not about what's fair, it's [about] what's right – right for the company." Amber was able to challenge it through her union because the AWA had not been offered properly – she had not actually seen it before she was put on it. But after winning her case for back pay, she was taken off her Sunday shift which had attracted double-time rates. One day, a few months later, she was told not to come in the next day because the store was closed – for "rebranding".

Therein lies the problem for many casual workers. In theory, workers are still protected from "unlawful termination" if they are sacked for refusing to sign an AWA. It is expensive – a case will cost upwards of $30,000 to run through the federal court – so if you are not wealthy or in a union, it is at best a threat. But for casuals, if you do not sign you can just find that your rosters are changed, your hours are cut back until it is barely worth coming in to work any more.

At retailer Spotlight, new employees were offered AWAs that abolished penalty rates, overtime rates, rest breaks, incentive-based payments and bonuses, annual leave loading and public holidays. For those who worked Thursday nights and Saturdays, this would cost $90 a week. In return, they received an increase in their base hourly rate of pay of two cents an hour. That was OK, said Spotlight management, because that is just "the starting point … Our store managers negotiate the rates with the staff depending on the skill of the person and market forces." But if the starting point for "negotiations" is $90 a week less, then most workers are going to be hard pressed to get near what they would have been automatically entitled to under the old system.

Workers at a Melbourne call centre operated for Lufthansa were told to sign AWAs which cut their base pay by between 3 and 10 per cent, and reduced penalty rates and loadings. To allegedly offset this, the agreement provided a complex bonus scheme in which, to get the full bonus (at management's discretion), workers had to achieve 110 percent of the performance targets and not take more than one day of sick or carer's leave. The Equal Opportunity Commission of Victoria said that there was "considerable potential for the proposed performance bonus scheme ... to discriminate against employees who need to utilise their leave entitlements because they experience personal illness and/or have parental or carer responsibilities."

The examples mount. Yet the advocates of WorkChoices tell us that it is bringing higher wages: real wages (that is, the purchasing power of your wage after allowing for price rises) have risen by 16 per cent since 1996. But that is barely the long-term growth rate in real wages anyway. Most of the increase has been obtained by managers and professionals with the top 10 per cent of incomes. For the median worker or the low paid, real wages have increased at barely 0.4 per cent a year in recent years.

Most recently, in the first six months of WorkChoices, average real wages (measured by the wage price index) fell by 0.6 per cent. At the same time, in Queensland and Western Australia, there are major labour shortages. Employers are offering huge wages to get people to work in the resources sector. Yet, *on average*, real wages fell. It would be surprising if this situation continued, but nonetheless it is remarkable that this should have been the case in an economy with the tightest labour market in three decades. Something strange is going on, especially in the part of the labour market where workers do not have strong bargaining power. In part, this is because the protections that used to exist for those signing AWAs are no longer there. Under the old system, agreements were meant to leave employees no worse off than they would be under the award. If you lost your penalty rates or another entitlement, you were meant to be compensated – most probably through an increase in the base hourly rate of pay. Now you can lose any or all award conditions and not receive a cent in compensation.

The trouble is that it is hard to know what is happening in that less prosperous part of the labour market, because the government does not publish data letting us see into it properly. We know that average real wages fell most markedly in retailing and hospitality – where penalty rates are most at risk – in the first six months of WorkChoices. But that does not tell us the specifics of AWAs in those industries. We know that, before WorkChoices, wage increases under AWAs nationally were typically only 2 to 2.5 per cent – barely half the 4 to 4.5 per cent that workers obtained under union collective agreements. But nothing has been, or will be, published about wage increases under WorkChoices AWAs – except that 22 per cent of Work-

## The gap between work and choices

Choices AWAs provide for no wage increase during the whole period of the AWA, which may last up to five years.

This glimpse came when the Employment Advocate, Peter McIlwain, answered questions asked by the Senate Estimates committee last year. His office had examined a sample of 250 AWAs registered in the first month after WorkChoices took effect. It also showed that just over half had abolished overtime pay. This was interesting because it meant that overtime was being abolished much faster than previously. A further one-third of AWAs reduced overtime pay. This meant that, in total, 82 per cent of AWAs either reduced or abolished overtime pay. The story was no better for other conditions of employment. Most AWAs abolished penalty rates, shift loadings and annual leave loading – all representing notable acceleration of the pre-WorkChoices patterns. Large proportions also abolished rest breaks, public holiday pay and allowances.

All these disappearing conditions, government commercials told us in 2005, were "protected by law".

These numbers only tell a small part of the story. They do not tell us about the differences between industries where workers are strong and where they are not. After all, AWAs are also used extensively in mining, where there is a severe labour shortage, and those AWAs – like the collective agreements they try to outbid – are very generous.

Yet, instead of publishing more detailed information, the government is now publishing no information at all. The Employment Advocate developed concerns that he had not expressed before about technique and interpretation. This decision to stop publication was one he came to entirely of his own accord, without input from the minister – nothing to do with the bad publicity generated by these statistics or how embarrassing they might have been to the cause of promoting AWAs or the government.

The Office of the Employment Advocate knows that it faces abolition if there is a change of government.

When the Cowra abattoir workers were sacked, they had few options. The most effective industrial weapon – going on strike – is impossible to implement if you have already been sacked. They could not seek reinstatement from the industrial tribunal because they had been sacked for "operational" reasons, and under WorkChoices that disqualified any claim for reinstatement, no matter how unjust, harsh or unreasonable the dismissal. But they, and their union, had one major weapon at their disposal: the media. Within hours, press and TV camera operators were outside the abattoir. The workers' plight was beamed into homes across the country.

David Peetz

The minister realised he faced a problem. This was just one of several cases in the national media of workers being sacked or abused under the new laws. He went on television to say that some employers, like the Cowra abattoir, had "jumped the gun". It seemed "quite possible" that the employer there had acted "contrary to the provisions of the law itself". The Office of Workplace Services (OWS) was told to investigate and speak to the company. The unions negotiated with management. Under media and political pressure, the company reinstated the workers. The Minister was triumphant: "This shows that the law works."

Except that the company had not broken the law at all in sacking the workers as it did. An OWS report to the minister eight weeks later cleared it of wrongdoing. Fortunately, through judicious use of the media, the workers had got their jobs back for the time being.

As with Cowra, much of the battle over WorkChoices is fought out in this symbolic domain. For the unions, the ability to mobilise media and create images of workers being disadvantaged has become a key tool in preventing employers from exploiting opportunities the law now gives them. No doubt many employers have decided that the cost to their reputation of adopting an aggressive approach would not, at the moment, be worth it. At least, that is the case for unionised workers who have the resources of a political savvy union movement behind them. Those who do not belong to a union, lacking media access, remain largely invisible and more easily exploitable.

For the government, image control is essential. It started badly. One of the early prosecutions, launched in March 2006 by the OWS, was against a group of workers. In early 2005 they had been placed by their employer in demountable accommodation that was infested with fleas and feral animals. It reeked of raw sewage. Not surprisingly, the workers struck for a few days for decent conditions, which they successfully obtained. Over a year later, the OWS, without the support of the employer, began proceedings against the workers, who faced fines of $20,000 each.

The symbolism was disastrously revealing. The minister ordered that the prosecutions be halted. Whenever a problem arises under WorkChoices, the standard response from the government has become: "Any examples of employees feeling they have been treated unfairly can take their claim to the Office of Workplace Services." Of course, the OWS can do nothing about many of the cuts in pay and conditions and dismissals under the Work-Choices spotlight because the law has made them legal. But the government wants workers to turn to its OWS, not to unions, for assistance, and it hardly helps the imagery if the OWS is so obviously enforcing the spirit as well as the letter of the law.

## The gap between work and choices

There are two other ways the government responds to evidence of mistreatment under WorkChoices. One is to confuse the issues. For example, after the OWS reported to the minister that the Cowra abattoir's actions were legal, the minister claimed (without any evidence) that what the corporation did would also have been legal under the old law. He contradicted himself again five months later when he argued to an industrial tribunal that the "operational reasons" provision must be a weaker protection ("lower threshold") than applied under the old law.

The other response is to seek to discredit the person making the complaint. Academics are a common target. When several workers who had been dismissed or disadvantaged under WorkChoices agreed to appear in union advertisements, the government pilloried the ads as "misrepresenting the position", justifying this by handing to journalists a series of short reports that had been prepared by the OWS without giving the workers concerned the opportunity to respond. The OWS investigations appeared very flimsy. One of the cases that appeared in the OWS material given to journalists concerned Optus technicians. With twenty-eight colleagues, Arthur Ledwidge was sacked for operational reasons a month after WorkChoices took effect, and given the "opportunity" to work as an independent contractor for Optus – provided he had the money to buy his own Optus van and cover his own worker's compensation, superannuation and leave. As the OWS found, there was "no evidence of breach of WR laws". Unable to meet his mortgage repayments, Arthur lost his house.

When the government launched a $55 million advertising campaign, "WorkChoices" was created as a single symbol. Yet the gap between work and choices, embedded subtly in the legislation's title (the *"Work Choices" Amendment Act*) is experienced starkly by many employees. Government spin has not been enough to turn around public opinion. The polls show that WorkChoices remains deeply unpopular with voters. The policy is opposed by a margin of two or three to one. Amongst voters who believe industrial relations is the most important election issue, the margin is four to one against the government. The government fell seriously behind Labor when WorkChoices was debated in Parliament, and was – in trend terms – behind in all three major polls through most of 2006, from the time WorkChoices took effect. WorkChoices represents a clear and present danger to the re-election of the government.

The man who owned the Cowra abattoir drives a Mercedes sports car. His private company was estimated in 2005 by BRW to be worth $120 million, placing him in BRW's top 500. He lives in the ironically named Bushranger's Hill, with what the Daily Telegraph calls "sweeping views" over Sydney's Newport and Pittwater. Around July 2006, after the workers were reinstated, he transferred $1 million through a "loan" from the abattoir to his private company. This came on top of another $800,000 he had transferred to his private company over the previous year. Then, in August 2006, he closed the abattoir permanently. Within weeks it was in liquidation.

The workers were left not only without jobs, but also owed an estimated $2.8 million in unpaid entitlements, about half of which were redundancy payments. The owner's private company then discharged the priority debt of the abattoir, making his private company the priority creditor – ahead of the workers, who had yet to receive any of their entitlements.

The image of the boss enjoying the high life and reinforcing his wealth while the workers face pay cuts, dismissal and disempowerment is an uncomfortable one for the government. But it is one that is becoming increasingly real. By the end of 2005, the wages share was at its lowest level in thirty-five years. The profit share, on the other hand, was at the highest level ever recorded. Between 1998 and 2004, the gap between the top one-tenth of wage and salary recipients (mainly managers and senior professionals) and the bottom one-tenth grew by 10.4 per cent. In the year to May 2006, average weekly full-time earnings rose by 2.8 per cent, well below the rise in prices, but among the chief executives salaries rose four times as fast.

The government said WorkChoices was about a new wave of prosperity. Higher productivity. More jobs. Abolishing the unfair dismissal laws, it said, would create 70,000 jobs, and now it claims credit for creating 100,000 – no, 200,000 – jobs. If this were the cause, of course, jobs must have contracted when the unfair dismissal laws were introduced. But when you go back and look at the figures, you discover that job growth after the unfair dismissal laws were introduced – 2.4 per cent in six months – was *higher* than the 1.6 per cent growth in the same period after the protections were abolished for four million workers.

And higher productivity? Seasonally adjusted labour productivity actually fell by 0.7 per cent in the first quarter after WorkChoices began. In reality, analysts do not pay much attention to one quarter's productivity figures, as they are highly volatile. They look at it over a complete growth cycle in the economy. But the only growth cycle completed under the government's *Workplace Relations Act*, the law that introduced AWAs in the first place, hardly gives cause for optimism. Labour productivity grew at only 2.2 per cent a year – below the 2.6 per cent that was achieved in the '60s and '70s under the traditional award system, now pilloried for its inefficiencies.

It is clear that WorkChoices is not about increasing productivity or prosperity; rather, it is about increasing the power of those who already have the most power and resources, and in doing so taking power away from those who have the least, and from those who would challenge the power of the mighty.

The greatest power rests with those who own and control the most resources. They use those resources to generate profit and more resources and power. In order to do so, they typically organise themselves into a collective of capital known as a corporation. This collective form has all sorts of benefits, including the granting of the status of an "artificial person", and the granting of limited liability, so valuable to people such as the owner of the Cowra abattoir. Workers respond to the power of capital by organising collectively into unions, since the power of an individual employee bargaining with a corporation is minimal, but the power of employees bargaining together is potentially quite substantial.

WorkChoices seeks to undercut this challenge to the power of corporations, by removing many of the protections that workers previously had as a result of the pressure exerted collectively by workers for over a century, lowering the starting point for negotiations (if negotiations occur), and making it very difficult – and sometimes illegal – for workers to bargain collectively. It seeks, in effect, to re-establish the great divide between the strong and the weak.

One mechanism for this is the targeting of trade unions. In no other Western democracy can a union be fined for seeking similar outcomes in different agreements ("pattern bargaining") or for including, in a collective agreement, provisions that protect against unfair dismissal. In no other Western country can a worker be jailed for six months for refusing to answer questions asked by government inquisitors about what happened at a union meeting where such seditious matters as pattern bargaining or union security provisions were discussed. As of 30 June 2006, twenty-nine people had secretly been questioned under threat of jail if they refused to submit or told anyone about what happened in the interrogation room. Some were denied the right to be represented by the lawyer of their choice.

The secondary target of WorkChoices is the independent industrial tribunals. Their powers have mostly been enfeebled or given to partisan government agencies or private contractors. The federal tribunal is left mainly with responsibility for administering the anti-strike laws targeted at unions.

And then there is another, unexpected target: the companies who refuse to play ball with the government, who wish instead to maintain constructive, cooperative relations with a unionised workforce. For many companies, maintaining good relations is the most sensible way to make a profit.

In no other Western democracy does the government micro-manage consenting relations between employees and employers to such a degree, fining

David Peetz

employers for making agreements that allow union officials on to their own workplace or permit union-provided training. While decrying the "paternalistic influence of ... third parties", the minister, at the stroke of a pen, declares provisions in collective agreements "prohibited content" and makes the users of such provisions potentially liable to large fines. A company like Smorgon Steel – lauded in the management literature as a company that has used a "partnership approach" to achieve "substantial improvements in organisation performance" – finds itself barred from government contracts because of retrospective rules that forbid such partnerships. It is, as the president of the conservative H.R. Nicholls Society says, the "old Soviet system of command and control, where every economic decision has to go back to some central authority and get ticked off".

Smorgon is immersed in government micro-regulation because it supplies steel to the building industry. The government has targeted unions in the construction industry with special legislation that goes even further than WorkChoices presently does. The construction industry is dangerous, so construction workers like to form themselves into unions. Each year, around fifty people who go to work in the industry one morning never come home. Like twenty-three-year-old father Nathan Park, killed on a Victorian construction site in September 2004 in an accident that was "easily avoided". The construction company, Melbourne Transit, failed to implement procedures that a Victorian county court judge said were "blindingly obvious". She fined Melbourne Transit $100,000. But the owner had already put that company into liquidation and so avoided any penalty. Shortly afterwards, the owner was operating again as a different company (such a valuable thing, the corporate form). Some $300,000 was collected by the union to pay into a trust fund for the education of Nathan's infant son. Rather than focus on such issues, the government established a royal commission, then a building industry task force, then an Australian Building and Construction Commission, all with severe punitive powers, all more concerned with prosecuting unions for closed shops and removing union banners from building sites than with prosecuting unsafe employers.

To get a small sense of the partisan nature of WorkChoices, consider the origins of the provision concerning "operational reasons" for dismissal. The Prime Minister stated that this provision arose from a dispute at the Blair Athol coal mine in central Queensland, owned by a subsidiary of Rio Tinto. Blair Athol management, according to the Australian Industrial Relations Commission, had created a "blacklist" of union members who were "singled out for termination" through a redundancy process. Mine management went about "demeaning" those targeted for termination, a practice "designed to force (unionists) to accept the redundancy package".

## The gap between work and choices

This case was pursued by the blacklisted workers under the unfair dismissal provisions of the old law. Following numerous cases, appeals and delays, most of the workers were reinstated and the case was settled after seven years. Reports suggest that Rio Tinto spent $20 million in legal fees, trying unsuccessfully to keep these sixteen unionists out of its mine sites.

Then along came the chance to rewrite the rules. Lawyers from Freehills, who represented the employer in the Blair Athol case, helped draft the WorkChoices legislation. No more Blair Athols.

Cowra is a small regional town, with a population of nine thousand. In regional areas, away from the resource boom districts, alternative opportunities may be hard to come by. There is a national shortage of nurses yet in Parkes, a hunded kilometres from Cowra, a nursing home gave five nurses a work choice: take a 22 per cent pay cut to become "care service employees", or be made redundant. That was legal, said the OWS. In a small town, if you take on your employer, you may also be hurting your chances of getting a job elsewhere. So there are stories from places like Coffs Harbour, Merimbula and Albury of people forced to sign AWAs that cut their pay, in ways that are mostly illegal but for which redress is quite impractical.

For women, the problems of WorkChoices are not restricted to regional areas. Women are more reliant on awards, and people reliant on awards have most to lose from WorkChoices. Workers on collective agreements will generally have the collective bargaining power to resist reductions in pay and conditions. But those who are entirely award-reliant, who until now have been subject to the collective protection of awards, are people who are without individual market bargaining power. They have suddenly had that collective protection taken away.

Women have more to lose from the attacks on institutions and from the shift to individual contracts. Unionism and collective bargaining have a bigger positive effect on women's pay than on men's. Conversely, individual contracting has a bigger negative effect on women's pay than men's. Women on individual contract agreements have an hourly wage one-fifth lower than men, whereas for women on collective agreements the difference is only one-tenth.

Throw this in with the welfare-to-work laws, which target sole mothers and the disabled, and we have an unpalatable mix. Because if a sole mother is offered a job on an AWA that has no penalty rates, no overtime pay, no meal breaks, no shift allowances, no leave loading, no redundancy pay and only pays minimum wage, and she knocks it back, she is breached and without income for eight weeks. Then where does she go?

David Peetz

WorkChoices killed off the ability of women and unions to pursue equal pay, parental leave and other important conditions through industrial tribunals. Indeed, some types of equal pay claims are now illegal. At the same time, actions that are illegal may become increasingly tolerated. Western Australia's Equal Opportunity Commissioner warned that one consequence of WorkChoices is a fear among workers about lodging complaints concerning discrimination. Stripped of the collective protections provided by the law – or at least, of confidence in these protections – it is women who are most vulnerable in the dysfunctional workplace.

But it is both easy and dangerous to fall into a sort of resigned torpor, to accept that all our rights have been taken away and we might as well just get used to it. In reality, workers still have many rights at work. There are a lot fewer than existed in the past, but they still exist. The problem for many workers is to know what rights they still have, and possess the confidence to exercise them. This is a special problem for non-unionists, who make up the majority of employees, as they are less likely to be informed about their rights or to have the ability to enforce them.

In one way, workers are lucky that WorkChoices came in when it did – during a resource-driven boom. For many occupations, there simply are not enough workers to meet employers' needs. But try explaining to the half a million workers presently unemployed that they are the ones with the upper hand in bargaining with a potential employer, and see what sort of look you get. Explain it to the sole parents or the disabled people on "welfare-to-work". The "boom" is uneven, many people are missing out (real wages are falling for about half the workforce), and economic growth is slow in several states. No boom lasts forever, and this one will come to an end as surely as every other one has. Then, even the workers who are momentarily protected from the effects of these laws, because their skills are in short supply, will find them biting hard.

In the long run, it is that fundamental shift in power – which eventually tears away the entitlements that workers fought so long to get – that represents the biggest threat posed by these laws. It is not what it does in 2007 or 2008 that comprises the worst aspects of WorkChoices; it is what it could do to the prospects of our children and our grandchildren. ∎

David Peetz is the author of *Brave New Workplace* (Allen & Unwin, 2006) and Professor of Industrial Relations at Griffith University.

# Big Ideas with Griffith REVIEW 2007

A series of forums chaired by **Julianne Schultz**, in partnership with the Art Gallery Society of New South Wales.

Sunday 18 March:
**The Trouble with Paradise**

Join this important discussion of the restrictions upon freedom of expression in the name of national security. With **Frank Moorhouse** and **David Marr**.

Early May:
**Hot Air: Confronting Climate Change**

A unique opportunity to see **Louise O'Halloran**, Executive Director of the Ethical Investment Association, one of 85 Australians trained by Al Gore to deliver his climate change presentation.

Thursday 31 May:
**Unintended Consequences**

**Noel Pearson**, Australia's most innovative and important Aboriginal leader, examines the agenda for future indigenous relations on the 40th anniversary of the referendum that granted Aboriginal people full citizenship.

ART GALLERY SOCIETY NSW

Booking is essential for these events:
Telephone: 02 9225 1878 or on the web at
www.artgallery.nsw.gov.au/membership/events

## Essay:
## Destination: Adelaide
## Author:
## Tracy Crisp

In the days when seatbelts were optional and parents smoked in the car without a second thought, Adelaide was a destination. We visited my grandfather. He gave us bags of copper coins and we spent them in department stores. Adelaide had movies and music, trains and a tram. It had traffic lights and Hindley Street and Sportsgirl in the Mall.

I came to university and thought I had arrived. I had black stirrup pants, a paisley shirt, new sunglasses and my own chequebook. I bought my first carafe of red. On hot days, I went to the Art Gallery. I saw Michael Hutchence, Bono and Annie Lennox. Live at Memorial Drive. Hoodoo Gurus in pubs. But only four years later, degree complete, the department stores weren't that big and Hindley Street wasn't that long. Jobs were too hard to find, too easy to lose.

I left my destination, and I was not alone.

Demographer Graeme Hugo says that "substantial" net migration losses from South Australia "reached record proportions" in the 1990s. We wanted adventure, higher incomes, jobs. We didn't know we were part of a trend which would have a significant impact on the growth and structure of the state. Hugo says "the effect of the net loss interstate has been amplified by the fact that it disproportionately contained the young workforce and economically productive groups" including a high proportion of young women.

Over the last decade, South Australia's population growth has been the slowest of all states except Tasmania. And, in a greying world, South Australia is greyer than most. Don't look at the statistics. Just look around.

What if these trends continue? In Series B of the Australian Bureau of Statistics' most recent *Population Projections*, the South Australian population is projected to peak at 1.65 million in 2032, then begin to decline and further age, so that by 2051 there will be around 1.58 million people living in South Australia, and around 30 per cent of us will be over sixty-five (compared with 15 per cent over sixty-five in 2004). Population projections are rooted in assumptions and are not intended as predictions or forecasts, but the scenario is not unrealistic. Those are not church bells you can hear – they're alarms.

In its 2003 paper, *A Framework for Economic Development in South Australia*, the Economic Development Board quotes Tom Peters as saying: "You can't shrink your way to greatness". Noting that "economic development has population consequences and vice versa" the board recommends "that the government formulate a State population policy as a matter of urgency".

Hugo writes: "While zero population growth and slow growth does not necessarily mean lower prosperity, the spectre of a declining workforce and population, and of the evolving age structure in the state are issues of concern. Accordingly, what is needed is a policy which weighs up the economic, social and environmental consequences of a range of population futures and selects a scenario which is most beneficial to all of these areas."

In 2004, the state government released *Prosperity Through People: A Population Policy for South Australia*. In his foreword, the Premier states that the population trends are considered " key barriers to the State's continued economic and social development". He says: "We must refuse to accept the inevitability of population decline and recognise the need to respond to the ageing of our population. I am confident ... that we can increase our population – and protect our environment – by ensuring development takes place within an overall framework of sustainability." The policy sets a population target of two million by 2050, with strategies focused on migration ("new" migrants and expatriates); fertility and ageing, and striking a better work–life balance to give flexibility and support to parents and mature-aged people; and labour force and skills development. This feeds into the government's strategic plan, *Creating Opportunity*, designed to create a dynamic, inviting state.

A destination and a place to stay. A place to which people will return.

In June 2006, the Strategic Plan Audit Committee rated progress of the population target as "unclear" (which means no data or no new data are available or measurement is problematic). The overseas migration target was rated as on track to meet the target in the timeframe, but there was little or no movement made on the interstate migration target. The committee reported that "the target will ultimately prove to be unachievable unless urgent and extensive actions are taken".

I left Adelaide one year after I graduated, one day after I married. We had one-way tickets and an idea that we wouldn't return. We didn't tell my mother-in-law that – there were tears enough – we said "five years, tops". And we left our half-finished boat in my father-in-law's shed. "We'll be back to pick it up," we said.

But my mother died in a car accident, and I found her absence too hard to understand. I tried for a few more years, but in the end I had to come back to the places she should have been, but was not.

I thought the stay was temporary, and that I would leave again. I thought we would buy a Norwood maisonette (an investment – Adelaide real estate was cheap), give it a lick of paint, grab the boat and be back on our way. But we stayed. It wasn't a decision we made – we just stayed. We read the letters then emails from our friends, and caught up with them for lunch when they came back from Melbourne for Christmas or brought fiancés home from London to meet their mums. They continued not living here, and we continued to stay.

Charles Landry, cultural planner, "international authority on city futures" and the state's second Thinker in Residence, estimates that, of Adelaide's one million inhabitants, "perhaps 250,000 are underachieving". In his report *Rethinking Adelaide: Capturing Imagination*, he says that "in Adelaide people with a high level of ambition find it hard to realise their potential. It feels as though the pool of risk takers and thinking people is too small to stimulate people to achieve more."

And more than the frustrations and thwarted ambitions of the entrepreneurial, professional and middle classes, Landry says that some of Adelaide's inhabitants are underachieving "desperately" and "leading a life that both drains them and Adelaide".

In *Extending Opportunity to All: A Blueprint for the Elimination of Poverty in South Australia*, the South Australian Council of Social Service notes that "almost a quarter of all South Australians are living in poverty … South Australians do want prosperity, more and better job opportunities, a better education for their children, and health and wellbeing. More than these, they seek to live in an embracing and genuinely inclusive community where the same opportunities are extended to all. The greatest barrier to this for South Australians is poverty."

Unlike the rest of Australia, where the gap between rich and poor has widened, "South Australians have become more equal in recent years, not because of the rising affluence of the worst off, but because of the declining relative standing of the best-off," says Dr Peter Travers from Flinders University. Landry explores the psychology of a city which allows, might even encourage, its inhabitants to "underachieve". Our culture, he says, is one of "constraint". In Adelaide, there is "a sense of trapped energy. A preference for order and perfectionism for which the Light plan of the city stands as the supreme emblem."

Someone once said to me: "Oh, I lived in Adelaide for a while, it was very repressed, all those lines on the footpath at the bus stops … and everyone stood in them!"

I didn't remember painted lines at bus stops. "But if the lines were there," I said, "why wouldn't you stand in them?"

She blinked, but didn't laugh.

"Yet it is a place that knows it needs to contrive opportunities out of nothing in order to survive with few natural resources," Landry writes. "So within this settled order creativity is occasionally allowed to burst out, exemplified by the Dunstan era."

At the moment, though, we are stifling our creativity and entrepreneurship. "A major challenge for Adelaide is confidence and the need to feel more relaxed about itself and less defensive. It could start by no longer promoting itself with adjectives such as 'sensational Adelaide' and projecting itself simply as 'Adelaide' – and allowing that to speak for itself."

Oh, yes please. That would be great.

"Cities can import resources and they need to; they can attract outside talent to refresh [their] inner gills and they have to; but most of all they need to achieve endogenous growth," he says.

"Harnessing the creative potential of local people has to be the defining core of Adelaide's reinvigoration." He put that bit in bold.

People say Adelaide is a difficult place to break into. Our defensive parochialism is notorious, our establishment infamous, our history littered with people who – depending on your perspective – either left in a huff or were driven out. Peter Sellars in the arts, Gary Ayers in sport.

When I first moved to Adelaide, I was seduced by my potential anonymity. I had been living in a provincial city, defined by my relationship to my parents, both of them teachers and one of them in politics. "Oh. You're Crispy's daughter," people said, not always with a smile.

In the city, I could drink and smoke and kiss whoever I liked and my parents would never know. But a million people isn't as many as you might think, especially not in a city-state. South Australians weave their way in and out of Adelaide. There's a city-versus-country divide, but there are 1.5 million South Australians, and 1.1 million of them live in Adelaide. We come here for appointments with the specialist, for trade school, to find a wedding dress, a job. Sooner or later you will know someone who knows someone standing next to you in the queue.

At the same time, you can know a lot of people in Adelaide, and still not know enough. In my first week at university, I learnt that the girls who carried dark green or navy blue Country Road bags would join the Foreign Affairs Department and had already been to France. I hadn't known that France was somewhere you could go. I was on the edges of the Adelaide Establishment where no one cared that I was the "daughter of Denis".

Whatever their weaknesses, networks do have enormous strengths. Adelaide's first Circle of Friends was established in 2002. Within a year, there were twenty-two, all supporting refugees and asylum seekers living in detention or finding their way into our community. And Adelaide's establishment is not impenetrable. Mike Rann, Jane Lomax-Smith, Robert Champion de Crespigny, Carole Whitelock – none of them are from these parts originally. And if that list sounds elitist, class is not a barrier to success in Adelaide. Robyn Archer, writer, singer, festival director, and Mark Bickley, Crows premiership captain, Chair of SA Great – they aren't establishment names.

Mark Bickley. I grew up around the corner from him.

I was in Sydney on the last day of Juan Davila's exhibition at the Museum of Contemporary Art. Breakfast in Glebe, then Crown Street, Hyde Park, a ferry, cicadas, humidity. A Sydney day. Until the MCA.

I had forgotten that Davila had painted Adelaide. "The Institute of Architects Bombs Adelaide" and "The Ruins of Adelaide City Council Real Estate Office at Victoria Square" took me by surprise. His essay, "The Ruins of Adelaide", reproduced in the newly-published book, jolted me.

"Colonel William Light's 1837 plan for the city of Adelaide has been a curse." Like his paintings, Davila's words are harsh. "This virtual city plan is a fortress – copied from Europe – to exclude disorder … Adelaide's master plan sanitises the city, violently excluding presentations of histories, ideas and behaviour outside the Anglo-Saxon experience."

Davila's Victoria Square is disorderly. Its foreground flooded, the Hilton and Town Hall toppling, the three rivers fountain being filled with urine from atop.

This is the place where – several times a week – my children and I get on and off the tram. It is the place where the Aboriginal flag first flew, and it is now flown here permanently. I have heard, in a welcome to country, that Light knew what this place meant to the Kaurna people when he made it the centre of his Adelaide.

It has two official names – Tarndanyangga and Victoria Square – but most people call it Victoria Square. Here is Davila again: "The declaration of dry zones – no drinking alcohol in the public spaces – as an affirmation of a will for order can be read as a perver-

## Destination: Adelaide

sion, given the dependence of the economy on the wine industry. It also targets those forced to drink in the city squares, unlike those who drink in grand settings." Can't argue with that.

I bought the Davila book, retreated to the airport, sat in the departure lounge. I smiled at the friend of a friend, at the person who seemed to recognise me although I did not recognise him, then chatted with two people I haven't seen for years. "So you're still living in Adelaide." I nodded, then said it back.

On the plane, I read Davila's essay again.

"The River Torrens area was appropriated and dominated by a free settler's concept of urban space, one which has denied people since the beginning – particularly minorities – the right to decide their own lifestyles ... The River Torrens is an odd refuge for children that are delinquents. It has become a scenario for the splendours of crime and also for its misery. The church and the accommodated classes in Adelaide favour charity: that is to say, to give to someone lesser than you that you never meet, of course."

I look out for the Torrens whenever I fly home, for the Festival Centre peaks and the Convention Centre glass. And on other nights, the Torrens' lights feel soft and warm.

For a view I love of Adelaide, I go time and again to the intimacy of Barbara Hanrahan's "Weird Adelaide", published in *The Adelaide Review* in 1988 and "sponsored by the SA Tourism Department".

Hanrahan gives us darkness: "Even in the daytime the streets of classy North Adelaide and Unley Park can be tunnels, enclosed by green leaves. And so quiet, so secretive, all the people shut away behind their high walls ... At night, Adelaide turns film noir, becomes a miniature Cornell Woolrich city, its empty side-streets black and creepy, with a feel of the back lot at Paramount or Universal."

But weird isn't always sinister. "The Spooner girls in their silver-spoon private-school uniforms, just the right degree of wrinkle in their socks, outside Sportsgirl in Rundle Mall. The frog cakes on their paper doilies in Balfours; the naughty R-rated moulds under the counter (ASK ASSISTANT) in the cake shop in Adelaide Arcade." And she rounds the picture out: "weirdness can have a distinctive beauty," she says of the Museum, Botanic Gardens, Beehive Corner, West Terrace Cemetery, hotels "and so much more".

In mourning the continuing loss of the artefacts of the everyday ("generations and generations of working-class people, quite disappeared"), Hanrahan foreshadowed Landry: "What we want now in Adelaide are writers and artists who work from the heart of those commonplace suburban streets, who recognise the weirdness of the ordinary, who record it before the version of it we have now is swept away. We want passion and intensity, an art that comes from places like Port Adelaide and Thebarton and Holden Hill; that stays unofficially weird."

While I am writing this essay, I bump into a friend just returned from a day's work in Melbourne and he says: "Is Adelaide a good place to live?" The question mark is a given. If you live in a place that people leave, you can't help asking yourself: is it me? Every now and then, you're forced to wonder: why do I live here?

Do people in Melbourne, Brisbane, Sydney, Perth have these conversations over their Saturday shopping brunch?

I live here because Adelaide is good for families. We can afford a better house than we could elsewhere. We're close to town and it's easy to get to the beach. Spring is awful, but autumn is glorious. The Fringe invigorates. I like living in a place that has been so good for women and has a deposit on soft drink cans. I cherish trips to Kangaroo Island, the drive-in at Gepps Cross. I like fishing from the Brighton jetty with my friend on Saturday nights (what a collection of squid jags she has), the pink pig statue on O'Connell Street, and our tall white-barked trees. It costs $2.50 to take a Port River "dolphin cruise".

And remember that first year of fire sculptures at WOMADelaide? A tinder dry summer, the smell of fuel, men from France speaking French. Constrained. But not.

People will come to Adelaide and people will leave. We'll never be Queensland, but we've got submarines, overseas students and the cusp of a mining boom. We make great chocolates, art and wine. London beckoned for Robert Champion de Crespigny, but J.M. Coetzee moved here asking "what kind of place is this … is this paradise on earth? What does one have to do to live here? Does one have to die first?"

If it really was death that brought me back, if that wasn't an excuse I made to explain my return to myself and to my friends, it's not death that makes me stay.

Six years ago, my grandfather, my husband and I drove past Gepps Cross and Bolivar, through Port Wakefield, then detoured to Port Augusta for home-made iced coffee with friends. Then back we went, out to the Flinders Ranges. They felt ancient, quiet and still. We stayed in the Blinman shack that my grandfather had stayed in every year for years. It was September and already hot. I was pregnant, so I couldn't have gin or beer or antihistamines. My grandfather showed us the wettest creek beds and the best rocks to climb. He showed us quandong trees and fossil beds. He told us the names of every flower we found, every bird

### Destination: Adelaide

we heard. We drank lemonade at the Parachilna Pub and at the end of the day, when the sky changed colour and the kangaroos grazed, my grandfather sat. And I sat next to him.

Six months later, the baby had been born, an unexpected congenital condition diagnosed, surgery proposed, done. My grandfather, then eighty-five, caught the train to the hospital every day for two weeks to hold my baby's hand.

And mine.

Five years after that, the baby is a boy starting school and my grandfather says: "That's where my Uncle Hal went to school." There is a photo of Hal and his classmates at the front of the school and when my grandfather gives that photo to me, I know that's why I left. And that's what brought me back. And that's what keeps me here. ■

---

Tracy Crisp is an Adelaide-based writer. Her memoir, "Scapho is Greek for boat" was published in *Griffith REVIEW 4: Making Perfect Bodies*.

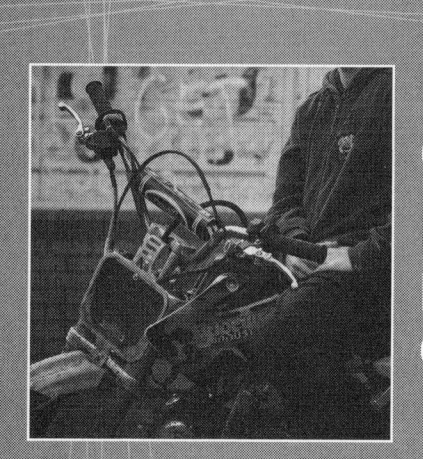

Reportage:
**On the ground**
Reporter:
**Natasha Cica**

*Image: 15 year olds Sam and Luke with their motorbike outside a local fish and chip in the outer Hobart suburb of Gagebrook, Tasmania / Photographer Peter Mathew.*

# On the ground

Glenn MacGregor's house has stunning river and mountain views, neatly netted fig trees in the garden, and a collection of cars including a Volvo and a Mercedes parked in the driveway. What do you assume about Glenn? What if I also mention he's a long-term resident of Bridgewater, a satellite suburb on the far north-eastern edge of Hobart that was built as a public housing broad-acre estate in the 1970s?

That mixed bag of facts won't gel for readers in Hobart. With its neighbouring estate, Gagebrook, Bridgewater has long been on the far wrong side of the tracks. These suburbs are notorious for scoring low on qualifications, skills, literacy, employment and income, and high on welfare dependency, substance abuse, crime, teenage pregnancy and family breakdown. In a state which has lagged behind the nation on many of these indicators, these estates have lagged behind the state.

The area's outgoing Labor federal member Harry Quick recalls that, when he started teaching in the local high school in 1990, it was "blackboard jungle stuff". By 1997, Bridgewater was considered to have Australia's lowest level of wellbeing. Whole streets of public housing stood vacant, houses smashed and torched. Housing Tasmania administrators remember people writing on their applications that they wouldn't live in Bridgewater or Gagebrook – no matter how desperate they were.

A decade later, these stereotypes persist. A few months back, *The Mercury* gave front-page coverage to a stone-throwing campaign by local kids against Metro bus drivers, and published a flame-licked arson map evoking last year's riots in the Paris projects. Locals maintain that the stories were sensationalised, that these were the actions of a smaller than ever handful of troublemakers, that Bridgewater and Gagebrook have changed. But I'm apprehensive as well as curious when I drive the twenty kilometres from inner-city Hobart.

"Are you sure you're a journalist?" asks Tony Foster, half joking, when I tell him I want to write a different kind of story. The mayor of Brighton – a municipality taking in Bridgewater and Gagebrook as well as more genteel neighbouring rural-residential areas – since the early 1990s, Foster spent his own childhood in public housing across the river. He's well known for throwing the arms and heart of Brighton open to the Kosovar Albanian refugees dumped there by Canberra in 1999. "I like having goals and bringing them to fruition," he says. In recent years, these have included a radical plan for total local water reuse that has let opium poppies, canola seed, market gardens and orchards bloom on Brighton's dry agricultural land, and a still-evolving blueprint for his municipality to become a hub for rail transport, and to attract industry and enterprise.

On the ground

Foster's biggest challenge has been the bad reputation of Bridgewater and Gagebrook. "Thirty years on, we still haven't been able to remove the stigma. It will happen, but it didn't take that long in other disadvantaged areas of Hobart with high levels of public housing built in the 1950s and 1960s," he says.

Like everyone else I talk to, Foster identifies the lack of basic infrastructure – transport, shops, services, sporting and recreational facilities – as a central, ongoing problem. A single visit reinforces this truth. Despite the postcard views of the Derwent River and Mount Wellington, the built landscape is bleak. The East Derwent highway slices the sprawling estates of purpose-built, grey-block houses into four awkward sectors dotted with lonely Metro bus stops, splotched with vandal-proof paint jobs. Bridgewater's shabby shopping centre is marooned on top of a hill, which heavy young mums with cheap prams and older pensioners struggle to reach on foot. There is a bargain store called Chickenfeed, a supermarket and a charity shop, its windows covered with metal grilles. In Gagebrook, homeboys on bikes cluster around the graffiti-smeared front of a fish-and-chip shop. Bigger blokes hot-rod around suburban cul de sacs, or fold their arms with attitude as I drive past front yards cluttered with car wrecks. I suspect they're up to no good. Druggies and dropouts for sure.

Hang on a minute. Exactly who has the attitude problem here? What do I think I'm doing, cruising like a tourist in my prissy Barina? On the edge of a children's playground, I pull over and get out, photographer in tow.

It's a good place to stop. The kids stare, then ask us what we're up to, then pose like Britney Spears or James Dean, and ask us to write down their names, or run away giggling, the same open/closed blend of honesty and shyness you'll find in any playground in Tasmania. We notice this playground's named in honour of someone determined to help Bridgewater and Gagebrook shift gears.

Domestic violence drove Chris Fitzpatrick and her young children from "normal" Hobart suburbia to these estates in the early 1990s. By 1996, she was running the Bridgewater/Gagebrook Urban Renewal Project (BURP), an organisation established with one-off funding from federal minister Brian Howe's "Building Better Cities" program, whose management team also included representatives of the local police, high school, businesses, council and housing. Fitzpatrick saw a direct connection between social and economic exclusion and low self-esteem. Determined to build that esteem, Fitzpatrick mobilised her community through BURP to communicate and collaborate in a remarkable exercise of DIY civil society.

An early Fitzpatrick target was a gang of teenage boys who were living in unsupervised groups in public housing units and wreaking havoc in the neighbourhood. Fitzpatrick sent a message to the gang leader, "Billy", saying she wanted to do a deal. His return message said he'd be at her house at seven o'clock the next night. Exactly on time, he knocked on her door and asked what she wanted. She said she wanted to talk.

Billy said he thought he'd come for a drug deal, and she answered that no, she needed him to talk to young people about what they wanted. "I'll pay you – this is called consultation," she said.

The next morning, Billy left a piece of paper for her under a rock. On it he'd written: "We'd like to play sport ... we'd like a place to go where no one will move us on." Fitzpatrick acted on these suggestions and Billy and his gang came on board. The bottom line, says Harry Quick, was: "If you're part of the community, you shouldn't stuff the community up, and we'll exclude you if you won't be part of the process."

By the late 1990s, BURP had set up sports teams and facilities, adult literacy classes, computer training, women's self defence lessons, mural painting, tree planting, a needle exchange program, a community festival, house painting, gardening, landscaping and fence painting schemes. It employed young people to look after their schools and vacant housing in the holidays, orchestrated winning entries in the Hobart Christmas Pageant, Rock Eisteddfod, Southern Men's Basketball tournament and Tidy Towns competition, and supported a home purchase assistance program for public housing tenants. Vandalism and property crime dropped dramatically, as did housing vacancy rates. *The Mercury* started running good news stories about Bridgewater and Gagebrook. For the first time, residents took real pride in themselves and their neighbourhood.

Tragically, Fitzpatrick died three years ago of cancer. (Local lore has it that, shortly before her death, a former member of Billy's gang called her from East Timor, telling her three of them had made it into the Australian army, thanking her for saving them from jail, and saying boot camp was bad but no harder than growing up in Bridgewater.)

Fitzpatrick's partner Gary Nasers now runs BURP. Today the organisation is mainly self-funded, with some support from Brighton Council and Housing Tasmania. Nasers is the first to admit Fitzpatrick's death left a big hole, and that despite the sense of community she undoubtedly engendered, Bridgewater and Gagebrook still score disturbingly high on most measures of socio-economic exclusion. But Nasers is positive about the future. He thinks BURP should now focus on developing education, training and employment opportunities, especially for young people. "It's very hard, labour intensive work," says Nasers. "You need a true comprehension of

On the ground

what damage is done by three generations of poverty and welfare dependence. You have to ask how you can break into that cycle. So we've paused a bit to explore how to do that. I'd like to see this community develop a pilot scheme for a broader, whole person, case management approach."

Nasers wants to set up a youth leadership program, and to develop a local plant nursery into a horticultural and agricultural skills training centre. More modest projects include the Turn Right program supplying a car, petrol and a mature volunteer adult to help young people clock up the fifty hours' supervised driving practice they need to get their P-plates, a model since copied elsewhere. A Hobart woman donated the first car, a local caryard supplied two more, then a battered Volvo appeared.

These are the vehicles in Glenn MacGregor's driveway – but the old Mercedes is his own. So is his house, situated across an empty paddock from BURP, where the former log truck driver now works as a volunteer. This puts him on the right side of a very new dividing line in Bridgewater and Gagebrook – between the approximately one-third of estate residents who bought their houses before Tasmania's property boom between 1999 and 2003, when median house prices doubled across the state and more than trebled in Bridgewater, so that a house that sold pre-boom for around $40,000 can today easily fetch $150,000 – and those who did not.

The stability of this prosperity shift for the "new haves" in Bridgewater and Gagebrook remains to be seen. Mortgagors and even established home owners in these suburbs – and indeed wider Tasmania – could prove unexpectedly vulnerable when the real estate bubble deflates and the economy stalls or slides. As University of Tasmania housing policy experts Michelle Gabriel and Keith Jacobs have observed, "structural economic downturns across Australia tend to be deeper and last longer in Tasmania" because of its "relatively marginal and isolated nature". And, as ANZ chief economist Saul Eslake argued in 2005, even in this economic boom time Tasmanians still rank relatively poorly on key indicators like income (20 per cent less than mainlanders), net household worth (31 per cent less), employment (57 per cent compared with 62 per cent nationally), long-term unemployment (one-third of total unemployed, compared with one-fifth nationally), children in sole-parent households (29.5 per cent compared with 23.3 per cent nationally) or households where no parent is employed (one-fifth of all Tasmanian children) and – critically for Eslake – educational attainment (44.1 per cent of working-age Tasmanians have not completed year 12, compared with 32.3 per cent nationally).

The "new have nots" are already feeing the pinch, not least of windfall envy. This boom has placed home ownership out of the reach of many Tasmanians, including the majority of Bridgewater and Gagebrook locals who missed out when prices were lower. House prices of $150,000 might seem like peanuts today in mainland or even mainstream Hobart terms, but unemployment in these suburbs remains far above national and Tasmanian averages, and household income, educational attainment and earning potential fall far below. Today, too, demand far outstrips the supply of public housing in these estates and elsewhere. Private rents across greater Hobart and Tasmania have soared, private sector vacancy rates are tight, and the state government has sold off substantial housing stock without (yet) delivering adequate replacement. Having traditionally enjoyed less "housing stress" than all other Australians with the exception of residents of the Australian Capital Territory, market forces have put Tasmanians on an uncomfortable and unfamiliar par with mainlanders in relation to housing costs and homelessness. Hobart housing recently became the second least affordable of any capital city after Sydney, and there are three thousand families and individuals on Tasmania's public housing waiting list – a locally unprecedented number – many of whom sleep in tents or cars or depend on emergency shelter.

Some assert Bridgewater and Gagebrook were built thirty years ago to put some of the poorest of Australia's poorest state out of sight and mind. Maybe so, but no policy wonk or service provider crafting socio-economic solutions for analogous problems today – anywhere in Australia – can afford to ignore the unfolding lessons of this remote experiment in broad-acre housing. Estates like Bridgewater and Gagebrook were dreamed up at a moment of supreme optimism in the public sphere and faith in the welfare state. And they were doomed to fail, according to Keith Jacobs – not because that sentiment was necessarily misplaced, but because of the "tenure bias" in Australian housing policy, so that generous tax subsidies have favoured private home ownership, entrenching public housing as the tenancy of last resort, increasingly a ghetto for high-needs residents and without adequate resources to meet those needs.

There is a clear and growing need for more balanced and sustainable housing policy across the state and the nation, avoiding both neo-liberal and welfarist excesses and extremes. But the main message I took out of Bridgewater and Gagebrook is that top-down solutions must be complemented by community-driven initiatives. In turn, this demands more of Fitzpatrick's kind of attitude, working from the bottom up to bring out the best in what looks – to most – like the worst. ■

References and notes available at www.griffith.edu.au/griffithreview

Dr Natasha Cica is the director of Hobart-based management and communications consultancy Periwinkle Projects. She writes regularly for *The Age* and *The Financial Review Magazine*. Her essay "Talking on the terrace" was published in *Griffith REVIEW 3: Webs of Power*.

Divided Nation

## Essay:
## Disturbing undertones
## Author:
## Dorothy Johnston

Australian fiction writers have, until the last few decades, avoided settling in Canberra and writing about the city in their novels and short stories. In *Wild Weeds and Wind Flowers*, Ric Throssell's biography of his mother, Katharine Susannah Prichard, he notes her comment that the national capital was "like a town made by Pinocchio. All that neatness and prettiness, so far removed from the struggle for existence." Historian Keith Hancock recalled his impressions of returning after an absence in his autobiography *Country and Calling*. "Canberra, now that I saw it again, both irritated and charmed me. Charles Hawker used to say that it was a good sheep station spoiled."

The same put-down has been repeated in countless clichés since, from "soul-less city" to Prime Minister John Howard's air of surprise as he remarked, after the 2003 bushfires that killed four people, injured several hundred and destroyed 491 homes, that Canberrans were reacting just like other "normal" Australians to their loss.

The point – whether made subtly or not – is that, while Canberra may possess certain physical attractions such as clean streets, plenty of trees, jobs in the public service and a lack of congestion, the city will somehow forever remain a stranger to passion and grief; that matters which fully engage the human heart will be shed at its borders – like a coat, if hearts were worn on sleeves, but more like an emptying of the spirit and a form of voluntary evisceration. This activity, leading to a kind of death, spells death also to the creative imagination.

The first published novel set in Canberra, *Plaque with Laurel* by M. Barnard Eldershaw – the pen name of Marjorie Barnard and Flora Eldershaw – first appeared in 1937. There is an irony and aptness in *Plaque with Laurel* being about a writers' conference, whose characters converge from elsewhere (mainly Sydney) and return to other, more interesting and absorbing places at the story's end. T.A.G. Hungerford's *Riverslake*, set in a workers' hostel, was published

Dorothy Johnston

in 1953, then there is another long gap before Robert Macklin's *The Paper Castle* in 1977. In 1981, Blanche d'Alpuget's *The Turtle Beach* followed Macklin's example of combining various Asian settings with a Canberra base, and ushered in two decades during which prose fiction has flourished.

Clichés and misconceptions have not lost their force. During his decade as Prime Minister, John Howard has steadfastly refused to live in the Lodge. A ubiquitous form of synecdoche in which "Canberra" elides to "Federal Parliament" – as in "Canberra decides", "Canberra to blame" – makes it harder for anybody living outside to understand the place as a collection of citizens, or even to want to. Canberrans enjoy high incomes and education levels relative to the rest of the country. Over 63 per cent voted "yes" in the republic referendum, by far the highest percentage of any state or territory, and we consistently vote Labor in federal elections.

The Griffin Legacy Plan, which advocates returning to Walter Burley Griffin's 1918 blueprint as a guide to Canberra's development over the next thirty years, was unveiled by the National Capital Authority in 2004. If the plan is followed, a "curving sea" of buildings will accommodate an additional 60,000 people in central Canberra. An unspoken question behind this plan, as with all previous ones, is how the affected citizens will live up to it. It's between the grandeur of the democratic vision and the human falling back – perhaps falling back right inside the earth – that the idea of the Gothic is born.

When I moved from Melbourne to Canberra in the late 1970s, I'd published the odd poem and short story, but nothing substantial. I was working on a novel. I moved because my partner was offered a job in the press gallery and I worried, among other things, about whether I'd be able to write fiction in Canberra, what I would write about – whether my imagination was stuck somewhere in Victoria and, if not, how much of it might be transportable.

It wasn't until several years later, when my son became very ill, and spent time in the infectious diseases ward of the old Canberra Hospital, that I was able to answer part of this question for myself. A child lying near to death in a hospital above an artificial lake led to my first story about Canberra, "The Boatman of Lake Burley Griffin". It's a short piece in which the lake takes on an undertone of the River Styx, the boatman unable to find his way across. Our lake was flooded in 1963, drowning a farmhouse, sheep paddocks and racetrack. At the centre of the city said to have no centre, it seemed to me then – as it has often since – an instance of the gap, or hole, between nature and culture. In those terrifying days, it was also an unnavigable passage between life and death.

It is gaps, disjunctures, edges that don't fit that have come to interest me most in this city where I've lived now for more than a quarter of a century. And in those gaps, what can – and sometimes inspiringly does – grow up is a form of theatre, a parody of public faces and publicly acceptable facades.

The best known of these is the Aboriginal Tent Embassy. First erected in 1972, in protest against the McMahon government's refusal to recognise indigenous land rights, the tent embassy has achieved an almost permanent presence on the lawns opposite Old Parliament House, though a proposal for its replacement by an "education" building is being considered as I write.

The term "embassy" implies a sovereign state, yet this one has been condemned as an "eyesore", "disturbing undertone", "blight on the national capital" and "a squalid slum that should be removed". The embassy has made good use of Canberra's physical and political landscape: the nearby streets lined with luxurious embassies in Red Hill and Yarralumla have given the symbols of tents, Aboriginal flag and sacred fire an added potency. For over three decades, it has asserted its provocative status, a thorn in the side of successive governments. It has been forcibly and violently removed, only to return with greater strength. It has been listed on the National Estate by the Australian Heritage Commission. Funeral and wedding ceremonies have been held there. A long and honourable tradition of protest in front of the Parliament has been maintained.

This tradition was changed fundamentally by the move up, and into, Capital Hill. The new Parliament House, in spite of the planners' and architects' intentions, has turned out to be a much more effective fortress than the old one ever was. Soon after arriving in Canberra, I took part in a demonstration inside Kings Hall, against budget cuts to women's refuges. We banged garbage bin lids and made a nuisance of ourselves. Kings Hall in the Old Parliament House was a genuine meeting place. Paths crossed between the chambers, members from opposing sides brought together. The public was allowed to mingle. The Members' Hall at the centre of the new building is a pale replica. It is just a crossing space between the chambers, closed to the public, who must content themselves with looking down on their politicians from an upper level.

Dorothy Johnston

Our Parliament is even more of a fortress now, with bollards and prohibitions against walking on the roof. Yet demonstrations still occur on the lawns outside – huge, imaginative demonstrations, like the Sea of Hands, made huge to correspond with the long, green, undulating space. Gigantism and parody effectively evolved.

In 1988, the ACT achieved self-government. Our fourteen-member Legislative Assembly and successive chief ministers, Labor and Liberal, have caused headaches for federal governments and the National Capital Authority Legislation decriminalising marijuana and prostitution was quickly passed, and bans were removed on X-rated videos and magazines so that Canberra became a centre for the distribution of pornography. Assembly debates from this period make interesting reading, for the arguments back and forth over the image the capital ought to project and confusion about the purpose of its citizens. A kind of up-yours attitude has developed under the big foot of the Commonwealth which, from time to time, squashes the tiny territory's determination to make its own laws. As with the Tent Embassy, it is proximity which lends bite to gestures of protest or defiance. We are just under their noses. They can pretend to ignore us, but they can't.

A brothel called Parliament House in Fyshwick, one of Canberra's industrial suburbs, mirrors and pokes fun at its namesake. In Canberra, prostitution is zoned light industrial, which means it's legal in Fyshwick, Hume and Mitchell and illegal everywhere else. This is perhaps a comment on the absence of heavy industry. In these zones, there is no traditional manufacturing to dirty the air, or watch going out of business. Parliament House Fyshwick, so discreet during the day that you would never notice it, is built above a sandwich bar and bottle shop. By night, the name becomes a great neon circle in the darkness. At sunset, customers and potential customers begin to gather. They buy six packs at the bottle shop. They've parked their Commodores, utes and semi-trailers, and stand around them, cans and bottles in their hands, kidding one another while they work up enough courage to walk through Parliament House's door.

My other favourite brothel is called Club Goldfinger. It's situated on top of a discount tyre place in Mitchell. There's a large billboard at the front showing a beautiful young woman dressed in gold holding on to the Parliament House flagmast. She stands there proudly, our local Statue of Liberty. Underneath her, in big black letters, is an advertisement for the tyre place: four new tyres plus alignment $49.50, lube $39.95.

These plays of opposites tend towards the Gothic, albeit mostly in a light-hearted way. In my view, Canberra Gothic could well become its own sub-genre. I see myself contributing to it through my crime series and *The House at Number 10*, a literary novel set in an imaginary suburban brothel. Crime fiction is an interesting way to write about the layers – often absurdly separated – of this city, and to try to capture in words the contradictions – visual, physical, social and political – of living here.

It is appropriate to invoke the Gothic as a model because the most potent of our symbolic buildings rests inside, as well as rising above, a hill. Above ground, the flagmast and granite walls of the Parliament easily dwarf the surrounding landscape, and the human aspirations and endeavours they are meant to represent.

As Sir John Overall put it: "Griffin had deliberately decided against placing the Parliament on Capital Hill – the dominant natural feature of Canberra – to avoid the symbolism that would go with placing the politicians in a position where they could look over the rest of the city. But the winning design sought to remain true to Griffin's intent by burying the Parliament in the hill."

The Gothic tale, a child of the Enlightenment, both mimicked and mocked its parent. In 1788, as the First Fleet arrived at Botany Bay and the colony of New South Wales, with its projections towards a democratic future and a convict underbelly, was born, Immanuel Kant's *Critique of Practical Reason* was being published. At the same time, writes Evelyn Juers in "She Wanders: An Essay in Gothic": "Ann Radcliffe was working on her first piece of fiction, *The Castles of Athlin and Dunbayne* ". The novels which followed Radcliffe's example were often set in ancient castles, making much of locks and keys, as well as whispered secrets that led to untimely, nasty ends, and acknowledging the chthonic depths, the dungeons and hidden byways that were as important a part of a fortress as its towers.

Inside our Parliament, locked doors and secrets abound. Ravished maidens are in shorter supply, though Cheryl Kernot once blamed Canberra's artificial way of life for falling into bed with Gareth Evans. Whether newcomers arrive searching for an entry, perhaps believing it is assured them, or live with their backs turned to it, our castle's influence can be overwhelming. The fact that inland Australian light shines brightly on it, that it is seldom veiled in mist like Kafka's castle, makes it more, not less, mysterious. The clear, inland light promises truth. It suggests that nothing less will be forthcoming.

But underground is a different story. Under Knossos lies Daedalus's labyrinth. Under every seat of power lie doors and openings to a core of fear and other dark emotions, for which the Minotaur is a most powerful and enduring metaphor.

In spite of Romaldo Giurgola's design, and the democratic principles to which he and his team remained committed, I imagine Edgar Allen Poe would feel just as much at home inside our hill as Thoreau, Emerson or Kant.

Canberra's front parlour approach to visitors is also suggestive of the Gothic. Keep the parts of your house that visitors see admirably clean and neat for important guests, and on no account let your children play there. Shove out of sight into the back room, or the basement, what you don't want anybody gawking at, but can't quite discard.

The American Transcendentalists found Kant an inspiration as they developed a belief in the importance of intuition, and the individual's relationship to nature. It would be several decades before their philosophy found full expression and the classic phase of the Gothic novel came to an end. It would not be until the beginning of another new century that their teachings, coupled with Jeffersonian democratic ideals, would influence the young Walter Burley Griffin.

"Life in harmony with nature, the love of truth and virtue, will purge the eyes to understand her text," wrote Emerson in 1836. But fifty years later, giving his hundredth lecture before the Concord Lyceum, he spoke of "a war between the intellect and affection, a crack in Nature".

In Canberra, kangaroos hop down suburban streets. Once one took up residence in the park just down from our place. I suspect he'd lost his way and could not get back to Mt Majura or the O'Connor Ridge. Sometimes, having crossed a double highway from Black Mountain, mothers with joeys hop frantically along the lake. In November, bogong moths, migrating to the Snowy Mountains in their tens of millions, sometimes get blown off course. Perhaps mistaking Parliament House for the granite masses of their destination, perhaps attracted by the lights, they land on the building's roofs and walls, wing-tip to wing-tip, a fabulous velvet cloak. They play havoc with the air-conditioning and are a public nuisance. Once, on a windy spring night, I watched them lift and settle, lift and settle.

In mid-summer, when those who can afford it are down the coast, the city has that deep quiet of a country town at noon, when

## Disturbing undertones

nothing much happens out of doors. The light is so clear it hurts your eyes. As before, and starkly, what seems absent to outsiders is the human scale Griffin was keen on.

Firestorm, January 2003: trees exploding into and around the capital, fire annihilating whole suburbs that lay against pine plantations and the bush. Nature run amok and merciless, making us take notice, pay attention. The fires that killed thousands of kangaroos and possums exposed a wombat city underground, a city of vast, interconnecting tunnels, their mouths hard and unyielding as charcoal. With my family, I went out at the weekends to leave bright orange carrots at the tunnel entrances. A sentimental, futile gesture perhaps, but one that we wanted to make. In March, the autumn rains came. The rivers ran ash. Australia went to war with Iraq. People marched around Civic in tens of thousands to demonstrate against it.

When the time came to design and build a memorial to those who'd died in the bushfires, and to all that had been lost, residents decided on a small-scale tribute, on regenerated land in Stromlo Forest Park. Dedicating it in January 2006, Chief Minister Jon Stanhope praised the artists for responding "to the community's request for a memorial that is simple, natural and beautiful, a place of contemplation with running water, trees, and seating".

It is in acts of honouring the dead that the city's authentic monuments are growing. Griffin's land axis links Parliament House to the War Memorial, where a funeral service for the internment of the "unknown Australian soldier" was held in 1993. Historian Ken Inglis described this as "a climactic event in the making of a place in the nation's capital sacred to the spirit of Anzac". David Headon quotes novelist Christina Stead as calling the nation's capital "freer because it is unfinished and all its components not yet joined."

I cannot foresee a time in which they will be joined, nor do I wish for such a future for my city. The gaps allow unheralded surprises: spontaneous, troublesome, ignoble, courageous and human. ■

References available at www.griffith.edu.au/griffithreview

Dorothy Johnston is a Canberra-based writer. Her most recent novel is *The House at Number 10* (Wakefield Press, 2005).

Memoir:
**The fence**
Author:
**Shane Strange**

Image: Glenn Sloggett / Picket Fence, 2003 / from Lost Man / Type C print 80 x 80cm, edition of 15

# The fence

I am sitting on the white wooden-frame and wire fence that runs along one side of our house and separates us from our neighbours – the Bonds. I am ten. It is a hot day and the sun is burning the skin on my arms in ways that I won't know about until I am over thirty and having skin cancer cut out of them.

A flock of rosellas is eating the tiny berries off the hundred-year-old camphor laurel tree in our backyard. Their high-pitched chattering almost drowns out the sound of my Greek Cypriot Nana as she barrels down the long hallway of our large, colonial house, yelling in her accented English at my sister or at Gabby or at anyone.

Here, on the fence, I have escaped it – her anger that bears down upon us like judgement. Our shame, my shame. She complains that people don't listen to her, but they do. Thin-walled houses don't hide fury from the neighbours.

I am waiting for John Bond, the youngest of five boys and two years older than me. His dad works at the water treatment plant at Mt Crosby and comes home every weekday at the same time. He drives an old green Holden and he says "fillum" for film. "Just like a bloody Aussie," Gabby says.

All his five boys play cricket and hockey and chess. They're mad about the Beatles. They cram into two bedrooms in a postwar home on a small triangle of land that fronts on to a major road. All except Arthur, the oldest, who is a teacher and lives up north. They have a mango tree in the very back corner of their yard. They speak in big voices and go to church. They vote Labor and have pictures of the candidate on thin wooden posts in their front yard at election time.

My parents are divorced. I haven't seen my father since I was five. My mother works seven days a week in the tiny corner store that she owns, and we – my mother and sister and brother and I – live here with Nana and Gabby.

I want to play cricket with John on his backyard pitch. I want to wrap my hands around my favourite one of his cricket bats and hit the ball into the fence for four runs, or over for "six and out". I want to take the three-step run up between the fence and the bowling crease, trying, trying, trying to bowl faster, stronger, more unfathomable deliveries.

Or I want to make a tape on his tape recorder, where we pretend to be radio announcers and tape music from the radio in between our fake cricket

## The fence

scores and bad jokes. And I want his mum, Mrs Bond, to make us a cold glass of cordial and a vegemite sandwich for lunch and talk to me in her broad floating sing-song voice that complements the rosellas in the tree.

None of that will happen today because the Bonds aren't at home. They've taken the boys to cricket, or they're visiting relatives, or they're away for the weekend, together.

I know this, but it doesn't matter to me. I know I'll sit here for hours in the hot afternoon sun. I know I'll sit here until Gabby comes down and tells me to come inside and stop being so silly because they, the Bonds, have gone away for the weekend.

I imagine climbing the fence: put one foot in the wire and the other foot flat on the wood on top, two hands steady and launch myself over – free. The Bonds are my idea of normal people and I want to be normal.

Crammed into the long formal dining room of our big house, my uncle tells visiting relatives from England that: "You know, Aborigines are physically incapable of farting." He is a big man who hides his fear with intimidation. He's held on to his broad West Country accent, even though he's lived in Australia since he was fourteen. "Yes, they did a study in the '40s about it. Don't fart. Amazing, isn't it?" Everyone around the table is quiet, interested. Then my aunty says: "Ohhh, don't believe it" and my uncle breaks out a big "aren't I clever" grin. We all laugh. For many subtle reasons that I don't quite comprehend, it's a good trick.

My uncle and aunty and cousins live on a farm about half an hour out of town. My uncle is building barbed-wire fences to keep the cattle out of his cornfield. He's put a new electric fence around the farmhouse as well. When we visit, my sister and brother and cousins all sit in front of the low wires and listen to the tick, tick, tick as the current passes through, daring each other to touch it.

In the early '90s, my uncle and aunty joined a fringe right-wing party – the Citizens' Forum or something like that. They believed in abolishing land rights and keeping immigrants out, even though my family came to Australia on a boat in 1960.

My uncle died of stomach cancer when he was fifty-seven. He wanted to build an observatory on the hill behind his farmhouse so he could look freely at the stars.

At night, I emerge from a bath and the air is soft like cotton wool and smells of the jasmine bush that my mother has growing around a downpipe at the back of the house. I feel clean and contented as I walk through the kitchen, my hair cold and damp against my scalp.

In the TV room, I stop to look at something on the television. My family are all gathered there watching. I rest my hand against the back of Nana's armchair. Unconsciously, I lift my right foot so that it rests on my left knee while standing. It is a comfortable way to stand.

Gabby turns to look at me and then looks down at my legs. "Stop standing like that," he says. "You look like an Abo."

Sometimes he says: "You know how I can tell he's an Aussie?" It's a joke he uses a lot. "I can hear his chains rattlin'." Then he laughs and slaps his knee.

I'm leaning against the fence as John Bond tells me from his side that World Series Cricket is rigged. England and Pakistan are touring. He calls the Pakistani team "the Puds".

"Yep," he says. "Just gotta look at what happens when the Poms and the Puds play each other. How big's the crowd? Hardly anyone there. Right?"

One part of me sees his point.

"So," he goes on, "how do you think they get the best television numbers? Australia has to play in the finals. And they have to play the Poms."

That would, I think, be the best contest to watch, but I find it hard to believe it's rigged. How would they do it?

"Besides," he says, "nobody wants to see the Puds win."

I carefully note his argument. "Puds" seems like a useful word and, if I need to, I can repeat it at school.

On hot days, Nana spends most of her time sitting on the front veranda drinking coffee: first on one side of the house and then, in the afternoons, she moves to the other. Here she holds court. I like the way she reads her books, and makes cups of coffee, and absentmindedly twirls a lock of hair on her forehead around and around between two fingers. The perfume of the three frangipani trees in our front yard sweetens the air.

We receive visitors, friends from the migrant hostel days. English, all of them: the Brays, the Hensons, the Burns, the Munsons.

I listen to them talk: about the war, about the hostel, about the bloody Aussies and the way they do things. They never talk about why they left England. They never talk about the way the women in the village would turn

## The fence

away from Nana because she didn't speak English like them, even though she was fluent in three languages. Or the way my mother and uncle were teased at school for being "half-Wop". They never mention Gabby working three back-breaking jobs at once: milking cows, manning a pumping station and on weekends building dry wall fences for Colonel Ferguson, the owner of the country estate where they were tenants.

I look at Nana. She sits in her chair. She laughs, or chastises Gabby. Her voice is a round melody against all these plodding English accents. I know she thinks that people don't listen to her, but I think she is like a sun – sometimes fiery, sometimes benign – that we all revolve around.

Last year, after Nana went into a home, my mother suggested my wife and son and I should move back into the old, now empty, house. For weeks after we moved, I could hear the ghost of Nana pounding up the hall and, as we sorted through her possessions and the possessions of my childhood, I'd close my throat as I felt the grief well up and sit there like a stone.

A young couple live in the shabby rental house next door. There is a flimsy fence between us and them that I want to rebuild: higher and more sturdy. I hear a crash. She is screaming and crying.

"Why do you make me do this to you?!" he yells from the bottom of his lungs. He punches the back door, a loud crack. And she is crying and wailing something that sounds like "Why do you hit me? Why do you have to hit me?"

I visit Nana in the home. In her last months, she grunts and mumbles an incomprehensible language. Her mind, lost between English and Greek, compromises on something that is neither. She begins sentences with magical, half-enunciated words and stops to search for the next one and becomes baffled and annoyed that she can't find what that might be. She fiddles with my shirt buttons and implores me with her milky, barely seeing eyes to do something – which is, I think, to take her home. She wastes away and dies.

Gabby died on the TV room floor in 1997 of a heart attack, his dinner tray spilled next to him. He brought it out so he could eat while watching the cricket.

When I was fifteen, and John Bond went off to university, they tore down the old wood and wire fence and replaced it with a picket fence, largely built by Gabby and Mr Bond. I remember them arguing over everything, but the fence was built. It was harder to climb over, but that didn't seem to matter as much as it did. They also chopped down the old camphor laurel tree, and the mango tree for good measure.

Mr Bond lives alone in his house now. He is over eighty. His boys are all gone. Mrs Bond is in a nursing home. She has dementia. She doesn't recognise Mr Bond when he sees her, but he still visits her every morning.

I say "hello" over the fence when I see him. He asks me how my mother's recent trip to England went. She had gone back for the first time since she was twelve. I tell him and he says: "You know, I've sometimes thought that I should travel over to England, but it's always seemed such a long way away. Too big a place for me."

He asks me how I'm going living back in the big old house in Ipswich and I tell him it's alright. I'm managing fine. ■

---

Shane Strange is an Ipswich-based writer and reviewer. His story "Requiem" was published in *Griffith REVIEW 13: The Next Big Thing* and subsequently included in *Best Australian Stories 2006* (Black Inc, 2006) and broadcast on ABC Radio.

# 'Should Freedom of Expression Be Limited in a Time of Terror?'

Frank Moorhouse and Julianne Schultz in conversation.

In association with the Griffith REVIEW.

**NATIONAL LIBRARY OF AUSTRALIA**

Wednesday 21 Februrary, 6 pm
National Library of Australia, Theatre, Free
Bookings essential: (02) 6262 1271

Essay:
**The antidote of multiculturalism**
Author:
**Geoffrey Brahm Levey**

Image: Mikhail and Georgia from the 'Tenant by tenant' series / Source: www.keithsaundersphotography.com

# The antidote of multiculturalism

A cruel irony has marked recent Australian social policy. Reconciliation between indigenous and settler Australians – which involves a concept and a process that are essentially symbolic – was made "practical", limited to policies aimed at improving Aboriginal living conditions that the government should have been pursuing anyway. At the same time, multiculturalism – a set of practical policies aimed variously at improving the absorption of migrants and harmoniously integrating a culturally diverse society around liberal democratic values – has come to acquire powerful symbolic significance in debates about what it means to be Australian. Indeed, so laced with symbolism has "multiculturalism" become that the Howard government is now considering its own symbolic gesture of simply removing the word from governmental use.

Multiculturalism is the most recent of four basic models that liberal democracies have adopted in responding to cultural diversity. The first seeks to *exclude* cultural diversity. The "white Australia" policy is among the best examples of this approach. The second model is assimilationism. It has featured in almost every modern nation-state. Indeed, the term "nation-state" presupposes this idea. That is, not the idea that "for every nation, its own state" – which is a common formulation of self-determination – but the quite different idea that "for every state, one nation". Australia and the other Anglo-democracies fervently pursued this approach to "nation-building" until the last third of the twentieth century. The third model is liberal pluralism, although it goes by various names. On this model, people are allowed to follow their traditions under their own steam, as it were, unassisted by government. Because this model turns on the distinction between public and private spheres, all liberal democracies, to some extent, have evidenced it, even when committed to assimilation. Officially, the United States exemplifies the liberal pluralist model. An institution like SBS, for example, is unthinkable in the US. However, American public law and policy make extensive allowance for cultural diversity, which makes the US in practice more like the fourth model: multiculturalism. Here, as we know from the Australian case, government not only allows people to express their cultural attachments; it seeks to accommodate, support, and even celebrate such differences in accordance with liberal democratic values.

Multiculturalism in Australia was perhaps destined to become embroiled in issues of national identity. The adoption of the policy in the 1970s followed more or less on the heels of the demise of the "white Australia" policy. But the controversy over multiculturalism is also fuelled by a perception that it threatens social cohesion and the political integrity of the state – challenges for which a robust national identity has long been seen as the necessary

## The antidote of multiculuralism

answer. As the celebrated liberal John Stuart Mill put it in 1859, "Free institutions are next to impossible in a country made up of different nationalities. Among a people without fellow-feeling, especially if they read and speak different languages, the united public opinion, necessary to the working of representative government, cannot exist."

The question is this: if Australia has changed from "an outpost of the British race", as it defined itself during the heyday of "white Australia", what exactly has it changed to? In particular, what does its commitment to multiculturalism – in policy if not in word – mean for its national identity?

Scholars tend to debate these sorts of questions about national identity in terms of three vying approaches: "thick" or ethnic nationalism; "thin" or liberal nationalism; and "state neutrality" or post- or civic-nationalism. The three approaches also frame the public debate on Australian national identity. All three categories are relative to the context being explored: what today is considered a "thick" identity in Australia, for example, is likely to be considered a "thin" if not anorexic identity elsewhere.

On the "thick" conception, multiculturalism is considered to be damaging to Australian national identity. Australia is said to have a distinct Anglo-Australian character and identity, which has great capacity to integrate newcomers. Advocates such as John Hirst and Keith Windschuttle point to the fact, for example, that intermarriage rates across ethnic and mainstream Australians are high, increasing with each generation. Welcoming intermarriage in a post "white Australia" era indicates how the prevailing "thick" conception of Australian identity has changed since the days of the "white Australia" policy. Today, "thickness" is claimed not so much in terms of a strict ethnic nationality or a bloodline of ancestry – the "crimson thread of kinship" in Sir Henry Parkes' immortal words of 1890 – but as a cultural heritage open to all.

"Thick" conceptions of Australian national identity have the virtue of recognising the deep and abiding influence of Anglo-Australian culture on the institutions and patterns of life in Australia. However, the accounts are problematic in that they tend to do what they accuse Australian multicultural policy of doing – namely, essentialise ethnic group identity and membership, rather than allowing for their internal diversity and dynamism. As John Hirst, historian and chairman of the Commonwealth Government's Civics Education Group (responsible for designing the civics and citizenship program taught in schools), put the accusation in his 2001 Barton Lecture: "Multicultural policy envisaged a world of distinct ethnic groups. This was more and more make-believe." The same claim is made today by the conservative commentators Janet Albrechtsen, Piers Ackerman and Andrew Bolt – albeit, ironically, with the shrill rider that multiculturalism has succeeded in making "distinct ethnic groups" a reality.

In fact, Australian multicultural policy is highly individualistic. From the early 1980s, the policy had begun to be framed in terms of addressing "all Australians" rather than only migrants or "ethnics". This phrasing – repeatedly used throughout the national multicultural policy statements – is deliberate and clear. It is each individual Australian who enjoys the rights (such as those to cultural identity and respect, and to access and equity) and bears the responsibilities (of abiding by Australia's liberal democratic institutions) under the policy. Lest there be any ambiguity, the *National Agenda* goes on to state that: "Fundamentally, multiculturalism is about the rights of the individual."

In contrast, it is Hirst who ends up treating ethnic groups monolithically, yoking the fate of members of ethnic groups to the choices of their co-ethnics. He cites figures to highlight the increasing assimilation of migrants across the second and third generations and thus the supposed pointlessness of multicultural policy. For example, among Greeks: "Ninety per cent of the first generation were Orthodox, 82 per cent of the second; 45 per cent of the third." Yet these figures also show how large proportions of this community in each generation wish to observe their faith and traditions. They beg the question of why these people should not be entitled to cultural consideration where necessary and appropriate. Further, why should the cultural interests of present generations be answered on the basis of the (anticipated) cultural interests of (some among) future generations? Indeed, even for those migrants seeking to assimilate, the extensive access and equity provisions and institutions covered by multicultural policy would still seem to be warranted. Those wishing to jettison their old identities no less than those who wish to retain them are entitled to protection from discrimination on the basis of their ascribed group membership.

Why does Hirst not see this? Why is he so concerned to dismiss multicultural policy as misguided even where it might serve the interests of many members of migrant groups? Perhaps the answer is that his thinking about multiculturalism – like that of many other advocates of a "thick" conception of Australian identity – has been based on the assumption that it necessarily denies the reality or importance of Australian culture. As he puts it: "The migrants were and are in no doubt that there is an Australian way of doing things, an Australian culture. This is the second way that the multicultural label for Australia is misleading. It suggests that there is simply diversity; that there is no dominant culture. Migrants who want to get on and be accepted know better."

It is the post- or civic-nationalists who are most concerned to deny the reality or political importance of a distinct Australian culture and identity. In many ways, their arguments are the mirror image of the "thick" conceptions. Indeed, the two camps tend to provoke and sustain each other. Where the "thick" conceptions contend that multiculturalism undermines Australian national identity, post- and civic-nationalists believe that invocations of a national identity are antithetical to multiculturalism and Australia's cultural diversity. They reject the idea of a national identity in both ethnic and cultural terms. To this extent, they express the traditional tensions between liberalism and nationalism. They believe that Australia's commitment to liberal democratic values, together with its cultural diversity, requires that the state should be neutral with respect to ethnocultural matters, though they differ on what this entails.

Some argue that Australians should simply dispense with the idea of a national identity altogether. For example, in their book *Mistaken Identity: Multiculturalism and the Demise of Nationalism in Australia* (Pluto Press, 1988), Stephen Castles and his associates conclude: "We do not need a new ideology of nationhood ... Our aim must be a community without a nation." Others, like the late Donald Horne, argue that Australian identity should be grounded only in political or civic values, such as tolerance, individual liberty, equality, reciprocity and a commitment to democratic institutions. And still others – Laksiri Jayasuriya and Andrew Theophanous, for example – suggest that Australian identity should be centred rather on the principle and practice of multiculturalism itself. Ironically, this last idea found expression in the National Multicultural Advisory Council's report that prepared the ground for the Howard government's *A New Agenda* in 1999: "Australian multiculturalism will continue to be a defining feature of our evolving national identity." Former Labor Party leader Mark Latham also picked up on this idea in the 2004 election campaign: "The challenge is to modernise our multicultural policies, to make them relevant to our multicultural identity."

Post- and civic-nationalist arguments have the virtue of seeking an inclusive definition of Australian identity and culture that acknowledges the cultural diversity of the Australian people. Yet these approaches are flawed and seem destined to fail. First, as several liberal nationalists have argued, "civic nationalism" is a misnomer in that it ignores the many ways in which liberal democratic states already and inevitably endorse particular traditions. They insist on a particular language or languages as the *lingua franca* of state business and societal intercourse; organise their year in terms of a particular calendar; recognise certain public holidays; prescribe what narratives are taught as history; and draw on particular cultural motifs and stories for the official symbols, insignia, flags, and anthems of the state. Some have gone – and do go – much further than this in mandating particular cultures Moreover, the putative "political" or "civic" values of democracy have deep cultural imprints and a jagged, if not always a sharp, cultural edge. The reason that limits of toleration are often so controversial is precisely because liberal democratic values are anything but culturally neutral: they are friendly to some traditions, not so friendly to others.

Second, national identity can and does play an important role in generating and sustaining social solidarity and cohesion, a sense of belonging and a commitment to the commonweal. Such features are legitimate interests of democratic states, and would seem to be all the more imperative in culturally diverse democracies. In *Veil Politics in Liberal Democratic States* (Cambridge University Press, 2003), Ajume Wingo makes the case that universal values and even constitutional principles are far less important for motivating ordinary citizens to accept democratic practices than are the symbols – including, stories, rituals, monuments and memorials – that a polity draws on or develops. These symbols – or "veils" as he calls them – are typically the stuff of nation-building. To reject national identity as obsolete, then, or to define it as if it could be ethnoculturally neutral, is to forsake or ignore one of the most powerful political forces available for bringing people together as a community.

Attempts to fashion a new Australian identity on multiculturalism itself fare little better. On the face of it, this approach seems to be a category mistake – that is, it mistakes political and administrative measures that variously allow, accommodate and integrate the realm of diverse identities for an identity itself. Yet, as Benedict Anderson famously observed in *Imagined Communities* (Verso, 1983), all national identities are constructed and imagined, so why not an identity imagined around multiculturalism? The difficulty is at once semantic and symbolic. The American metaphor of the "melting pot" helps to illustrate what a national identity focused on multiculturalism is up against. The image of the melting pot misdescribes American society where, as Wingo puts it, "the U.S. population is increasingly a collection of distinct subpopulations, with more diversity between ethnic, linguistic, or cultural groups than within those same groups". Yet the fact that the "melting pot" is a myth is irrelevant, says Wingo; what is important is that it offers a powerful symbol of unity that well serves the legitimate interests of American democracy in creating a sense of solidarity.

Compare the Australian case. Australian society and culture are highly integrative – or so we are told. Intermarriage rates are high; the title of "new Australians" is or was eagerly bestowed on migrants; the nomenclature of hyphenated identities is still uncommon. "Multiculturalism", the proposed focus of Australian identity, is thus also mythic, on this account, in misdescribing Australian society. Yet, unlike the metaphor of the "melting pot" in the United States, the proposed national myth for Australia semantically conveys diversity and difference rather than unity and solidarity. "Multiculturalism" lacks the rhetorical force of the "melting pot" for nation-building purposes.

## The antidote of multiculuralism

I stress that the difficulty here is more rhetorical than substantive. As a public policy based on liberal democratic notions, multiculturalism is indeed concerned with integrating a diverse society on fair and prudent terms. Nevertheless, while polls have consistently shown that the overwhelming majority of Australians support multiculturalism, it is also the case that many Australians are unable to warm to the term. By the mid-1990s, even Jerzy Zubrzycki, one of the architects of Australian multicultural policy, was calling for the term to be dropped, although he continued to support the policies for which it stands. And, of course, now the Howard government reportedly is in the process of removing the word from government policy. For all these reasons, it makes more sense to construe multiculturalism as a set of principles, policies and programs in the service of an Australian national identity than as the locus of that identity itself.

This brings us to the intermediate position of "liberal nationalists". Their "thin" account of national identity acknowledges both the legitimate national interests of liberal democracies and the need to make some room for cultural minorities. The debate at this level is largely about the precise calibration of the "thinness". For example, the Canadian political philosopher Will Kymlicka argues in *Can Liberal Pluralism be Exported?* (Oxford University Press, 2001) that "nation-building" in liberal democracies is legitimate where it is limited to creating and maintaining what he calls a "societal culture": "I call it a societal culture to emphasise that it involves a common language and social institutions, rather than common religious beliefs, family customs, or personal lifestyles ... Citizens of a modern liberal state do not share a common culture in such a thick, ethnographic sense ... if we want to understand the nature of modern state-building, we need a very different, and thinner, conception of culture, which focuses on a common language and societal institutions."

Kymlicka allows that liberal democracies also engage in nation-building by developing a national media, national symbols and holidays, and majority group heroes and events. Yet others including Australian philosopher Chandran Kukathas draw the legitimate boundaries of national identity rather more narrowly.

To my mind, liberal nationalist approaches – for all their good sense – wrongly dismiss, or lose sight of, the place of national character in national identity. The inclination to do so is understandable enough given the obscene ways in which such notions have been politically exploited or socially expressed in modern history. However, as liberal nationalists know better than most, nationalism itself can serve both illiberal and liberal goals; the task is to distinguish its legitimate roles and uses. The concept of national character also is often challenged on the grounds that the attributes highlighted are stereotypical and contradicted by competing images and stereotypes. Consider one of the most celebrated portraits of the Australian character, Russell Ward's *The Australian Legend* (Oxford University Press, 1958): "According to the myth, the 'typical Australian' is a practical man, rough and ready in his manners and quick to decry any appearance of affectation in others."

Kukathas in his book *Multicultural Citizens* (Centre for Independent Studies, 1993) cites Ward's portrait and then Jonathan King's opposing assessment that Australians are "lazy, arrogant, racist, urban money-grabbers who have surrounded themselves with the myth that they are outback heroes". Like many other commentators on the subject, Kukathas notes the "difficulties in trying to tie down any notion of a 'national character'" and moves on.

And yet, as everyone knows, the French really are different from the Germans. Canadians are different from Americans, and Australians are different from the Brits and even the New Zealanders. As people are imprinted with their national cultures, they tend to exhibit distinctive habits. That many do not exhibit their "national qualities", and that there may be contradictions, is neither here nor there, in human affairs, the only surprise should be if it were otherwise. I suspect that liberal nationalists – who tend to travel a lot – might grant this much at a cultural level, while insisting that issues of national character should be separated from the state and quarantined from the business of liberal democratic government. But national character will perforce find expression through a society's governing institutions – how could it not do so?

All three schools of thought misunderstand the place of national character. The crucial point about national character is not that it doesn't exist, or that it should be confined to the non-political sphere, or that it should be politically promoted. Rather, the point is that national character cannot be the object or intention of political administration without doing it violence. Any deliberate attempt to represent national character will wrench out particular aspects, and the accounts offered can, at best, bear a passing relation to it. The resultant image is bound to be a kind of grotesque.

If national character is not to become national caricature, then it must be left to its own devices. It will find its own expression. Consider, for example, the new Parliament House in Canberra. That ordinary Australians and visitors can walk up grassy banks and literally stand over and on their political representatives and leaders in the Senate and House of Representatives not only exemplifies a characteristic Australian attitude to authority and an egalitarian temper; it emerges from this attitude and temper. Or, still at Parliament House, take the public uproar that followed a regulation in 2005 requiring security guards to cease using the expression "mate" when addressing politicians and the public. A Member of Parliament taking umbrage at the informality had prompted the move. The public's sense that acceptable norms had been breached came only when the guards were told to be more formal. National character, because it *is* character, expresses itself just in and through what we do and find "natural" or acceptable.

A second dimension of national identity that liberal nationalists underplay concerns what may be called the crucible of civil society. Because they seek to render nationalism compatible with liberal democracy, and thus to make room for cultural minorities, they tend to focus mainly on the legitimate boundaries of state action and access to the public sphere. National cultures, as we have seen, are "thinned" out in terms of which ethnocultural aspects are deemed to be appropriate for government involvement. Other cultural aspects – regarding food, dress, speech, surnames, leisure activities and family size – some of which were once pursued by states in their more assimilationist days, are deemed to be the prerogative of ethnic groups or their individual members. Thus we are presented with two domains: a national culture that is the province of the state; and ethnocultures that are the province of migrant groups and individuals. The possibility that a national culture might also be constructed and fomented in civil society seems to be ignored or denied. Hence Kymlicka's comment: "The 'melting pot' image was never accurate. Immigrants do indeed integrate into common institutions and learn the dominant language, but they remain, visibly, and proudly, distinctive in their ethnic identities and attachments." Integration, let alone assimilation, is countenanced only in the restricted terms of the national or societal culture that is the compass of the state.

This picture of integration is just as unrealistic as the assimilationist model. In Australia, as in other liberal democracies, there are myriad interactions among migrant groups and between them and the dominant cultural majority that result in cultural absorption and integration of one form or another. For obvious reasons, this absorption is mostly in the direction of the patterns of the dominant culture. John Hirst cites the stories of a Greek husband rejecting his wife's request for the family to acquire a goat as un-Australian, and of a proud Sri Lankan, Bekaboru Kiyanahati Balapan Koyako, coming to the realisation, in meeting other Australians, that he badly needed a shorter name (he chose Kojak). These are great examples of how national cultural integration is mediated in civil society, beyond the state. There are many other examples of the inductive power of Anglo-Australian culture at work in civil society, including the norms governing queue-forming, social space, voice-raising, speech turn-taking, spitting and belching, and the polite reluctance to use the car horn on anything but the most urgent occasions.

The mistake, of course, is to think that the integration is always in the direction of the cultural majority. The impact of Aboriginal culture on Anglo-

Australian culture – including vocabulary, motifs and art – is clear, if too little appreciated. Anglo-Australian culture also has been changed in various ways by successive waves of migrants, from the rise of soccer as a popular sport, to so-called "new Australian cuisine", to the now national preference for coffee over tea and wine over beer. Judging by the entries in metropolitan telephone directories, the conventions regarding the complexity of surnames have also been greatly extended.

So a national culture is forged in the hurly-burly of civil society, as well as in the institutions overseen by the state. In Australia, Anglo-Australian culture remains dominant, and one cannot begin to make sense of Australian institutions and life without understanding this. Still, in many ways the Anglo-Celtic Australian culture of old is increasingly becoming an "Anglo-meltic" one in terms of the general patterns of Australian life. That is, Anglo-Australian culture – while still dominant – is being modified.

The continued and overwhelming dominance of "Anglo-Australia" on the country's institutions and norms helps to explain, why the metaphor of the "melting pot" has had such limited currency here. After all, one might assume, given claims about the highly integrationist nature of Australian society, that the "melting pot" better captures the prevailing circumstances in Australia than in the United States. Indeed, Hirst concludes his lecture on exactly this note: "The marrying and partnering of people of all sorts across all boundaries is the great unifying force in Australia. The United States of America never saw such a rapidly melting melting pot. It will produce before too long a new people, who will have darker skins, much better suited to this place and our sun."

In its traditional meaning, as made popular in the United States in the early twentieth century by the English-Jewish immigrant playwright Israel Zangwill, the "melting pot" stood for a kind of democratic assimilation in which all the various immigrant cultures would combine to produce a "new American" identity. Hirst certainly suggests this meaning by his vision of a "new [Australian] people". And yet, while he entertains a changed skin colour, all but one of his examples of cultural absorption involve migrants accepting the established Anglo-Australian way of life. The one exception involves a Vietnamese busker in downtown Sydney playing the didgeridoo. Unimagined, and perhaps unimaginable, are true-blue Australians playing the sitar. As Hirst himself notes, "new Australian" was the standard term bestowed on recent migrants in the postwar period, and it presumed their acceptance of the Australian way of life as they found it. For Zangwill and the "melting pot", the idea of a "new American" involved a genuinely new identity; Down Under, being a "new Australian" meant that one was on route to becoming an "old Australian".

## The antidote of multiculuralism

Multiculturalism in Australia has relaxed some of the pressures and expectations on migrants to travel this route. However, *pace* many of its critics, multiculturalism has not radically transformed the landscape of Australian national identity. If there are changes in the future, they will have little to do with multicultural policy, and everything to do with the thinking and feeling of Australians at the time. In the meantime, we would do well to remember – or learn – that national identity is multifaceted and has different domains.

Some years ago, the American political philosopher Michael Walzer (*Political Theory*, vol. 12, 1984) described liberalism as the "art of separation". We in Australia need to master this art a bit better than we have. There are aspects of national identity having to do with Australian character that will naturally affect the way we govern ourselves, but which we can scarcely do anything about without warping them. There are aspects of national identity which are duly the province of government, such as the inculcation and transmission of a national language, the teaching of the nation's history, and the establishment of national institutions, holidays and memorials. And there are aspects of national identity that properly belong in the realm of civil society and beyond the business of government, such as how people dress, call themselves, or spend their leisure, what languages they speak to each other, and even in what accent they speak their English. Here, among the myriad relations of Australians, will also be forged the habits and sentiments and character of the Australian people.

Most of the time, our political leaders intuitively respect these different boundaries of national identity. The recent campaign to tie Australian citizenship more tightly to English language proficiency, however justified or efficacious such a move might be, treats an aspect of national identity that is properly the prerogative of government. Too often, however, our leaders entertain ideas of legislating the Australian character rather than national identity, and thus brook corrupting both. Or, with shades of Orwell, they seek to dictate the cultural choices of Australians in civil society in the name of "our values" when they are decidedly not *our* values. Multiculturalism, understood as a set of policies integrating a culturally diverse society based on liberal democratic norms, helps to preserve the liberal art of separation. It is the antidote and not the poison. ■

Geoffrey Brahm Levey is editor of *Political Theory and Australian Multiculturalism* (Berghahn Books, 2007), and co-editor of *Jews and Australian Politics* (Sussex Academic Press, 2004), and *Secularism, Religion and Multicultural Citizenship* (Cambridge University Press, 2007). He teaches at the University of New South Wales.

Essay:
**Beyond pity**
Author:
**Robert Hillman**

*Image: Najaf Mazeri at his store in Melbourne / Courtesy of Najaf Mazeri.*

# Beyond pity

I first met Zarah Ghahramani on Tehran's Revolution Boulevard in June 2003, just down the road from the northern campus of the city's university. She was dressed in the tunic of all young urban women in the Islamic Republic of Iran: dark scarf drawn tight over her head, lightweight coat (pale blue this day) reaching almost to her ankles. She asked me in her accomplished English whether it would not be too impolite to inquire what I was writing in my notebook. I told her that I was gathering material for newspaper articles on Iranian politics. "I thought as much," she said without explanation, then offered her hand and spoke her name. As we walked along in the gathering dusk for a minute or more, I could only assume that Zarah had made a habit of approaching people who looked as if they might have a newspaper to report to in the West. But why? At the intersection of Revolution and Azari, where we might courteously have parted, Zarah stopped and made some comment about the rowdy traffic. Then she added that she had a few things to say about Iranian politics herself. Would I listen?

We sat at a kiosk in the Laleh Gardens not so far from where we'd met, and Zarah told her story over two hours. All around us, Tehrani mums and dads feted their children on the peculiarly flavourless ice-cream that Iranians favour, while young men in mock-Benetton tops engaged in air-courtship (the right motions, but no action) of young women dressed like Zarah. Fairy lights blinked on the garden's laurels and date palms.

Sitting hunched over the table, Zarah kept her voice low, and folded and refolded the straw of her Coke into a compact wad. She spoke with astonishing candour of her involvement in reform politics at Tehran University, where she was no longer permitted to study; of imprisonment, torture, severe sexual abuse. As I learned later, her scarf concealed the regrowth of hair shorn from her head in Tehran's Evin Prison eighteen months earlier: she had torn her scalp to shreds with her fingernails while awaiting her daily interrogations and had kept her hair short after her release while the wounds healed.

Before approaching me, she'd satisfied herself that she was not being followed and filmed. She knew she was watched. Her days and nights were vexed by the need to take care: any infringement of Iran's rigid dress code would be harshly punished, any expression of political dissent would see her returned to Evin for a very long time, or until her interrogators judged her so cowed by certain refinements of the torture she'd already endured that she could no longer imagine rebuking her government.

# Beyond pity

Her story could have been told with variation by thousands of young Iranian men, and without variation by a few young Iranian women. She'd been twenty and studying languages at university when first detained by state security agents late in 2001. Tehran University had been at that time a centre of student activism. Hundreds of young men and women had raised their voices in the streets around the campus, demanding freedom of choice in what they read, in what they wore, in what they wrote. Zarah had been one of the leaders of the protests, intense in her political convictions, but not truly aware of just how hard the other side played the game. Twenty-nine days of interrogation in Evin, much of it in a blindfold, had demonstrated to her the savagery of the regime when roused. By the time her interrogators had finished with her, she'd been prepared to confess to anything at all, and confess she had. She had worked as an agent of the United States of America; she had accepted money from anti-regime organisations in Europe and the United Kingdom; she had committed "immoral acts" with leading male figures in the protest movement; she had attempted to subvert the rule of law in Iran. Her confession was nonsense, but she signed it.

"That is what happened," said Zarah at the conclusion of her story, and she added, with a bestowing gesture of her open hands, "for you to use."

Over the next two weeks, Zarah nudged me and my partner, Anni, north, south, east and west in Tehran, then took us down to Shiraz and Isfahan. She introduced us to writers, artists, movie-makers, businessmen, and to her many friends and relatives. Her account of her ordeal was confirmed everywhere. In Shiraz we visited her particularly close friend, Eva, who had shaved her head herself to satirise the regime's phobias, and to dramatise her solidarity with Zarah. Her own boldness notwithstanding, Eva was worried for her friend, and Zarah's family was more worried still. Watching Zarah indoors amongst those who cared for her, bare-headed, laughing, lampooning the regime, I could see what it was that made her friends and family so anxious. Her attachment to the liberty she craved was too intense, almost mad. Her face flashed the rage of the humiliated. Her interrogator in Evin Prison had warned her of the torments to come if she were re-arrested. One day, I felt sure, she would carry her rage outdoors to spite him, and would pay all over again.

"Come to Australia," I urged her. "Apply for a study visa."

"Would that be possible?"

"Maybe. We should try."

"Then they win," she said, and dismissed the idea.

Anni and I returned to Australia after our month in Iran, but remained in contact with Zarah by hotmail and regular calls from her friend's mobile phone. What she said to me and what she wrote made it more apparent than ever that she was living on borrowed time. And this was something she would have acknowledged herself if she could have set aside her contempt for the people who had harmed her and think straight for a moment. She spoke of her lapses from the conditions of her release from Evin, and conceded that they were becoming more frequent. She was not supposed to talk to anyone involved in anti-regime politics, for example, but she did. She was not supposed to go anywhere near the university, nor attempt to use its library, but she did. She was not supposed to sign any of the reform petitions circulating in the university precinct, but she did. My response was always a version of "Stop it!"

Then one day, a year after my return to Australia, Zarah sent an me an email to say that she wanted to get out of Iran and would accept any help I could provide. What had changed her mind? "My father," she said. He had taken her by the shoulders and made her stand in front of a mirror. "Look!" he'd said. He wanted her to see what Evin and the relentless surveillance since her release had wrought on her face and figure. She obeyed her father: she stood there and stared. But it wasn't the erosion of her beauty that had persuaded Zarah to flee to Australia; it was the grief in her father's eyes, reflected above hers.

At the time of Zarah's imprisonment in 2001, Najaf Mazeri was crossing the Timor Sea in a ramshackle shrimp trawler. He shared the deck with a consignment of eighty-five men, women and children, most of them Afghans like him. The trawler was, strictly speaking, the property of the people it was carrying, for although the passengers didn't know it, the fees they'd paid to an Indonesian people-smuggler included the total cost of the vessel. The sum of those fees was the equivalent of $127,000.

The joint owners of the vessel only become aware of their status as informal title-holders nine days into their voyage from an anchorage off a beach on the southern coast of Java. They had been led to believe that the derelict trawler would convey them a short distance to a much larger and newer vessel somewhere out in the ocean. This vessel was never found, and the trawler's taciturn captain frankly declared he had no knowledge of its existence.

Najaf's journey to Australia began in the northern Afghan city of Mazar-e-Sharif in March 2001, a few months before his Timor Sea voyage. By the age of thirty-one, he had survived a rocket attack on his house by the *mujahideen* forces opposing the Russian invasion of his country, casual, indiscriminate shelling by the Russians themselves, and a relentless Taliban vendetta against his tribe, the Hazara. He had witnessed the last few seconds of his younger brother Rosal's life as the boy succumbed to a shrapnel wound that had left a hole in his mid-section through which the earth on which lay was visible, and the death of a beloved older brother, Gorg Ali, felled one quiet day by a single shot as he was gathering honey from the family's beehives. Najaf himself had recovered from a shrapnel wound that had torn the quadriceps of his left leg.

The prospects of Najaf remaining alive in Mazar-e-Sharif were poor once the Taliban took control of Afghanistan. Talibs were killing young Hazara males pre-emptively to forestall any rebellion by their sworn enemies. Acting pre-emptively themselves, Najaf's relatives and friends gathered three thousand American dollars, borrowing from money lenders, selling livestock and emptying their pockets to pay people-smugglers to convey their favoured son to Australia. If Najaf found safety, the family's bloodline would survive.

Najaf arrived in Australia knowing that he would have to argue for his right to remain; Zarah, after the expiry of her study visa, knew that she would be obliged to argue the same way: "Where I come from, the state has the right to imprison, torture and kill people it dislikes. It dislikes me." Both invoked treaties and statutes, studied definitions and made their case. The argument prevailed for Najaf; Zarah, three months after her application for a Temporary Protection Visa, is still awaiting a result but has met with a sensitive and sympathetic response from Immigration thus far.

Despite her argument with Iran's regime, Zarah had expected to live her entire life in her homeland, regardless of who governed it; for Najaf, any life remote from his kinsmen was inconceivable until menace made him think again. Australia was not a deeply meditated destination for either; its unnewsworthiness was an attraction of sorts. As to what they would do in Australia if they were permitted to stay, neither had much idea. Make a living if possible, yes, but beyond that it was all vague. Certainly there were no plans to radically redefine their lives, no plans for any crowd-pleasing embrace of a foster fatherland – Aussie Zaz, Aussie Naj. Their resettlement strategy was one of minimal change, as far as possible. They had, after all, entered Australia the way one might enter a sanctuary: at the gallop, exhausted after so much dodging and weaving, grateful to have doors swing open. A certain period of grateful prostration follows admission to a sanctuary, but the more persistent mission for Zarah and Najaf was to live the lives they had already imagined, only more securely.

Impediments to the refugee's mission vary from nation to nation, culture to culture. In Australia in the twenty-first century, the resettled Muslim is up against what appears to be an orchestrated program of state-sponsored harassment. At regular intervals, one government minister or another offers views on the psychology, philosophy and priorities of Islamic militants, often followed by suggestions of ways in which the community's "good Muslims" might help isolate the "bad Muslims". Ministers use every opportunity to remind the electorate that "bad Muslims" have no idea of where to draw the line, feel licensed to cut the throats of their promiscuous daughters, amputate the hands of robbers, apply the lash with reckless abandon and stone young women to death for the sin of having been raped.

Further advice is offered to a third category of Muslims – those who are good, but not good enough: they are advised to take a long, hard look at themselves; to stop abusing their women; to stop listening with any sympathy at all to Islamist rowdies and firebrands; to learn English quickly, and in general to make a greater effort to assimilate.

Reminding us of how poorly people fare under strictly applied Sharia law, which is part of the official harassment, is rather like declaring one's total disgust with Herod's slaughter of the first-born. Very few Australians are likely to mount a defiant defence of Herod or of Sharia law. Why mention it and its sanctions at all? These government sermons are presumably addressed to the non-Muslim majority of the Australian electorate, to establish the "bad Muslim" as the common enemy – the "other". It can't hurt to identify yourself (as often as possible) with those who abhor the slaughter of the first-born.

Najaf's and Zarah's experience of Australia has been shaped by this climate of harassment, but not entirely in the way that might have been expected. Najaf has had scant experience of anti-Muslim disdain, and Zarah none at all. It has been their well-wishers who have pressured them to play down the more evident features of their heritage. And no well-wisher has been busier than me.

Once released from Woomera early in 2002, Najaf was free to take up his craft of rug mending. He lived cheaply in a share house in inner-Melbourne, travelling by public transport to the premises of carpet merchants. He'd sit cross-legged, plying a curved needle to frayed rugs and torn *kilims* for up to fourteen hours a day. His mastery of his craft and his knowledge of the rugs of Afghanistan were recognised as exceptional. He'd woven rugs himself in Mazar-e-Sharif after a long apprenticeship, and his feeling for wools and dyes and the quality of loom-work fascinated his patrons.

## Beyond pity

The level of ignorance about Afghani rugs amongst Melbourne's dealers at first surprised, then appalled, Najaf. He assumed that only the most studied and conscientious of people would ever set themselves up as sellers of fine rugs. Much of what his employers sold was uninspiring – rugs made of poorly cured wools, dyed with cheap chemicals that aged badly, the patterns over-expressed – but he also came across fabulous works that entranced him. When shown a perfect rug, he passed his arched hand lightly over the surface again and again, testing the touch of the wool against his sensitive inner-palm. Then he would turn the rug over and study the naked weave, moving his head left and right like a snake charmer mesmerising a Cobra.

Najaf's wife Hakema had farewelled him from Mazar-e-Sharif with no great conviction that she would ever see him again. The villages and cities of Afghanistan are full of tales of husbands, sons and brothers who set off, as in a folk tale, to find their fortunes and are later reported shot, imprisoned or drowned in the ocean.

Soon after leaving Woomera, Najaf telephoned a friend who relayed his message to another friend who finally told Hakema and Najaf's now two-year-old daughter Maria that Najaf was alive and that he'd discovered the land of Australia, right where it was supposed to be on the map. Najaf hadn't been permitted to send this message (innocent though it was) from the detention camp – a prohibition designed to prevent any clandestine communication between terrorists. Now letters were written, prospects discussed: the government of Australia was probably going to let him remain, Najaf wrote, and within three years he would be able to bring his family out. And what news of the new land? A friendly place, certainly. Australians liked Afghani rugs – an excellent thing.

Najaf was able to open his own rug shop in 2004, a small place in High Street, Windsor, next to an Indian restaurant. He imported rugs directly from Afghanistan through the agency of a friend in Mazar-e-Sharif, stipulating that the rugs must be of the highest quality. Clients were impressed with his wares, but more impressed with his sense of beauty; he spoke of his rugs – of the best of them – as if they expressed the poetry of a people. His clients became his friends – friends (such as me) who worried aloud what more poorly informed Australians might make of his Afghani attire. Our concern followed the periodic censure of the "bad Muslim" by the Prime Minister, the Treasurer, the Minister for Immigration and Multicultural Affairs, the parliamentary secretary to the Minister for Immigration and Multicultural Affairs, the Attorney-General or the Minister for Foreign Affairs.

After each of these ministerial sermons, Najaf was encouraged by his nervous Australian friends to project himself as one of the Prime Minister's "99 per cent" of worthy Australian Muslims, not one of the small number of bad guys occupying so much of the government's time.

Hakema and Maria, now six years old, joined Najaf in Australia in June 2006. Hakema was a little shocked at her husband's new, Western look, and encouraged him to grow his beard once more and return to a traditional style of dress. And so he did, to the distress of his Australian friends. He watched the news, *The 7.30 Report* and *Lateline* on the ABC each evening, preparing himself in case a government minister had another rush of blood to the head. He became adept at reading the body language of prospective customers who wandered into the shop, he with his menacing beard and Hakema at the back of the shop in her equally menacing veil. "Don't worry," he would say, amused and patient, "I am not a fundamentalist."

Well before Zarah left her homeland in 2004, it had been claimed that Muslims of a certain sort were capable of drowning their own children on the high seas, if that was what it took to gain entry into Australia. Further revelations established that this dire practice was a local political concoction, but some Australians – perhaps many – remained persuaded that, under the right circumstances, Muslims would sacrifice their children.

Before she left Tehran, I kept Zarah well informed of the toxic anti-Muslim atmosphere building in Australia. My indignation tended to override my judgement. After all, I lived in an area of Melbourne where Muslim women from a dozen countries went about their business traditionally garbed and I'd never witnessed a single incident or insult. If I'd thought about it a bit longer, I would have realised how capable these women were of looking after themselves. I might have reflected on my own experience of living and travelling in Muslim countries, and recalled the wit, humour and cool mockery of male posturing that I'd noticed often enough amongst Muslim women.

Without intending to, I was contributing to Zarah's anxieties about the reception a young Muslim woman, a citizen of the pariah state of Iran, would meet in Melbourne. This had the perceptible effect of nudging her along a path she would have negotiated herself, but with more care and reflection. Her spiritual allegiance was divided between the Muslim faith of her father and the Zoroastrian faith of her mother, but preparing for her journey to Australia, she opted for Zoroastrianism.

Still severely traumatised by what she had endured in Evin prison, Zarah's attempt at recovery in Melbourne was hindered every time a government minister censured Australia's Muslims. She had enough political savvy to discern the government's strategy and, left to her own counsel, would have coped nicely. But she had to contend with both my pique and my concern:

"Did you see that stuff on the news? Costello?"

"Of course, Robert."

"Don't take any notice of him. It's crap."

"I know."

"What he said, that's not what all Australians think."

"Yes, I know."

"Still, better keep an eye out."

"An eye out?"

"You know, just be careful."

"You want me to be careful?"

"Yes."

"Okay. Careful of what?"

My concern for Zarah extended to her wardrobe. I was most relaxed when her choice of clothes matched that of every other casually dressed young woman on the streets of Melbourne: low-cut jeans, broad belt, simple top. Then, perversely, I began to worry that she looked too much like every other young woman. When we went to meet publishers to discuss a book we'd written together, I almost suggested that she wear a head-scarf with her jeans.

I was not only unwittingly amplifying the government's invidious message, I was on the verge of suggesting that Zarah perform the unspoken obligation of all immigrants to Australia: to be exotic and different – "colourful", in fact. We have come to approve of the exotic complement to the Australian way of life; we attend the festivals of colourful newcomers, celebrate their enrichment of our cuisine, endorse their right to be a little bit different. But we ask them, the colourful newcomers, to accept that we are not interested in changing anything. Colour is fine, but we want it as ornament, hundreds and thousands sprinkled on a blancmange, the blandness beneath untouched.

Najaf told me of a time in the Woomera Detention Centre when anxiety over his wife and baby daughter, still in Afghanistan, reduced him to despair. He wandered about the camp looking for a place where he could suffer in privacy. He had only one shoe; the other had been left floating somewhere on the Timor Sea. It was spring in the desert, but spring that year was unseasonably cold. He settled against a brick wall, drew the grey blanket from his bed around his shoulders and, without thinking about it at all, began to sing a shepherd's song of Northern Afghanistan:

Let us go to Mazar, oh my beloved

Let us see the red flowers bloom,

The red flowers of Mazar

Go tell my sweetheart her lover has arrived!

She is a daffodil. A buyer has come to take her.

Go tell my love that the unending days of love have arrived,

For her sweetheart has come, her true love has come.

Come, oh my beloved!

My desire for you has made me mad

Your wine-coloured lips have made me mad

But while I wait to drink from your glass

My heart is full of fear.

The place Najaf had chosen was under the balcony of the office where immigration officers spent the day. As he sang, one officer, then another and another strolled out on to the balcony, attracted by the song. Before he'd finished singing (the song repeats its final five lines as a chorus and can go on for some time), six people were standing on the balcony, smiling down at Najaf. He grew self-conscious and stopped singing.

"Go on!" one of the officers called.

Najaf waved his hand and shook his head.

"Go on! You sing beautifully!"

"Finish," said Najaf, employing one of his twenty words of English.

"Sing it again!"

"Finish," Najaf repeated. He got to his feet and went in search of a more genuinely private place. He walked on his one shoe, his blanket still drawn about his shoulders.

I have now retreated from my insufferable supervision of Zarah's resettlement in Melbourne; I have stopped worrying about what Najaf wears, says and does. The Damascus moment came for me a few months ago when Zarah asked me about the term "thought police", which had appeared in a newspaper article on the war in Iraq. I summarised Orwell's *1984*, and the conversation led to a discussion on torture – a subject Zarah knew more

## Beyond pity

about than the average person. When I spoke of Room 101, Orwell's vision of the ultimate hell, Zarah nodded and unconsciously put her hand to her head – an associative mannerism she has whenever the subject of interrogation comes up. "We have one in Evin," she said, and went on to explain that the chamber had been established by Savak, the Shah's secret police, and was preserved by Iran's present regime. I waited for her to say more, but she didn't. "You didn't go there?" I eventually asked, and Zarah laughed, not with mirth. "I'm sitting here talking to you, aren't I?"

In the days that followed this conversation, I thought of Zarah in her tiny cell in Evin Prison – a prison the size of a city. I thought of her seeking a way she could rest that spared her back and shoulders and arms, where the lash had landed, that spared her bruised legs and ribcage. A few floors below, Evin's version of Room 101 was awaiting her, for all she knew. Her great hope was that she would be asked to confess and sign a document of some sort. At her final interrogation, the document was offered but, before agreeing to sign, she suggested to the interrogator that he simply have her killed. The interrogator declined.

What did I think I was doing in trying to shield a young woman with such wherewithal from the foolish bluster of our politicians? I should have been thinking of the grit and anger and spiritual ambition that Zarah had brought with her to Australia. I should have been thinking, too, of Najaf's daring and intelligence, not his wardrobe. I had to concede that I had adopted a version of the Australian multicultural conceit: genial assimilation. A cynical reworking of that conceit informs the repeated rebukes of Muslims, but even in its uncorrupted form – expressed as a collage of variously pigmented folk singing *We Are Australian* – the conceit adds to the sentimentality sloshing about. It does not add to the nation's vigour.

The vital life of any nation, I have come to believe, is better served by the arrival of immigrants who take a look around and decide to change things, just as they may have wished to do in their first homeland. Or, if they are happy with what they find, well and good. At least let them be free of the pity of people like me. ■

---

Robert Hillman is the author of five books, including the award-winning autobiography *The Boy in the Green Suit* (Scribe, 2003). His book with Zarah Ghahramani, *My Life as a Traitor*, will be published by Scribe in July; his book with Najaf Mazeri, *The Rug-maker of Mazar-e-Sharif*, will be published by Insight in May. His memoir, "The Ballad of Frank and Hazel", was published in *Griffith REVIEW 10: Family Politics*.

# Essay: Explorers, writers and other creative strangers

## Author: Joanna Kujawa

*In homage to Lech Paszkowski and all creative strangers*

In the immigration office in Paris, I had one chance to convince the person in charge why I should be allowed to stay. Someone in the waiting room cried as he was handed his deportation papers. People of all nationalities, and their children, waited their turn. When it was my turn to face the immigration officer, I was determined to show that all was fine, that I was worthy of staying, that I was non-threatening. But something betrayed me to the woman in charge. She looked at me with professional suspicion.

"Why are you here? We have enough people from your country, from every possible country, staying here illegally. You have no money, I suppose?"

"But yes, I do. A little. Just enough," I whispered.

"Just enough for what? And how have you earned your money without a working visa?"

How could I explain to her that I dreamed of a fuller life? This was inexplicable within the confines of her world. That people worked illegally because they could not work otherwise. That I walked the streets of Paris whispering verses from Baudelaire wanting to breathe the air that Modigliani and de Beauvoir had breathed. In her eyes, I was an Eastern "barbarian" at the gates of Paris, who came to deceive and take other people's jobs. My imagination ran wild. Was it the stamping of Cossacks' horses on the Eastern steps that she heard when I was answering her questions? Did she disapprove of the freezing winters drowned in glasses of vodkas drunk by my ancestors? Was it something about my Eastern European face? Eyes too big to be fully civilised? Or was it the "red curse" that worried her?

Under any other circumstances, I would not identify myself with these symbols, but then I wanted to throw them back at her to mock her suspicion and rejection. To mock the system that categorises people, a system too restrictive to define anything of significance about another person except as an "intruder" with low economic assets. How could the questions on an immigration form encompass the qualities of Slavic vitality I love, or the writers who created the cultural narrative in which I grew up, or the adventurers and revolutionaries who shaped my imagination?

Similar incidents happened in North America. There, people put me into the category of vodka and sausages when they tried to be friendly. My American friend with a degree from Berkeley was surprised that there was "Polish literature" despite Czeslaw Milosz, a Pole and the 1980 Nobel Prize winner for literature, teaching at her university for decades.

An ironic reversal of roles took place some years later in Southeast Asia, where I suddenly became a "rich Westerner". My young, soft-spoken guide took me to remote temples in Cambodia and confessed on the last day of my trip how angry he was about "serving rich Westerners" like me. He believed (wrongly) that I had enough money to smuggle him out of the country to find a better life in the West. I understood his dreams. Like myself years earlier, he too religiously studied French and English. He wanted to see the world and be a writer.

I knew that feeling. After the incident in Paris, I knew that there was a very long and treacherous bridge that a stranger and a foreigner must cross. A bridge crowded by rigid rules of "rich" and "poor", of desirable and not. I knew that the bridge led to another side of being, an open-ended and creatively intuited belonging unfolding in front of me. This thought exhilarated me.

I wanted to explore other possibilities of being and belonging.

Some questions, however, still needed to be answered because how does one describe an experience as diverse as belonging without reference to the traditional notions of "sameness" of territory, language and history? These are not only intellectual questions; they are, rather, natural promptings as one experiences belonging beyond bureaucratic formulas and social expectations.

Twenty years, four continents and three passports after my Parisian experience, I came across a historical account of Polish adventurers and artists in Australia before World War II. I learned that, since its very beginnings, Polish immigration to Australia was different to that in North America – or anywhere else for that matter. I discovered this – the wonderful gift of another writer, Lech Paszkowski – in a book he wrote – *Poles in Australia and Oceania 1790–1940* (ANU Press, 1987). I found this book by sheer chance as I was researching my PhD. And, through Paszkowski's book, I found the roots of my nomadic belonging. Paszkowski claims that Australia has always attracted the most adventurous spirits. This was welcome news. I felt at home with them here. The Poles he wrote about came, stayed or left, but always left a mark with their lives, with their unorthodox choices, and with their indefinable forms of being and belonging. Often misunderstood, they sometimes became Australian icons, such as Paul Strzelecki, known for his explorations of Gippsland and Tasmania as well as for naming the highest mountain in Australia after a Polish patriot, Thaddeus Kosciuszko.

It is not clear why Strzelecki left Poland, but theories suggest his involvement in one of the splendid, but disastrous, uprisings in which Poles seem to specialise. Another version is that he was a restless spirit, in romantic and financial trouble in Poland. Indeed, Strzelecki had a romantic interest in Poland: a young woman called Adyna who patiently – if naively – waited for him as he voyaged the world, measured and mapped blank spaces on all continents, accepted honours from the Royal Geographical Society in London and published acclaimed books about his geographical discoveries in Australia. Until her death, he wrote her "dashing" letters, and I suspect that she enjoyed the vicarious pleasures of travel and adventure from his letters.

Then there is the wonderful, nomadic Bronislaw Malinowski, an anthropologist and ethnologist who travelled from Poland to Australia, Papua New Guinea, Mexico and Africa. His most important works were written about his research in Australasia in the early twentieth century. On a prolonged stay in Melbourne, he romanced and married Elsie Masson, the daughter of a "local professor" – as he wrote in a letter to his relatives in Poland. They went off together to the Trobriand Islands, off the coast of New Guinea, to conduct the first anthropological study of the islanders. It was a prolific time – Malinowski wrote about intimate aspects of the lives of the islanders, including the classic *Argonauts of the Western Pacific*, *Coral Gardens and their Magic*, *Myth in Primitive Society* as well as two detailed and illustrated books on sexual life of the islanders.

Paszkowski's book revealed smaller "stars": tiny jewels of stories about Polish adventurers in Australia, such as the colourful Sygurd Wisniowski and Joseph Sabatowski.

Wisniowski was an incorrigible globetrotter. During the 1860s and '70s, he travelled incessantly to North and South Americas, Papua New Guinea, New Zealand and

Australia. Australia was his favourite destination, and he made a fortune in the goldfields near Ravenswood. As the story goes, he soon lost it in a shipwreck, and again devoted himself to travelling and writing. His memoir, *Ten Years in Australia,* was published upon his brief return to Poland, and his novella about Maori communities in New Zealand (*Tikera or Children of the Queen of Oceania*) was translated into English and published in Auckland in 1972, nearly a century after it was written.

Sabatowski, on the other hand, was more a patriot and a revolutionary than a globetrotter. I like the story of his life because of his puzzling end and obsessive commitment to fight Polish oppressors at that time: Russia and Prussia. He left Poland after the failure of the January Uprising against Russia in 1863–64 only to join the Turkish army to continue fighting Russia, then the Austrian army to fight Prussia and then the French army to also fight Prussia. Freud would no doubt have a theory about him, as after years of fighting wars and uprisings, Sabatowski eventually settled in Sydney and became a gynaecologist.

Long before I read Paszkowski's book, I already had my favourite explorer: Joseph Conrad (1857–1924), writer and sailor – my teenage idol. His beginnings carry the drama of adventure. He was born Jozef Korzeniowski, his parents exiled by the Tsarist Russian government for their political activities as Polish patriots, so his uncle, Stefan, a nobleman with lands in the Ukraine, became his father-figure. Young Korzeniowski dreamed of exotic travels and wanted to be a sailor – an unusual choice for a young Polish nobleman. His uncle, however, agreed to send him to a school in southern France to follow his dream.

In France, Korzeniowski got involved in shipping guns for a revolutionary cause, fell in love with an unsuitably mysterious and revolutionary woman, went into debt and attempted suicide. His uncle saved him from his financial – if not romantic – trouble, and Korzeniowski went on to London where he gradually progressed from first officer to captain, and became a British subject. He sailed the seas of South-east Asia (the geographic setting of many of his books) and South America (*Nostromo*), as well as the Congo River in Africa (*Heart of Darkness*). By his own admission, he was hot-tempered, swore in Polish while riding horses, and spoke with a thick accent: a bizarre mixture of his native Polish and a dialect of southern French. For me, as a teenage girl in communist Poland, he was an irresistible combination

Joanna Kujawa

of the adventurous and creative aspects of a life lived passionately.

From Paszkowski, I learned that Korzeniowski also travelled to Australia and had a few stopovers in the ports of Sydney and Melbourne in 1879, 1888 and 1889. All the stopovers had a literary history. In 1879 the young seaman sailed from London to Sydney, and while waiting there to join another ship heard about the scandal of the steamer *Jeddah* whose crew abandoned 953 Muslim pilgrims when it seemed the ship was sinking. The news created a great upheaval among officers and seamen and became the theme of his masterpiece *Lord Jim*. He described Sydney Harbour as "most beautiful" in *The Mirror of the Sea*, and some of the personalities he met in Sydney – including an Australian mate, Charles Born – became characters in his books. In 1888, Korzeniowski returned as the captain of *Otago*. His name was so horrifically misspelled in Sydney newspapers that by the time *Otago* reached Melbourne he had changed it to Conrad.

The metaphor of the explorer is not only my personal passion; it has always played powerfully on our collective imagination. Perhaps the first explorer, wanderer and "migrant" of a sort was Homer's Odysseus. His journeys have inspired a kaleidoscope of interpretations throughout the ages. The ancient Greeks saw him as a courageous warrior tested by the gods for his brilliant trickery. To the Romans, he was the epitome of a "deceitful" foreigner who, through his insidious plan, destroyed the city of Troy. After the displacements and tragedies of the World War II, Theodor Adorno and Max Horkheimer thought that Odysseus was the despairing exile who is always out of his cultural context in the world.

My encounters with Jerzy Zubrzycki and George Smolicz, two intellectuals who left Poland during World War II and eventually settled in Australia, suggest yet another interpretation of the "exile". Both Zubrzycki and Smolicz managed to creatively transform the traumatic experiences of war in a way that helped to shape and enrich Australian multiculturalism. Zubrzycki told me that when he arrived in Australia he aimed to correct the errors of pre-war Poland, which had failed to embrace all ethnic and religious groups in the 1930s. He wanted to prevent the same situation being repeated in Australia. Throughout his career at the Australian National University, he worked to implement multiculturalism as an integral part of Australian life.

Smolicz crossed Central Asia and the Middle East, and lived in an endless string of camps for war refugees as a child refugee. His experiences inspired him to reform the Australian educational system in a way that would allow children of all backgrounds to learn about their original culture and language. He envisioned Australia as a country of infinite cultural richness. That is the cultural contribution of explorers.

Indeed, many of the Poles who arrived here more recently, such as award-winning composers of scores for Australian films (Cezary Skubiszewski), poets (Anna Walwicz), designers (Kajetan) or actors (Jacek Koman), call themselves explorers. They belong because of their intellectual and artistic contribution. Their journeys often led to Australia through several other countries, each a space of learning and contribution. They are all interesting strangers who, through their journeys, redefine what it means to belong, whose "souls are about larger belongings" not confined to one land or language.

Bruce Chatwin once said that the appeal of explorers and nomads lies in their "irreverent and timeless vitality". And the most potent image of the explorer is of someone who, with great courage and creativity, responds to the challenges and complexities of life that arise – someone who encompasses the courage, enthusiasm and drive of the adventurer and the reflective and creative qualities of the artist that are eventually integrated into a larger society. The explorer is not a poetic or an exotic term. It is the "newcomer", "migrant", "exile" seen from a different, more complex vantage point, and allowed to participate creatively in their new society.

There is yet another journey to undertake – not only by the "newcomer" but by the host society as well. That might be even the more challenging exploration. It asks the society to give up prejudice, a presumed and often unconscious sense of superiority and rigidly defined ways of belonging "here". In this version of explorations, Odysseus arrives at a new land knowing that not only he, but the entire population of that land, will share this journey, taking the known and familiar to uncharted shores of new visions and self-discovery. ■

Joanna Kujawa was awarded a PhD by Monash University for her thesis "Migration, Belonging, Alienation" in 2005. She has published short stories and essays in Australia, Canada, the United Kingdom and Poland. She currently lives in Melbourne.

Memoir:
**On becoming a Jew**
Author:
**Lee Kofman**

*Image: Jewish children walking to the Jewish Synagogue in Flood St, Bondi. / Photographer: Peter Rae / Source: Fairfaxphotos.com*

# On becoming a Jew

*If you ever forget you're a Jew, a Gentile will remind you.*

– Bernard Malamud

Brooklyn laundry, 2002: Sometimes I am asked how it feels to be a Jew in Australia. For years I had not considered myself a Jew. I was a woman, writer, lover, feminist, social worker and serial immigrant with a hyphenated national identity – Russian-Israeli-Australian – but I hardly identified as a Jew. I ate pork, lived outside Caulfield, had a multicultural circle of friends, and when I first arrived in Australia on the eve of the millennium, I was charmed by the gentle Australian men. I ended up marrying a Jew, but only by default. His upbringing and education were more those of an Aussie.

Recently I participated in an academic literary colloquium, reading my piece about a true story that happened to my mother in a Brooklyn laundry shortly after she immigrated to America.

My orthodox mother, unmistakably Jewish in a wig and opaque stockings despite New York's sticky summer, was waiting for her laundry to dry. The smells of fresh soap and stale clothes mixed in the airless room. A girl – maybe twelve, maybe a bit older, her raven-coloured hair braided into two neat plaits and her denim mini-skirt revealing the strong legs of an adolescent – stuck her tongue out at my mother while her own mother wasn't watching. It might have been a mistake, but she did it again. Then she gave my mother the finger. My mother tucked her head into her book.

The girl's mother walked out to smoke. Only my mother and the girl remained now in the stuffy laundry. The girl came closer in feline movements too adult for her age and whispered: "Bloody Jew, piss off. Bloody Jew …" She nudged my mother, just a little bit, with her arm.

After I finished my reading, people approached me, saying how shocked they were upon hearing my story: Surely nowadays things like this hardly ever happen …

As I drove home alongside the azure beach of the most liveable city in the world, where kangaroos, Greeks, Jews, Italians and Aussies all reside together, I doubted that my writing had done justice to my mother's feelings. I wondered what this particular incident had meant to her. Had it registered also in her mind as an accident in the modern, liberal world?

Strangely, it wasn't this incident itself, but the reaction of my peers, that made me do some soul searching. It occurred to me that, as my mother stretched her words along the New York–Melbourne line, putting on a cheerful bravado – "I whispered to her, but very firmly: 'You little bitch, if you don't stop now, I'll call the police'." – I had responded to her story with the same shock and disbelief as the university audience. On that drive, I also recalled her brief silence which followed my reaction – unusual for my chatty mother.

From my car window, I watched palms and beach-going people. How lucky I was to live here, in serene Melbourne. In the mid-1980s, when I was a child and my family emigrated from Russia to Israel, my mother had felt similarly privileged. After her years in the Soviet Union (where everyone was equal but some were less equal, especially if they happened to be Jews, and where as a Masters graduate she had to work cleaning parks because of KGB persecution), she had arrived in the Jewish land foolishly expecting to find utopia.

We lived then in an immigrants' hostel: five people in two tiny rooms with iron beds. My mother insisted on keeping the door unlocked until one day my father, whose Hebrew was the best of all of us, read us a newspaper article about Israeli jails. My mother and I both gasped in disbelief: Jews as thieves? Murderers? Rapists? There is no such a thing … but the doors were locked from then on.

I thought of my mother who, heavy-bodied but agile, climbed the Golan Mountain in her long dress and sneakers, and who in Jerusalem's eastern part of mosques and Allah Akhbar talked to a local Arab about the meaning of life. My mother who, even while locking the doors, still passionately loved every centimetre of that land for so long. Yet, seventeen years after our arrival, disillusioned with Israel's institutional corruption and politics, again she fulfilled her Jewish role of wanderer.

She came to America still believing in utopia. Despite the obvious hardships of being an immigrant in her early fifties, she embraced the American system with enthusiasm. Another phone conversation comes to mind.

"I took a taxi and the driver was Russian. Of course he turned out to be an ex-engineer … Anyway, I asked what he thought of America. "It's not America," he replied. "It's Americhka!"

"I'm not sure I understand."

"I'll give you an example: here if your income is under a certain amount you get a tax refund at the end of the year. Can you imagine a law like that in Israel? This is exactly what he meant. Darling Americhka."

I was still driving. And thinking. And watching the pale-blue sky embroidered with sunshine. I never tire of Melbourne's beauty, just as my mother is utterly taken with New York's dense foliage and art galleries. While struggling to find employment and an affordable apartment, she still cultivates, with her tireless energy, love for this tough city. She passionately appreciates whatever it bestows upon her: markets, convenient public transport, good education for my brothers. The city is like her new beloved. That day in the laundry, I now believe, was his first betrayal.

Caulfield, 2000: I told the laundry story to my Israeli friend, who has been living in Melbourne longer than I. Both of us have witnessed several anti-Jewish and anti-Israeli verbal attacks since migrating, but agreed that in contemporary Australia it has never been the norm. We have never felt particularly singled out.

My friend thought I was over-reacting.

"What are you saying? That the West is incurably anti-Semitic? That Jews will never find a refuge? What do you expect? You said yourself, there is no such thing as utopia. It's not always about Jews: it's human nature to dislike outsiders. Luckily we live in a place where most people are tolerant."

I walked away even more disturbed, thinking I was turning into a true diaspora Jew, infested with paranoia a la Woody Allen.

Having spent most of my life in Israel, accustomed to being a majority in that country, I was naturally less preoccupied with my ethnicity than the Jewish community in Australia. Isaiah Berlin, an English-Jewish philosopher, once said: "In Israel I don't particularly feel a Jew, but in England I do."

Diasporas tend to perceive their countries of origin as symbols for their particular yearnings, rather than as complex realities. The Jewish diaspora is no different. As the Israeli-Australian anthropologist Dr Cohen puts it: "Many Israelis living in Australia feel that the local Jewish community likes Israel (as central to their Jewish identity), but dislikes Israelis. The community doesn't like seeing them leaving the country, even though they themselves live here. This is the paradox."

Consequently, Israeli migrants often develop dubious relationships with the Jewish diaspora. It is the same with families: technically, you are of the same blood – but not necessarily organically compatible. I owed the Jewish community, though. As a new immigrant, I struggled to find decent employment with my Israeli qualifications and work history. A major charitable Jewish organisation gave me my first chance, employing me to run a fundraising campaign based, of course, in Caulfield, where everybody knew everybody and Yiddish was spoken as much as English.

Raising money that went into water recycling and tree planting in both Israel and Australia was an exercise of real value. I plunged myself into the work, admiring the generosity of the community members who donated their time and money. Yet I wasn't organically compatible. As an ex-Soviet child brought up on everyday portions of uncontested patriotism, I grew up suspicious of any rhetoric, and everything to do with Israel was uncontested in Caulfield.

## On becoming a Jew

I knew from first-hand experience how Israel was imperfect, based in an impossible location and dealing with impossible problems. Its people – both Arabs and Jews – were busy surviving rather than simply living. Every day you hadn't exploded, or been shot, or robbed of your money by the taxation office or an unfair employer was a good day. In such extreme circumstances, the reality was shifting constantly from beautiful to horrific and vice versa. People were corrupt and courageous, selfish and kind. Living in Israel was like riding a roller coaster day after day. But I couldn't really talk about this at work.

I felt so ambivalent in Caulfield, where people took on astronomic mortgages just to live amongst other Jews creating a quasi-*shtetl*, and sometimes remained single in the absence of a suitable Jewish spouse, spending weekends at Jewish functions amongst the same people they had known since school. If that was what it meant to be a Jew, then I definitely wasn't one.

"There is something you don't get," a thirty-something Australian-Jewish woman told me. After spending her youth in Jewish schooling, at Jewish functions and in Jewish neighbourhoods, she had broken free and moved to Byron Bay.

"We huddle together, because we're a traumatised community. Our parents and grandparents are mostly war refugees, some raised us in houses stuffed with canned foods, just in case another war broke out."

Indeed, the Holocaust has been deeply internalised as a lingering residue within the subsequent generations of Jews. Though memories of it are often loudly invoked, writes the academic and writer Eva Hoffman, it is rarely discussed, unpacked or processed. Unable to come to terms with its impacts and legacy, we replay in our minds a tragic narrative which neither empowers nor enlightens us.

It is not only the tragic past that never really loosens its grip on our present; we are also trapped by the looming, hypothetical future. Memories of the Holocaust become a constant reminder to stay on guard. Holocaust survivor Primo Levi wrote of the Holocaust as "a fundamental, unexpected event, fundamental precisely because unexpected, not foreseen by anyone. It took place in the teeth of all forecasts; it happened in Europe."

This unexpectedness has understandably caused a lot of fear in generations to follow, but has also engendered a rhetoric. For the post-Holocaust Jewish community, Israel is the embodiment of the hope "Never again!" so questioning the country's ways can be seen to undermine Jews' own security.

Gradually I started realising how much pain there was in Caulfield, disguised with merry *klezmer* tunes.

I was forming a counter-argument to my Israeli friend. Jews are not merely other outsiders. Since the Romans threw us out of Israel, for centuries we have missed out on the normalising experience of possessing a home that most other diasporas had at some stage. This perpetual homelessness, the lack of origins, also made the Jews more suspicious in their "host countries" – it turned them into extra-outsiders. Stalin is known to have said that the Jewish lack of a homeland made them "mystical, intangible, other-worldly".

Our national psyche has developed differently based on this constant oscillation between prospering in the host countries, then being persecuted for this same prospering and other prejudices, and moving on again and again. This odd condition finally culminated in the Holocaust.

A plane to Melbourne, 2004: I lived far from Caulfield, in a beachside suburb, and finally found work within my profession in an Australian workplace. But my Jewish fate pursued me there, beating its wings on my window, knocking its head off. It began with fleeting, singular incidents, just as in my mother's story.

On a plane to Melbourne, my future husband chatted with an Australian businesswoman about the events of September 11. "Well," the woman said, "it was all obviously planned by the Jews. Don't you see they control the world?" She had no idea he was one of them.

I laughed upon hearing the story. The woman was an insignificant exception in Australia, a country proud of its multiculturalism. To be sure, though, for a week I surfed Australian internet forums debating current affairs. To my surprise, conspiracy theories about Jews were alive and kicking. I wasn't sure what it meant to be a Jew, but many had ideas on what we were after. Jews were greedy, wealthy (on my social worker's salary, being a Jew suddenly sounded rather appealing …) and controlled American politics – especially in the Middle East. Interestingly, in 2004 only about a quarter of American Jews voted for Bush, and the US right-wing extremists actually accused American Jews of spreading socialist values.

Historically speaking, in turbulent times Jews have often found themselves in the midst of the conflict. Sometimes one could even say it was of their own doing, as in the Russian Revolution, but more often they were scapegoats. In the Middle Ages, there was a widespread belief that Jews enjoyed killing Christian children and poisoning wells to spread the plague. The blame has continued well into our times: *New York Times* researcher George Johnson has observed that the main targets of conspiracy theories in the twentieth century were Jews.

So, in the new millennium – as the West and Islam are clashing – Jews are at centre stage, stuck in between as usual. Christos Tsiolkas's uneasy book *Dead Europe* (Vintage, 2005) portrays this reality, with its freak show of Jew-hating characters across various countries and strata. As I followed my

## On becoming a Jew

gloomy internet search results recalling my husband's story, one of the book's characters came to mind – the Sarajevo survivor who blamed Americans (or, more precisely, American Jews) for the civil war in her country. She spoke about 9/11 in a similar vein to the businesswoman on the plane: "I was glad to see those Jews jumping from those burning buildings. They deserved their towers to burn."

Over the past five years, there has been an unprecedented revival of anti-Semitism worldwide. In Germany, someone wrote on a memorial to the Holocaust victims: "Sixty years later, and we are still guilty? No!!!!" Sami al-Arian, a Palestinian-American professor, declared recently that God considers all Jews "monkeys and swine". At a conference in October 2005, the Iranian President repeated the Ayatollah Khomeini's idea that Israel must be "wiped off the map". The West was outraged, yet most in the Muslim world haven't expressed a public condemnation of this statement. The most reasonable response from the Middle East actually came from the Palestinian chief negotiator Saeb Erekat, who told the BBC: "What we need to be talking about is adding the state of Palestine to the map and not wiping Israel off the map." And in Newcastle, Australia, where I spent a few great days participating in a writers' festival, "Jews must die" was spray-painted on a synagogue.

The world was tightening in on itself, even in my remote beach suburb. Politics suddenly seemed very personal. Yes, perhaps Jewish paranoia belonged to Caulfield, whereas I was secular, cosmopolitan, ethnically androgynous. But I could feel my crooked Jewish nose lengthening like Pinocchio's. Just like him, I was lying – mainly to myself – and had been doing so for many years. It's not that I wasn't a Jew – I had just never *wanted* to be one. After all, so many times we have been dispossessed of our belongings, exiled, tortured, burnt alive (the lucky ones were forcefully baptised), gassed, during pogroms our children's heads were smashed on stone and women were raped, and much more. Why would I want to be a Jew?

But I couldn't run away for much longer. I was becoming a Jew, despite myself.

As my husband finished telling the story from the flight, he added: "I have a solution to cure the world of anti-Semitism. Let's open a Jew Zoo."

"A Jew Zoo?"

"Yes. Let's put some Jews in a zoo so people can visit and observe them regularly. Perhaps they'll see we're human beings."

Moscow hospital, 1981: Simon Klimowitsky, a Melbourne-based Russian poet of Jewish origin, says even the Jews themselves cannot be sure who they are. They are hybrids – the most enigmatic ethnicity.

Indeed, as a nation, we make an odd one. We are much older than our fifty-seven-year-old country that contains about one-third of all the Jews in the world. A million more Jews live in the United States than in Israel. Overall, we are spread across about a hundred countries, as far-ranging as Zimbabwe and Kazakhstan. And no such a thing as a Jewish look even exists, despite Chagall's famous paintings of curly-haired people with melancholic eyes. We can be red-haired, blue-eyed, possess chiselled Hellenic noses, or appear Ethiopian, Indian and in rare cases Asian.

What is the invisible ribbon binding us all? How does one feel Jewish? In search of a common ground, we are often reduced to the Holocaust and the Israeli–Arab conflict, but we have so many other facets. Our diaspora, amongst the most hard-working and high-achieving of minorities, has lent itself to competing ideologies and spiritual pursuits from communism to Buddhism to capitalism and has produced a legacy of thinkers like Einstein, revolutionaries like Trotsky, writers and artists like Bashevis Singer, Modigliani and so on. So who are we? What is our common denominator?

The Australian academic Ien Ang, interviewed by Mary Zournazi for her book *Foreign Dialogues* (Pluto Press, 1998), observes the Jewish psyche through a literary lens: "Self-hatred is prominent in a lot of Jewish literature … [self-hatred] relates to an experience where you are constructed as a foreigner or a stranger."

The word "Jew" – just like "woman" – is loaded, implying double standards for its carriers, being perceived as a perpetual outsider even in their immediate environment. Perhaps being a Jew is indeed like being a woman. To borrow from Simone de Beauvoir, one is not born, but rather becomes a Jew. Jewish identity is shaped largely in response to the world's reactions to us. Like women, Jews share a history of discrimination across nations, generations, cultures and languages. We have always stood out, despite the best efforts of some to fit in.

I suggest renaming anti-Semitism "anti-assimilationism".

The first time I became a Jew was when I was about eight, still living in communist Russia, and was admitted to a Moscow hospital for heart surgery.

In hospitals, as in any place where death is in such close proximity to the living, the national psyche lies bare, undisguised by rhetoric. The free Soviet public health system was in fact so expensive that people who could not afford to bribe every nurse and doctor in the clinics and hospitals died. In the children's ward, we lay for hours with no one to change our chamber pots, brush our knotted hair which had become breeding grounds for lice or give us pain-killers. Yet that common despair didn't lead us to any particular bonding. We kept to the rituals of our ages and cultures, and so I was utterly excluded as the only Jew. When I returned after the surgery with my upper body enclosed in a dressing and my chest itching painfully, I tried to fall asleep, to get through the night somehow.

## On becoming a Jew

"The Jewish princess has come back," said the oldest girl – who soon would die. "I have an idea. Let's sing all night so she won't be able to sleep. I've got lots of new lyrics. If you sing, I'll let you copy them tomorrow." They sang and sang, the whole night.

On that night, the longest in my life, I was becoming and unbecoming a Jew, all at once. For the first time, I realised the full extent of the gap between me and them, but I was also determined to bridge it.

I wanted to sleep well for the rest of my life.

Kryal Castle, Ballarat, 2005: Cruising through a world full of prejudice and hatred towards you, you feel it imprint itself on your psyche. After experiencing the extreme, you are then more prone to extremes yourself in order to escape. Some, like me, find consolation in utopian cosmopolitanism at a cost of denying their roots, whereas others isolate themselves from the outside world, cultivating some sort of superiority – even though both choices originate from the same desperation, the same need for refuge and "never again".

On my wedding night at Kryal Castle, I asked my mother to give a speech. She walked to the stage past coats of arms adorned with crucifixes and past our French, Pakistani, Jewish, Chinese, Italian and Australian guests in her Orthodox Jewish outfit – a surreal vision of true multiculturalism.

"I'm so delighted," my mother announced, echoing underneath the Gothic ceiling, "on this great day to be amongst all the Jews ..."

"Mama," I shouted, "not everyone is Jewish here." As though she didn't know.

"But Jewish people are the best."

The following week, when I called friends to apologise for this incident, most said they understood what she said to be a joke. I wasn't convinced. I grew up with my parents reacting to the world mainly through a Jewish "prism", watching titles of American movies to see whether the director was Jewish and favouring books on Jewish topics. Perhaps my refusal to be a Jew was also rooted there, in that childhood of forced division.

Every Jewish closet, 2006: is full of skeletons. So is mine. I still struggle to reconcile the image of my distressed mother in the Brooklyn laundry, and that of her speaking triumphantly at my wedding. It is easier to love her in the laundry than at Kryal Castle, just as it is easier for me to visit Caulfield occasionally and enjoy the succulent Yiddish and kosher bagels than live or work in the suburb. It is easier to forgive those Russian girls from the hospital, especially as some of them are dead by now, but it becomes increasingly difficult to keep dismissing the current political climate in which the hydra of anti-Semitism is growing anew its ancient, horrific heads.

It is also impossible to keep dismissing my origins. Nowadays, as the racial and religious tensions rise, we are all – even against our wills – becoming a bit more Jewish, or Muslim, or American, or Australian, or whatever.

So I am a bit Jewish nowadays, and follow a more consistent version of cosmopolitanism with regard to Jews too – it's not about me and them anymore, Caulfield versus the beach. I take more interest in our history and follow current affairs more intently. And, perhaps for the first time, I let the pain of being a Jew into my life. Resistance and logic fade and I am flooded with an overwhelming sadness for our not-so-distant past of exiles, pogroms, for the six millions and for the present of the Promised Land which has been turned into chaotic, bleeding ground.

I am also sad about what the future might bring in light of increasing fanaticism and war.

Brian Castro wrote in *Griffith REVIEW 8: Our Global Face* that real thought is always in between, inseparable from the complexity of feeling, suffering from contradiction. I agree with him that contradiction is the experience of truth. I experience it now. At the same time that I am becoming Jewish, I also feel most acutely the urgency to preserve my old beliefs in some mysterious commonality of human nature, hoping – perhaps naïvely – this can be an antidote to the storm of hatred brewing all around.

I began this essay with the question of how it feels to be a Jew in Australia. I want to believe that nowadays I am more able to answer it.

I still maintain I'm immensely lucky to live here, in a country whose greatest downfall (or perhaps advantage?) is that it is laid back. I believe this even in the aftermath of the Cronulla riots: I see them not as a rule, but as an ugly exception. I am lucky in this spacious land where people still smile at strangers on the streets. But the word "lucky" is not synonymous with feeling safe, and means instead arbitrary and incidental. Lucky is a fragile word. And this, I guess, is my point – there is a fragility embedded in being a Jew that none of us can ever escape, no matter what colour our skin is or what we believe.

Isaiah Berlin once said: "I do not think that there is a country where Jews feel totally secure, where they do not ask themselves: 'How do I look to others?'" Most likely, this same uneasiness is what I am inheriting as I am slowly becoming a Jew. ■

---

Lee Kofman is a Melbourne-based writer. Her essay "Hamlet in the classroom" was published in *Griffith REVIEW 11: Getting Smart*, and she also contributed to *The Lure of Fundamentalism* and *Webs of Power*.

Divided Nation

# Essay:
# Of Middle Eastern appearance
# Author:
# Randa Abdel-Fattah

"Do you ever wish you were fully Aussie?" This question was posed to me by a teenage girl in a Sydney school last year.

"What do you mean by fully Aussie?" I asked.

"Um ... like Anglo, you know?" There was no malice or sarcasm intended. The girl was sincere and simply curious as to whether I yearned to be liberated from what she saw as the shackles of my hyphenated identity as an Australian-born Muslim of Palestinian and Egyptian heritage, and take refuge in the more convenient and *legitimate* hyphenated identity of Anglo-Aussie.

My first reaction was to laugh. Unfortunately, her sentiment could not be attributed to a naïve, schoolgirl view of Australian identity and citizenship. It was the kind of construction of Australian identity I have been hearing for some time now – from politicians, journalists, radio hosts, public figures, none of whom can hide behind the excuse of puberty or inexperience in life.

When the political rhetoric is spun, and demands are made for citizenship tests, and Australian values are invoked to justify an "us and them" mentality, and some migrants are deemed less Australian for their inability to speak English, and a ban on the *hijab* is called for in secular schools, and the deportation of an Australian citizen of Egyptian background is demanded because of outrageous comments he has made, it becomes blatantly obvious who our government and spin doctors have identified as the so-called ideological threat to Australian values.

"Muslim" and "Australian" are widely perceived as mutually exclusive and bipolar opposites. One does not need to adopt a victimisation complex to arrive at this rather obvious conclusion. Muslims – whether Australian born, migrants or converts of convict ancestry – are the new Public Enemy Number One. Such an enemy is constructed because, like it or not, we have been undertaking a rather urgent and almost parasitical soul-searching exercise since September 11. Our status as Australians feeds off the un-Australian status of others. We can only be truly Australian as a measure of those we deem to be truly not. As somebody who readily falls into the category of "other", I am curious as to why Muslims – and indeed people who fall under the crude misnomer "of Middle Eastern appearance" – are on this end of the deep and bitter wedge that has been forged in Australia. There is a fracture in our society and, rather than feel optimistic about it healing, I feel increasingly apprehensive about it worsening.

Is it because the criminals who attacked America on September 11, 2001 professed to be Muslim (although their actions clearly abrogated any such claim)? The language of the "Coalition of the Willing" has only ever been coloured with statements about the "terrorists attacking our way of life" and "our values". By the crude logic of shock-jocks and politicians anxious for votes, the purported alliance of the terrorists with Islam renders Australian Muslims and Australians of Arabic background (because the misconception is that every Arab is a Muslim) equally suspect as antagonistic to "Australian values".

There have been various attempts to define Australian values. A fair go, egalitarianism, gender equality – all values critics have pointed out are universal human values, certainly not values over which Australia can claim intellectual property rights.

However, the way in which the debate plays out demonstrates that it is not a generalist values debate. How Muslims view labour laws, free trade, the environment or capitalism has never been at the heart of the issue. The values debate has ostensibly focused on women's dress and attitudes to certain social norms (such as alcohol, a day at the beach or sexuality). Integration, fitting in, assimilation: it doesn't matter whether you belong to a union or recycle your plastic; whether you wear a bikini to the beach, can join in a jovial who-got-more-pissed-on-the-weekend Monday morning water cooler conversation or date are the pivotal points that rate you on the one to ten scale of What Makes You Aussie.

That is why that young schoolgirl asked me whether I ever *wished I was fully Aussie*. I had just explained that observant Muslims don't drink alcohol or take drugs, don't have boyfriend/girlfriend relationships and don't wear bikinis or swimsuits to the beach or pools. There were a lot of don'ts in my talk and the girl, rather than seeing these as a matter of personal choice, took pity on me. But her assessment of me as different and weird accurately reflects a widespread wariness amongst the general population of overt religion. It is the place of observant Muslims in a secular society that conjures up this irrational fear and the perception that Muslims represent an ideological affront to a secular lifestyle. It is not a Muslim's spiritual beliefs in heaven and hell, the big bang, creationism or Darwinism. It is the *hijab*, the beard, the call to prayer, the fasting during work hours, the praying during lunch breaks, the self-discipline against indulging (even in moderation, even in tiny small doses!) in all things dear to secular life – sex, drugs, alcohol – that seems to me to be the point of divide.

I don't think the divide that has made Muslims feel like "the other" is based on race, colour or culture. It is a divide based on religious observance. Italians and Greeks may go to church on Sunday or wear a cross around their necks, but most date, enjoy a drink and have the appearance of religious anonymity. The religious observance is not explicit, and that is why their "integration" is perceived as a success of multiculturalism, whereas the Australian-ness of a non-drinking Muslim bloke who steps out of work to go pray at lunchtime, or a woman at the bus-stop with a suit and *hijab* on, is circumspect.

Well, what about orthodox Jewish women, I hear you protest. They cover their hair with a wig and only expose it to their husbands as a symbol of modesty. And what about nuns who also wear a veil? And Mormons, who have strict dress codes and also do not drink? It is most interesting. So many similarities between Islam and other faiths and yet for every five or more documentaries a week about Muslims, Muslim women or the veil, there are virtually none about the almost identical principles of modesty found in Judaism, or Paul's admonition to women in Corinthians that their hair should be cut off if it is not covered.

It is Islam and Muslims who have the public fascinated and on edge. Perhaps it is because of the increasing size of the Australian Muslim population. Do we accept people as Australians as long as we can manage the size of their minority status? The less noticeable they are, the more acceptable they become?

Time and time again, the values debate has centred on the role of women in Islam (perceived as oppressed) and the role of women in the West (championed as liberated). In the recent past, Prime Minister John Howard has called for "some Muslim migrants to learn English and treat women better in order to fit in with Australian values". He later defended himself, saying he was referring to a small section of the Muslim population.

The qualification was laughable. If the Prime Minister was so genuinely concerned about women's rights in religion, he should not have stopped at Muslims. What of Orthodox Jewish men who each day say, "Blessed art thou, O Lord our God, King of the Universe, who hast not made me a woman"? No headlines about that. And is

Christianity so innocent? According to Ecclesiastics 25:19, 24: "No wickedness comes anywhere near the wickedness of a woman ... Sin began with a woman and thanks to her we all must die." Women are still struggling to be ordained in Australia's supposed utopia of female liberation. Our society is palpably silent on the exploitation of other religions to deny women their rights. And yet, when a Muslim displays a patriarchal, misogynist attitude, the public and our politicians are outraged, as though – God forbid – there are no sexist, chauvinistic non-Muslim men.

That our sports heroes have been embroiled in shocking scandals involving the degradation (and alleged rape and sexual assault) of women is forgotten. That there have been gang rapes perpetrated by Anglo-Australians (whose ethnic identity is never revealed) is ignored. That there have been reports of date-rape drugs being administered on cruise ships is met with silence.

The hypocritical way in which the Sheikh Hilali affair unfolded is a case in point, for whilst the Sheikh's comments were undoubtedly appalling, the reaction of the Prime Minister, politicians and the media exposed a superiority complex on the part of those who raise Western standards of masculinity as the model yardstick. The "us and them" card was whipped out. *We* respect women. *We* believe in equality. *We* stand for liberation. *They* believe differently. Was the ferocity of public indignation elicited by the words in the sermon, or by the fact that the person giving the sermon was Muslim? After all, comments that imply that women invite rape by the way they dress have been made by members of the judiciary. Barristers routinely seek to tender evidence as to the way a rape victim was dressed in order to impugn her credibility. No public or political frenzy there.

The impact this marginalisation has on Australian Muslims frightens me. It is simply naïve to think that the political discourse and Aussie! Aussie! Aussie! Oi! Oi! Oi! rhetoric is aimed at empowering Muslims – migrants and the Australian-born – or inspiring a sense of citizenship in them. It is no stretch of my cynicism to see the rhetoric and puffed up chests of "our values or go home" as an appalling vote-grabbing exercise. Stir up the politics of resentment under the pretence of a celebration of Aussie pride. The result is alienation, defensiveness and, amongst young Australian Muslims, confusion about one's identity and place in the only country one knows as home.

I know of such confusion because I have felt it many times. The kind of identity politics that has been thrown up by the pressure to define Australian values and identity hit me straight in the eye on my trip to Sweden last year. I was invited as one of the authors to speak at the Gothenburg Book Festival in September 2006, and it was there that I befriended a Swedish journalist and rap artist who was raised in Sweden but born in Lebanon to a Kurdish mother and Lebanese father.

While we interacted with other international guests, one person asked Nabila: "Do you feel Swedish?"

"Yes," she replied. "Until you asked me."

When we reflected on her response later that day, I asked her: "What about your Kurdish and Lebanese background? How does it impact on your identity?" She gave me a nonchalant smile and then shrugged. "To be honest, I'm tired of defining myself. Am I Swedish? Am I Kurdish? Am I Lebanese? I'm all of these things, and none. Sometimes I'm more Swedish than Kurdish, sometimes I'm more Lebanese than Swedish. In the end I'm just me."

Her answer resonated with me. It so perfectly encapsulated an ideal space within which to position one's sense of self. As idealistic and naïve as her expression of self-definition was, I longed for the freedom to detach myself from hyphens and labels and the need to prove loyalty to one part of my identity at the expense of the other – something that seemed to underpin the values debate back home. At times I felt intensely Australian, my chest swelling with pride at the sound of an Australian accent in the streets of Gothenburg. Listening to Suad Amiry talk about her marvellous book, *Sharon and My Mother-in-Law* (Granta, 2005), I felt intensely Palestinian and craved to walk the streets of Jerusalem again. Eating at an Egyptian restaurant in Stockholm, I instantly connected with the owner and reminisced with him about the chaos and magic of Cairo.

The inconsistency in my emotions and devotions used to faze me. It used to arouse in me a sense of disloyalty and insincerity. But Nabila showed me that there is no weakness in loving many things with equal strength. I returned to Australia conscious, for the first time, of the utter fluidity of my identity. I don't need to feel "fully Aussie". Not because I am not of Anglo background (I don't believe Anglo equals Australian), but because it is an impossible demand of a country founded on immigration to expect a pure demarcation between citizenship and heritage. One's past, whether ancestral or as a migrant, necessarily shapes one's present. The issue is the place of this construction of self in Australia's future. ∎

Randa Abdel-Fattah is the author of *Ten things I Hate About Me* and the award-winning, *Does My Head Look Big in This?* Her essay "Living in a material world" from *Griffith REVIEW 8: The Lure of Fundamentalism* won the 2005 Victorian Premier's Alfred Deakin Prize for an essay advancing public debate.

Essay:
**Retro-assimilation**

Author:
**Anna Haebich**

Image: Audrey and Sasha from the 'Tenant by tenant' series / Source: www.keithsaundersphotography.com

# Retro-assimilation

Nostalgia for an assimilated nation haunts public debate on national identity and nationhood, as well as related issues of race, ethnicity, indigenous rights and immigration. Commentators on both sides of Australian politics deny that the Prime Minister is turning the pages of government back to the assimilation policies of the 1950s. They are right, of course. We celebrate cultural diversity and acknowledge indigenous rights, cultures and histories. Yet, although the word "assimilation" is rarely mentioned, there is more than a hint of its essence in official pronouncements on national values, citizenship and the practical integration of Aboriginal communities. The paradox of public denial of assimilation and hidden allegiance to its tenets can be explained as "retro-assimilation".

From this perspective, current visions of the nation can be seen as yet another example of nostalgia and clever marketing. Retro-assimilation mixes 1950s dreams of an assimilated nation with current ideas of nationhood using today's spin to create a new vision based on shared values, visions and agreements. Like other retro products, it uncritically exploits the surface of the past without regard for original meanings and significance. Retro-assimilation has strong appeal in today's climate of social turmoil, transformation and global threats; we are irresistibly drawn to its retroscapes, and nostalgic memories of safer and simpler times.

As we respond to the rosy glow of this past, few recognise in the scenes of happy Australian families, responsible citizens and the bogeymen of war, terrorism and alien "isms" the deliberate tactics of government campaigns. Like all quality retro products, retro-assimilation has a time-tested lineage. This dates back to the 1950s when the Menzies government avidly promoted the vision of an assimilated nation of Australian families living the "Australian Way of Life". Many senior conservative politicians grew up surrounded by these images, and fifty years later some remain in their thrall. In a world of retro-assimilation, the past is a grab bag of clichés used to sell the present. Nostalgic memories peddle solutions for current issues or camouflage unpalatable political agendas. While this may be ethical for designers and marketers, it makes for dodgy politics. Our national history deserves to be respected as more than a marketing ploy for the use of later generations. The retro past never really happened.

Peeling back the layers of retro clichés to find the "real" 1950s is a difficult task. The popular view – also espoused by retro-marketers – is of a golden time of prosperity when each family had a comfortable income, a car and a house in the suburbs filled with all the trappings of modern living. This dovetails with memories of a "decade of normality" wedged between the violence of the 1940s and the political protests of the 1960s – a time of stability, conservatism, peace, circumscribed gender roles, restrained sexuality and a conservative mass media. Some commentators – like Richard Bessel and Dirk Schumann in their book *Life After Death* (Cambridge University Press, 2003) – argue that this was a "strange" normality: shockwaves from the war forced a "desperate flight into normalcy" and determination "to move on and not look back". Many people sought security and stability in the family, popularised in imagery around the world at the time. Others see the decade as a social and psychological turning point, a pivotal period of global upheaval and dramatic change that transformed the world and determined the shape of events for the remainder of the century.

For poet W.H. Auden, the 1950s was the "age of anxiety". Below its shiny veneer of complacency and conformity lay the velvety darkness of anxiety and fear. The decade was a peculiar mix of contrasts – of rapid change and conformity and exhilaration and fear – that resonates with today's turmoil and transformation. The United Nations and the blockbuster exhibition "Family of Man" – which toured the world in the 1950s, with a comforting message of universal brotherhood and equality – promoted the ideal of an international family of nations, but the political and economic realities were different.

That decade had unprecedented global migration, extraordinary economic development, undreamt of prosperity, and a new world of consumerism and advertising and political spin. Despite the creation of the United Nations, with its promise of world peace, reports escalated of new theatres of war, political terrorism in decolonising nations and racial conflict in the wake of the emerging civil rights movement. Overshadowing everything else was the spectre of a world split by the competition between capitalism and communism and the terror of atomic global annihilation through their competing will to power. Fanned by US doctrine at home and abroad, this created a scenario of fear and delusion, and the Janus-faced paranoia about enemies at home and abroad.

Today we grapple with the black dog of depression, but the personal devil in the 1950s was anxiety. The drugs of choice today are Prozac and Zoloft, but back then the "miracle cure for anxiety" was Miltown (meprobamate) – a tranquilliser known popularly as the "happy pill" or "emotional aspirin". Within a year of its launch in 1955, one in twenty Americans was prescribed Miltown, over a billion tablets had been sold and the monthly production of fifty tons could not keep up with market demand. The drug was widely prescribed for mothers to bolster their role of maintaining peace and stability within the haven of the family. Miltown became the panacea for the anxieties of American life, its calming effects helping to prop up the increasingly precarious vision of a nation of happy families.

In Australia, mothers relied on the analgesic properties of the aspirin, phenacetin and caffeine contained in Bex and Vincent's Powders to get them through the day. These products could be purchased across the counter at any corner store, and their widespread use gave rise to the iconic 1950s housewives' remedy of "a cup of tea, a Bex and a good lie down". According to Hugh Mackay, the anxiety of the times penetrated the heart of the Australian family to shape the nihilistic view of the Baby Boomer generation: eat, drink and be merry because, with the press of a button, the world could be annihilated. Australia, like many other nations, was in a state of high anxiety as our leaders struggled to carve out a respectable place in the new world order as boundaries of empires, nations and alliances of power were redrawn. During the Cold War, we followed our new ally the United States, joining its war in Korea and exhibiting extreme hostility towards communists at home and abroad. As we renegotiated ties with Britain, we even volunteered territory to test twelve British nuclear bombs between 1952 and 1956.

Yet our leaders seriously misjudged world opinion when they took a conservative stand on colonialism and race in international debates, and Australia was condemned by near neighbours in Asia and Africa. We resented the loss of white dominance in the Commonwealth and then sulked when we were excluded from the Bandung Conference of twenty-nine non-aligned Asian, African and Middle Eastern nations in 1955, billed as the "first intercontinental meeting of coloured people in the history of mankind". We tried to keep our race-based immigration policies and discriminatory treatment of indigenous people hidden from world scrutiny, but were criticised in the UN and the world media led by communist Russia and China and new nations in Africa and Asia. The criticisms were couched in race terms, but UN debates also addressed the rights of indigenous peoples and at one point threatened the sovereignty of settler colonies like Australia. Instead, the International Labor Organisation passed the 1957 Indigenous and Tribal Populations Convention, which advocated assimilation of indigenous people into nation states as citizens with full rights of citizenship, while retaining some traditional rights to land and culture.

These pressures and anxieties pushed Australia towards a form of democracy that would satisfy new global expectations of modern nationhood. The vision of an assimilated Australia reflected the international discourse of equality and anti-racism, promised a shield from criticism and kept the nation abreast of international responsibilities. This vision also gave hope to an increasingly jittery and anxious public, who saw in it realisation of some of the principles they had fought for during the war. Nonetheless, the "white nation" status quo continued, and existing patterns of cultural, political and economic dominance and Australian sovereignty went largely unchallenged.

Of course, assimilation brought change. The entry of one and a half million immigrants between 1947 and 1961 – two-thirds of them from Europe – and the government's attack on racial segregation inevitably altered demographic, social and cultural landscapes. While the pressure to assimilate rested heavily on Aboriginal people and immigrants, successful assimilation depended on more enlightened attitudes and behaviours at home. The federal government embarked on a campaign of nation-building directed at Australian audiences, but with an eye to convincing critics overseas of its commitment to change. In developing the campaign, the government drew on the successful use of propaganda to forge national unity during the war years and new US techniques of nation-building, which used the tools of mass persuasion – public opinion polls, advertising and public relations – to "beef up" the nation through optimistic messages of material progress and assurances of citizens' security from threats from within and without.

The campaigns were mired in government rules and red tape, and the resulting pamphlets and films looked dull and uninteresting compared with the sensational reports on Aborigines and migrants in popular magazines such as *PIX* and *Australasian Post*. Campaign materials were produced in-house through the Australian National Information Bureau and the Australian Government Film Unit, survivors of the carve-up of the government's powerful wartime propaganda machine. The Department of Immigration had is own publicity section, and worked collaboratively with these two agencies. Aboriginal campaign materials were the product of often-fraught negotiations between the federal Departments of the Interior, Territories and External Affairs and state Departments of Aboriginal Affairs.

The official campaign presented images of the family and "the Australian way of life". This is a notoriously slippery concept: aspirational and mutable, loosely defined in terms of an outdoor lifestyle, the nuclear family, home ownership, suburban living, mateship and a fair go for all. The campaign film *The Way We Live*, pitched "the Australian way of life" to aspiring migrants through images of suburban housing, leisure, work, consumer goods, and services such as transport, health, education, financial assistance, cultural institutions and social organisations. Designed to counter images of "bush and billabongs", the film focused on urban living and Australia's growth potential.

If "the Australian way of life" expressed the style of the nation, the suburban middle-class family was its heart. This was both the goal of an assimilated nation and the vehicle to achieve it – central to the processes of nationhood. This ideal was represented in the government pamphlet *An Everyday Australian*, which showed a young suburban family: their brick home and its garden setting, modern furnishings and appliances, the family car, the husband leaving for work in the city, the wife at her housework, and the family enjoying the weekend cleaning the car and picnicking with friends. Without any distinction of class, race or ethnicity, this unit – male bread winner and dependent spouse and children – was the focus of domestic life, work, education, security, personal happiness and citizenship around the nation. The dream was embraced by many Australian couples who married young and quickly started families of two to three children, then set about buying their own homes.

Considerable effort was devoted to promoting the immigration program to Australians, and to attracting immigrants and informing overseas agencies such as the International Refugee Organisation. Just as Arthur Calwell promised, when introducing the program in 1947, that "our population shall remain predominantly British", so the campaign reassured Australians that immigrants would be British or readily assimilable Europeans and there would be no competition for jobs and housing or lowering of living standards and working conditions. In short, "the Australian way of life" would be maintained.

The campaign assured Australians that immigration would benefit the nation by providing much-needed labour for postwar reconstruction, industrial development and resource exploitation, and that national defence would be improved by building up the population in the north with migrant families. Results from opinion polls, introduced to Australia from the United States during the war, showed considerable bipartisan support for the immigration program – as long as national standards of economic development, employment, and law and order were maintained, and migrants were not too visible.

As Rowena MacDonald demonstrated in her 1996 exhibition at the Australian Archives Gallery in Canberra, *Selling a Dream: Promoting Australia to Postwar Migrants*, the campaign used images of family life, the beach and boundless prosperity to lure migrants to Australia. On arrival, migrants were handed pamphlets that outlined the benefits of Australian citizenship and, for migrants from Europe, the special qualifying conditions for "naturalisation" – five years' residency, the renouncing of allegiance to their home nation and the ability to speak English. Australian governments placed great importance on naturalisation, seeing it as proof of successful assimilation and a marker of migrant loyalty and commitment. But, despite government efforts, many migrants remained ambivalent and in 1957 only 32 per cent of those eligible had opted for Australian citizenship.

Most of the campaign was directed at convincing Australian audiences. They were targeted in the film *No Strangers Here* (1950) based on a 1945 American film, *The Cummington Story*, which depicted the experiences of a refugee family in a typical Australian town and proffered the advice: "These are ordinary people like ourselves ... you saw how a friendly helping hand helped them settle in all the faster" so "the newcomer need never feel a stranger". During the Commonwealth Jubilee Year in 1951, the Jubilee Train criss-crossed Victoria and South Australia distributing 15,000 copies of the pamphlet *Why Migration is Vital for Australia*. Four years later, Australia celebrated the arrival of its millionth postwar migrant, an attractive young British housewife. However, such a reassuring symbol of Australian immigration was not a matter of chance: the young woman had been chosen carefully by the Chief Migration Officer in London according to criteria drawn up by the Department of Immigration in Australia.

The centrepiece of the campaign was the prestigious annual Citizenship Convention, which was attended by up to four hundred prominent political and community leaders. The conventions were a public demonstration of consensus about immigration and its core doctrine of assimilation. At the launching ceremony in 1950, Prime Minister Sir Robert Menzies proclaimed that "a man, woman or child who comes here to settle is either not accepted and is therefore not admitted, or he or she becomes an Australian – a member of this community, a member of our nationality, a member of our brotherhood, and in the best sense of the word, a member of our family". The gatherings were also a channel for information and a rallying place for citizen support. Migrants played only a minor role at the conventions prior to the 1960s, but were invited each year to stage cultural performances once discussions had closed. In the Convention's 1961 tableau *We the People*, immigrants were woven into its narrative of the nation, which progressed by stages from the first settlers to the gold rushes, Federation, the two world wars, pioneers of aviation, sport stars, and finally migrant contributions to Australian development. Aboriginal people were not mentioned at all.

The Good Neighbour Council also played a key role in the campaign through its national network of 300 local branches and 10,000 volunteer workers – the majority of them middle-class white Australians. The branches sponsored naturalisation ceremonies, film evenings and public lectures, and provided an example of good citizenship to their fellow Australians by offering practical assistance to migrant families that was well meant but often patronising.

Considerably less government time and money was spent promoting Aboriginal assimilation. There was no funding to set up a national infrastructure of prominent community leaders and local citizens; the federal government demurred on the grounds that Aboriginal affairs was a state responsibility and the states cried poor. Of course, the Aboriginal population, estimated in 1950 at 80,000 – 1 per cent of the national total– was tiny compared with the numbers of migrants, but there were important international sensitivities to be considered. Changing entrenched racism to facilitate assimilation was a huge challenge. This Aboriginal assimilation campaign was the first of its kind in Australia, and the only concerted effort before the reconciliation movement of the 1990s. Campaign materials included pamphlets and films with the telling titles *Our Aborigines*, *Assimilation of Our Aborigines*, *End of the Walkabout*, *Fringe Dwellers*, *The Skills of Our Aborigines*, *One People* and *Aborigines and You*. The government also endorsed in 1955 the celebration of an annual National Aborigines Day, and two years later appointed a group of senior Protestant church officials to head up the first National Aborigines Day Observance Committee.

Hundreds of thousands of pamphlets were distributed overseas and in Australia. In 1959, some 80,000 copies of *Fringe Dwellers* were sent out, and between 1961 and 1963, around 135,000 copies of *Our Aborigines* were distributed to government departments, church organisations, schools and universities, businesses, trade unions and community groups around Australia. The pamphlets presented an optimistic narrative of assimilation that began with an account of traditional Aboriginal life, then moved to the beneficial influence of government policy and legislation for dispossessed communities, and came to rest with images – surprising for the times – of Aboriginal suburban citizens and families participating in a new, modern Australia. The message was that, with a helping hand from other Australians, Aboriginal assimilation was possible.

The pamphlets also explained the steps being undertaken to extend full citizenship rights to Aboriginal people and highlighted the significance of Aboriginal children in achieving the goals of assimilation. In *Fringe Dwellers*, two-thirds of the images were of children with captions that reinforced the message that "the programme of assimilation throughout Australia concentrates particularly on children. For many of them and in due course, for their

## Retro-assimilation

children, hopes of assimilation are high." Rather than the government's dull lectures, it was probably the dramatic reports of civil rights protest in the United States and Aboriginal activism at home that drove popular support for Aboriginal citizenship which culminated in the 1967 federal referendum when 91 per cent of the electorate voted yes – the highest ever recorded for a referendum in Australia – and endorsed the repeal of the race-based clauses of the Constitution.

Ironically, the pamphlets were riddled with the same paradigms and language of race that they set out to erase. This is hardly surprising after years of forced segregation, countless myths and misinformation about Aboriginal people and widespread blindness to the depth of racism in Australia. This language made the pamphlets comfortable and familiar for local audiences, and community interest ensured they were put to good use. The pamphlet *Fringe Dwellers*, issued in 1959, was added to the University of Queensland's library collection; it was displayed in the Glenray Technical College's "aborigine room"; at Bingara in New South Wales, the local newsagent put twenty-five copies in his shop window; and the NSW Department of Railways' bus tour to Taree distributed them to passengers who later attended an Aboriginal corroboree. The Kogarah Presbyterian Church in Sydney included the pamphlets in a course on assimilation for teenagers, along with a display of photos, leaflets, artworks, artefacts and school books from Ernabella Mission and screenings of slides and such films as *Men of the Mulgas, Children of the Musgraves, Namatjira the Painter* and *End of the Walkabout*. The senior class at Ulverstone High School in Tasmania wrote essays that focused on the new facts they had learned and overlooked the message of assimilation: Aboriginal people were the original owners of the continent; white settlement had driven them into remote arid lands and fringe camps; they lived in terrible conditions, suffered from poor health and died young; and they were generally worse off than black people in the USA, Britain and Africa, despite Australia being a rich country and signatory to the UN Declaration of Human Rights.

Readers overseas picked up on the racialist content, paradigms and language. At the United Nations in 1959, Soviet President Nikita Khrushchev used an image of an Aboriginal camp in *Fringe Dwellers* to attack Australia. The Chinese press quoted directly from the same pamphlet to describe how Aboriginal people were removed from their homelands to make way for economic development and dumped on wastelands where they survived "only on the fringe of hope and often on the fringe of despair". The photograph of an Aboriginal camp in *One People* in 1961 prompted criticism of Australia in the Moscow newspaper *New Times*, which was published in eight languages. Then, in 1963, Moscow accused British colonists in Australia of the near total annihilation of the Aboriginal people. In 1961, Australia's Department of External Affairs ruled that *One People* was "thoroughly unsuitable for overseas readers", as it was riddled with inaccuracies, contradictions, stereotypes, negative impressions and poor editing, and failed to adequately answer questions raised overseas concerning Aboriginal legal and political rights.

Materials to promote assimilation to Aboriginal people were produced by the relevant state government agencies, since Aboriginal affairs was by law their responsibility. Compared to the rather benign tone of the information booklets distributed to migrants, these materials were aggressively didactic, patronising and racist. *Dawn* magazine, launched by the NSW Aboriginal Welfare Board in 1952, relentlessly pushed the message of Aboriginal assimilation from its cover image of an Aboriginal Stone Age man juxtaposed against a modern city, through to the text and images of its feature pages and editorials. By 1965 *Dawn* had a circulation of 15,000, but by this stage Aboriginal readers were finding their own uses for the magazine – identifying lost relatives in its pages of photographs, writing letters critical of the government that were sometimes published and, in the case of future activists and writers like Kevin Gilbert, honing their writing skills in the pages for young Aboriginal writers.

Materials produced by the Department of Native Welfare in Western Australia were riddled with racist and patronising assumptions that demonstrated just how out of touch their creators were with Aboriginal opinion. The instructional primer *Citizens* (1964) contained cartoon drawings depicting Aboriginal families in conventional suburban homes and participating as citizens by voting, having a drink in a hotel, and seeking police assistance in upholding their rights. Dubbed the "How to drink" booklet by government officials, *Citizens* was used to launch the campaign to introduce drinking rights in the south of the state in 1964. Departmental training films seriously under-estimated the visual literacy skills of Aboriginal audiences accustomed to watching television and commercial feature films. One short film included a cartoon segment where stick figures carrying flagons of wine tumbled out of cars into a suburban house that suddenly exploded while a prim voice warned: "Loud parties will cause trouble." The several films about domestic work and infant care simply ignored Aboriginal women's accumulated knowledge and skills. The films *Good Food Good Health* and *A House in Town* produced in 1969 for the department's Home-maker Service aggressively instructed Aboriginal viewers in the routines of suburban domestic life and roles of the nuclear family.

## Retro-assimilation

The government's optimistic message of assimilation also appeared in the popular press, sometimes in articles by "Special correspondents" written in distinctively government styles. However, there were other stories that contradicted the official line by depicting the hardships and even the impossibility of assimilation. During the 1950s, the popular *PIX* magazine published some surprising articles about migrant and Aboriginal experiences in between its titillating pictures of bikini-clad girls and quirky human-interest stories.

The hard work and sacrifices of migrants were recounted through stories of families living in self-built garages on suburban lots while husbands and wives worked long hours at mind-numbing factory and industrial jobs to make ends meet. A moving article in 1957 described the tragic plight of casualties of migrant assimilation – "vagrant migrants … a lost race of despondent, neurotic misfits" who had "gambled their lives in a new world and lost. Maladjusted, beset by language problems, burdened by horrible memories that they just can't forget." Even the self-congratulatory stories of Australia as a haven from the horrors of war and communist life and the patronising accounts of Australians trying migrant coffee and foods differed from government publications in acknowledging the memories and cultures that migrants brought with them.

*PIX* also carried a range of stories that drew attention to the place of Aboriginal people in a modern Australia. There were the idiosyncratic weekly cartoons created by Eric Joliffe that depicted Aboriginal people as primitive desert dwellers who made surprisingly modern – and therefore humorous – comments about topical events such as the drudgery of housework, the H-bomb, domestic disputes and the vanity of women. Traditional Aboriginal life was represented in stories of exotic savagery from a distant Stone Age past, and was sometimes linked through outmoded explanations of racial and cultural decline to Aboriginal fringe camps of the 1950s. There were also stories of outstanding Aboriginal people, notably the artist Albert Namatjira, whose declining fortunes were recounted, like the intertwined lives of the star-struck lovers in the movie *Jedda*, within the familiar narrative framework of the tragic life of people forced to live between two cultures – a narrative that was profoundly pessimistic about the possibility of assimilation.

These stories of migrant and Aboriginal people were filtered through the lens of mainstream journalism, but there were alternative newspapers and publications where their voices spoke more directly to readers. Ethnic-language newspapers could be seen as countering the goals of assimilation or providing a passage into a new assimilated way of life. They were usually business-oriented, containing useful information on ethnic-owned services and ethnic professionals for new arrivals and the growing ethnic communities.

Anna Haebich

The pros and cons of Aboriginal assimilation were discussed in a plethora of small pamphlets published by churches, mission societies, student groups and Aboriginal political organisations. The Coolbaroo Club, a Perth-based Aboriginal political and cultural organisation, published *Coolbaroo News* (later *Westralian Aborigine*), a broadsheet that showed Aboriginal people participating as modern citizens selectively negotiating their way through the challenges of assimilation. The Federal Council of the Aboriginal Advancement (later the Federal Council for the Advancement of Aboriginal and Torres Strait Islanders) supported a program of Aboriginal rights while it attacked assimilation policy. In 1963, Council Secretary Stan Davey published a pamphlet entitled *Genesis or Genocide? The Aboriginal Assimilation Policy*, which criticised the policy for endeavouring to destroy Aboriginal identity and for failing to achieve equal legal status for Aboriginal people or to meet international standards. He challenged readers who condemned "elimination by extermination" in Nazi Germany and communist Russia, asking whether they thought this should be "condoned in Australia because of a different method of achieving the (same) objective".

Assimilation was a seductive solution to the threat posed by global challenge to "white Australia". While the imagery and rhetoric of assimilation created the impression of a new nation of equal citizens, the mechanics of assimilation reinforced the inequalities of the status quo. The marketing of assimilation through the powerful images of Australian life and Australian families distracted the public from the fact that there was no level playing field, only players who always won and those who rarely could. Confronted by our own global fears and anxieties, we remain susceptible to the repackaging of this phoney dream as a solution to today's dilemmas. But where will this leave us? If nations who do not know their history are destined to repeat the past, what happens to those who pin their hopes to the retro-marketing of a phoney dream? ∎

Notes are available at www.griffith.edu.au/griffithreview

Anna Haebich is Co-Director of the Centre for Public Culture and Ideas, Griffith University and is writing the first Australian cultural history of assimilation, *Imagining Assimilation*. She is the author of the award-winning *Broken Circles: Fragmenting Indigenous Families 1800–2000* (Fremantle Arts Centre Press, 2000). Her memoir, "A long way back" was published in *Griffith REVIEW 6: Our Global Face*.

Divided Nation

# Essay:
# On being invisible
## Author:
## Anita Heiss

As a Wiradjuri woman with an education, access to health, employment opportunities and a platform, I am incredibly privileged. I sit within the top 1 per cent of the bottom 2.5 per cent of the nation. I am, by any definition, an exception – but I often feel my community is invisible.

In the non-Indigenous world, though, I am normal. I have the basic human rights that anyone expects. I write now, and because of that privilege I am at times visible.

On a Qantas flight from Sydney to Los Angeles in 2003, I overheard a conversation between an American tourist and a Melbourne man. The tourist said: "I've just been in Australia and I met a fourth-generation Australian. That's pretty good, isn't it?" The man responded: "Well, you just don't get any more Australian than that!"

I turned to my Wiradjuri colleague and said: "Try four thousandth generation Australian!" Clearly our long history – tens of thousands of years of existence – doesn't count.

Aboriginal people are generally not on the Australian identity radar. We are invisible. Yet there are many hyphenated Australians: Greek-Australians, Italian-Australians, Chinese-Australians, Lebanese-Australians and "real-Australians". "Real-Australians" can trace their family heritage back to the convicts and prostitutes who made up the First Fleet, the original "boat people", reluctant refugees to the "great southern land" from 1788 onwards.

It is clear to me that the national identity is struggling for clarity – and has been since 1770 when Captain Cook planted the Union Jack at Possession Point and claimed the east coast of Australia under the doctrine of *terra nullius*, even though there were people here.

Since then, Australian identity has accommodated convicts and settlers who became "landowners" – the backbone of the country, raising cattle and sheep and doing it tough in droughts and floods. Australians fought wars that weren't theirs and from those wars identities were created. Each year, Anzac Day remembers the Australian and New Zealand troops who died at a beach on Gallipoli Peninsula in 1915. Aboriginal Australians are, for the most part, not considered within this tradition, or in much of the written history of Australia's participation in world wars, although they also fought.

The Anzac identity created by action outside Australia was followed by the locally produced identity of the surf lifesaver, the iconic tanned and buffed male affectionately known as the "Bronzed Aussie". Aboriginal Australians are not considered within this beach identity either, although many of us are coastal peoples and certainly bronzed.

Australian identity took a different direction in the 1980s when Paul Hogan created Mick "Crocodile" Dundee – the Aussie cowboy, a fish out of water in the big smoke. Hogan then started to "throw a shrimp on the barbie" as part of a campaign to tempt Americans to our shores. At this point it was clear that cultural identities were being created for tourism and entertainment. And, although Aussies had never thrown a shrimp on the barbie before – they ate prawns cold or covered in honey and sesame seeds at the local Chinese restaurant – all of a sudden they were told that part of the new national identity involved barbecuing crustaceans. And so they did.

Aboriginal Australians were not a part of this campaign either, although the middens up and down the coast are testament to our taste for crustaceans.

The backyard barbecue as a symbol of national identity has been challenged as multiculturalism has impacted deliciously on the culinary output in our cities (it is hard to find anything more exotic than a Chinese restaurant in a small country town). "Modern Australian cuisine" fuses different ethnic traditions by adding Asian spices to European staples. Real Aussies can't be accused of being racist: they enjoy "foreign" foods.

But if the adage of "you are what you eat" is true, then Australians are confused about their identity. "Aussies" are often regarded as a laid-back, easy-going and fairly hospitable people. And to a large extent they are. However, many forget that their history includes racist policies. This underbelly still exists, and means that intolerance is rife.

Such intolerance based on race found expression in the riots at Cronulla Beach in Sydney's south on December 11, 2005. Following the assault of local lifeguards by Lebanese-Australian men, locals retaliated. Anglo-Aussies (hiding behind the flag) stood their ground

## On being invisible

against the Lebanese-Australians (hiding in gangs). I don't think it was the Skips versus the Lebs: it was Idiots versus Idiots. Regardless, the lines were drawn by the self-appointed identity police on who was, and who wasn't, Australian. The mob of violent, shirtless drunks chanted "F*** off, Lebs" and bellowed *Waltzing Matilda* – attacking those who "appeared" to be un-Australian – of "Middle Eastern appearance".

The same proud Aussies sent inflammatory SMS notices to each other, encouraging their mates to gather at Cronulla. Messages to "bash Wogs and Lebs" were reinforced by slogans on posters and placards that read "ethnic cleansing" and "Aussies fighting back". Active, blatant racism became the Australian way of life in Cronulla. One poster read: "Free snags – no tabouli". Even culinary fusion was out.

I've always wondered why media commentators don't use the phrase "of Australian appearance". Maybe no one wants to admit what it would mean: looking and behaving "white". If the Cronulla riots are a guide, it means Anglo, drunk, violent and with a mob mentality.

Amidst the boozing, brawling and bellowing in the name of protecting the "values", authenticity and icons of being Australian, no one asked the "first Australians"

how they felt about the chaos at Cronulla. Placards that read "We were here first" made us laugh. But then we didn't expect them to carry a placard reading "We were here second".

Well-known local spokesperson for Aboriginal affairs Merv Ryan has long been active in ensuring that the Sutherland Shire's Aboriginal culture is preserved and the spiritual connection of the 1,700 local Kooris to the land – and beaches – is acknowledged. He has been an active participant in establishing a Reconciliation Statement with the council, and regularly performs the "welcome to country" ceremonies on behalf of the Dharawal Nation.

Ryan remained quiet at the time of the riots, although he encouraged young Kooris to stay away, out of sight of the mob. At a local community forum after the riots, all he said about the "Take Our Beaches Back" slogan was: "These people are claiming this beach because they've been here for 230 years. We've been here for 60,000!" A relevant point, delivered with dignity. Ryan forced the audience to think.

I wonder what kind of national response there would have been if thousands of Aboriginal flags – rather than Australians flag – were waved that day. If the focus had been on claiming land and values, not attacking and excluding.

My conclusion from the surfside identity wars is that, more than ever, the national identity needs grounding. Otherwise we remain a society of intolerant, violent, directionless idiots, waving the Union Jack because we don't have a flag that captures the spirit of our diversity. Many of us have no genetic or cultural affiliation with Britain – I am Aboriginal with Austrian heritage.

The Prime Minister's conclusion was to put assimilation back on the agenda. Aspiring Australians have to assume "Australian values" – values diametrically opposed to Aboriginal values; competition not cooperation, the individual not community and so on – and learn history as well as English. Did those on the First Fleet have to adopt Aboriginal values and learn the language? No, the obligation has always been to learn the language of the second peoples.

An editorial in *The Australian* on September 16, 2006 declared: "What we are witnessing in small pockets of Muslim migrants now is an aggressive denial of Australian culture." What Australian culture? Going to the beach where people get bashed? Taking BYO grog everywhere you go? Taking sick days because you can? Playing pokie machines in RSL clubs? Having snags instead of tabouli? What "Australian culture" is being referred to in this one-sided debate?

What is happening in 2006 is scarily close to the policy of assimilation designed in 1951 and amended in 1965 at the Native Welfare Conference. It stated in part: "The policy of assimilation seeks that all persons of Aboriginal descent will choose to attain a similar manner of living to that of other Australians and live as members of a single community – enjoying the same rights and privileges, accepting the same responsibilities and influenced by the same hopes and loyalties as other Australians."

The same doctrine of assimilating Aboriginal people in the twentieth century is being redeployed in the twenty-first century, now targeting immigrants. Again, Aboriginal Australians remain outside the discussion.

I travel the world teaching and performing, and the way Aboriginal Australia is perceived internationally concerns me deeply. When I ask my mainly American students, how many have seen *Crocodile Dundee*, most raise their hands. Many expect me to tell the time by the sun, live in the desert, speak pidgin, throw a boomerang, cook bush tucker and dance on cue, in part because of that film.

I look at my Dolce and Gabbana watch and tell the time. I teach in the coloniser's language and use it to my own ends as an educator and author. I tell them I cook kangaroo three times a week, hunting for it at the supermarket – where most urban-dwelling Aboriginal people gather their nourishment in the twenty-first century. I tell them to deal with it. I contain my frustration over the reality that the urban blackfellas – one-fifth of Australia's Indigenous population lives in greater Sydney – remain invisible.

In the classroom, I can at least redefine what Aboriginal identity is, and how it evolves. But redefining the national identity is another story. It always comes back to who is and who isn't Australian, and who was here first.

Canada and the United States hold their Indigenous populations in far higher esteem, defining them as "first peoples". That doesn't happen here. That would mean admitting the colonisers – the Anglo-Australians – were the "second peoples", and let's face it, second place is rarely celebrated. No one remembers who won silver; we only remember who came first. Admitting "second" status would concede too much about this country's real history and identity, add to confusion over who is and who isn't Australian, who's more Australian, and who – in the case of the Idiots versus Idiots at Cronulla Beach – has to the right to say "Go back to where you came from".

The Aboriginal and Torres Strait Islander Commission (ATSIC) was Australia's national representative, policy-making and service delivery agency for Indigenous people for fifteen years. For all the criticisms levelled at it, ATSIC performed at least one major role well until it was disbanded in 2005. That was to keep Indigenous Australian issues on the political radar. Since its abolition, Indigenous voices in Australian politics have virtually disappeared. The hand-picked advisory body, the National Indigenous Council (NIC), simply ensures that the Government's flawed way of doing things continues. The NIC is required to provide expert advice to government on improving outcomes for Indigenous Australians, but it is what the Minister for Families, Community Services and Indigenous Affairs Mal Brough has described as "a replacement for ATSIC and not a representative body. It is not involved in specific funding proposals or program/planning matters in individual communities or regions."

Blackfellas are so invisible in Australian politics that the government is under no pressure to do anything about the modern-day black deaths caused by "Syndrome X" – a combination of diabetes, end-state renal disease, strokes, hypertension and heart disease that is killing Indigenous Australians at a terrifying rate. Indigenous Australians die twenty to twenty-five years younger than the rest of the population. Why isn't this issue considered to be a national Australian health crisis? If Syndrome X affected the self-defined "real Australians", this would be a matter of national concern. It would be headline news until an appropriate and acceptable course of action was found. But being invisible, and separated from the rest of the country, we're told that Syndrome X is an "Indigenous health issue". It's not: it's an Australian health issue.

If we were visible on the national identity radar, it would be part of the national agenda, but while we remain invisible we don't matter.

Poet and activist Sam Watson, co-founder of the Black Panther Party of Australia in 1971, was also active in the anti Springbok mobilisations (1971) and the Aboriginal Tent Embassy (1972). A Brisbane-based Biri Gubba and Munnenjarl man, he has firm views on Australian politics and why Aboriginal Australia remains invisible: "This entire nation of Australia is based on a culture of lies, mass murder and violent denial. White people look at Aboriginal people and they are confronted with the full horror of their own crimes. That is why they now look and refuse to see …"

And so, while we don't appear on the national identity radar, and we have no role in the Australian political infrastructure or agenda, what can we do to become visible? What avenues are open to us to have a say in the society where we exist and participate every day, but are almost unrecognisable? What forums allow us to represent ourselves and our identities and communities? How can we tell our stories and our shared histories? How can we make polticial statements that hopefully will effect social change?

The last platform we have left is the arts. Our writers, storytellers, filmmakers, playrights, new media artists, musicians and visual artists are using their skills, creativity, knowledge and opportunities to make us more visible, not only to the rest of Australia but to the entire world.

Historical and political issues are being covered as a means of highlighting facts around the stolen generations – facts denied and ignored by the Commonwealth Government. But award-winning books – Doris Pilkington's *Follow the Rabbit Proof Fence* and Larrisa Behrendt's *Home*, Albert Holt's *Forcibly Removed* and Glenyse Ward's *Wandering Girl*, Edna Tantjingu Williams and Eileen Wani Wingfield's *Down the Hole*, to name a few – are writing us into Australian history and, one hopes, the national psyche at the same time.

## On being invisible

Musical anthems – Archie Roach singing *Took the Children Away* and Bobbie Randall's *Brown Skin Baby* – resonate. Theatre-goers here and abroad flocked to see plays on the stolen generations like Dallas Winmar's *Aliwa* and Jane Harrison's *Stolen*. Our filmmakers are helping to make us more visible by shaping the way history is remembered, politics is lived and the nation's conscience is guided.

Filmmaker Glen Stasiuk was inspired by his family's history and the respect he felt for the "black diggers" who were invisible in the Anzac identity. The writer, producer and director of *The Forgotten* says he "had members of my family fight and die in both world wars, and my great uncle was one of the first Aboriginal soldiers to receive a war medal. This film is for them and all the other Aboriginal people who have fought for our country and not gotten the recognition that they deserved. Not a lot of people know about the contribution made by Aboriginal people, particularly during the earlier wars. I hope *The Forgotten* can help get these stories across."

Visual artists have also made us visible around the globe. The opening of Musée du quai Branly in Paris showcased Indigenous arts and culture to a global audience. The commissoned collection including works by Lena Nyadbi, Paddy Nyunkuny Bedford, Judy Watson, Gulumbu Yunupingu, John Mawurndjul, Tommy Watson, Ningura Napurrula and the late Michael Riley. Our art is held in high regard elsewhere, and these artists have become part of the 1 per cent of the bottom 2.5 per cent who are seen.

The project was curated by Brenda L. Croft from the National Gallery and Hetti Perkins of the Art Gallery of New South Wales. Croft says: "The great ironies about Indigenous visual art and culture being used to sell Australia to the world, and it being the essence that overseas visitors consider to be quintessentially Australian, is how undervalued it is here on home soil. One of the world's leading architects, Jean Nouvel, considered contemporary Indigenous art from Australia as his only choice for including as a major architectural component of his vision for the Musèe du quai Branly – yet we continue to hear how many of our most significant cultural activists – for that is what our artists are – continue to be preyed upon by unscrupulous commercial dealers, who reap the profits from the artists' creativity.

"Imagine Ricky Swallow, who represented Australia at the last Venice Biennale, living in poverty, being kept virtually hostage in a room, 'encouraged' to keep painting, not benefiting from the massive markups placed on their work. Yet our people generously continue to share their vast repetoire of visual language and cultural heritage with the rest of the world, patiently waiting for the day when outsiders will finally get it, and recognise we exist, not only as artists, but as humans beings, and Australians, too."

Jon C. Altman, Director of the Centre for Aboriginal Economic Policy Research at the Australian National University, says even racist Australians can – and do – appreciate Aboriginal art. But they do so with detachment: "The Australian nation loves Aboriginal art and associated financial spin-off benefits to the tourism sector and commerce, but fails to see that arts success is predicated on land rights, or that artists need a degree of cultural and geographic distancing from townships to succeed."

But the distancing, detaching and everyday examples of how we remain invisible continue. Delivering the 2004 Lambie Dew Oration at Sydney University, long-time supporter of Indigenous health and literacy projects Jeff McMullen said: "As I was looking around this Great Hall, looking at all these portraits, I was wondering how long it will be until we have a portrait here of an Aboriginal leader. Where are the signs and symbols of the ancestors here in this sandstone hall? When you work with Aboriginal people, you have these thoughts. What is missing in this Australian story?"

What is missing from the Australian story is the first Australians. ■

---

Anita Heiss is an academic and author whose books include *Dhuuluu Yala (Talk Straight): Publishing Aboriginal Literature* (Aboriginal Studies Press, 2003) and *Who Am I? The Diary of Mary Talence, Sydney, 1937* (Scholastic Australia, 2001). Her next book, *Not Meeting Mr Right* will be published by Bantam in 2007.

Just click to listen to what people like **Frank Moorhouse**, Murray Sayle, Robyn Williams, Peter Doherty, Jeff McMullen, Ian Lowe, Chris Sarra, Joanna Mendelssohn, Gideon Haigh and other writers have to say.

If you are unable to make it along to one of our events, catch up with what was said with the audio files now available on the "News and Events" page of our website.

www.griffith.edu.au/griffithreview

**Griffith UNIVERSITY**

Essay:
**Blow-ins on the cold desert wind**

Author:
**Kim Mahood**

Image: Permanent residents / Photographer: Kim Mahood

# Blow-ins on the cold desert wind

Each year I drive from my home near Canberra to the Tanami Desert and spend several months in an Aboriginal community that has become my other home. The trip takes a week or two, allowing for the incremental adjustments that make my arrival one of recognition, pleasure and ambivalence.

There was a year I did it differently, flying directly to Alice Springs and travelling the thousand kilometres of corrugated and sandy desert track squashed into the back of a troop carrier with nine or ten elderly Aboriginal artists. We arrived in the early hours of the morning, less than twenty-four hours after I had left Canberra. The vehicle headlights lit a disorderly world of damaged houses, broken cars, lean furtive dogs and accumulated rubbish. This was a number of years ago, when I was still sorting out the uneasiness of my relationship to the place and people, and I felt the rise of old anxieties and discomfort. It seemed that, having departed from the orderly, over-planned surrealism of the national capital, I had arrived at its sinister twin. As I helped to drag tattered foam mattresses and assorted bundles from the back of the troop carrier, I thought of the plans and policies manufactured in the tidy hill-fort of Parliament House, and imagined them on their trajectory across the nation encountering a zone of refraction somewhere in the upper atmosphere, arriving as a mess of shattered fragments on this windy plateau. This image has stayed with me, a visual metaphor for the sustained capacity of remote Aboriginal Australia to subvert the best intentions of successive state and federal governments.

One of the results of moving on a regular basis between predominantly white urban Australia and predominantly black remote Australia is an awareness of the gulf of perception between those people for whom Aboriginal Australia is a reality and those for whom it is an idea. An idea can tolerate a number of abstractions. Reality, on the other hand, must tolerate a number of contradictions. The way in which these contradictions are bridged by both white and black is largely through humour, irony and a well-honed sense of the absurd – qualities generally missing from any public representation of white and Aboriginal interactions.

The whites who work at this interface talk about Aboriginal people all the time. The trajectory of every conversation, no matter where it begins, ends up in the same place. These conversations are full of bafflement, hilarity, frustration, admiration and conjecture. They are an essential means of processing the contradictions with which one deals every day.

The Aboriginal people talk about the whites too, but I doubt that it is in the same sustained and obsessive way. I can't be sure of this, and it is something I will probably never know. What I do know is that the Western Desert word for white person, *gardiya*, runs like a subliminal refrain under the currents of ordinary conversation. No matter how much time one has spent or how strong one's relationships with Aboriginal people, the word follows you about like a bad smell. It is not intended as an insult; it is simply a verbal marker to underline the difference between *us* and *them*.

It becomes an insult, however, if one is Aboriginal. In the volatile world of family and community politics, it is the greatest insult that can be levelled at anyone who is suspected of harbouring *gardiya* aspirations and values. To take on any form of authority over your peers opens you to such an accusation, as does the refusal to share vehicles, money and possessions. People of mixed descent are continually reminded of their compromised status, and children with white blood are frequently referred to as *gardiya*.

To be white exempts you to some extent from the network of responsibilities and obligations. It is accepted that you belong to an inexplicably cold and selfish branch of the human family, and refusals to share what you have are accepted with equanimity. However, the boundaries become more difficult to hold as relationships deepen, and negotiating one's place in all of this is a continuing process.

By the standards of white Australian society, the life I lead is extremely provisional. I don't have a regular job, I don't own a home and my annual income is in the bracket that attracts a low-income rebate on my tax return. In the eyes of the Aboriginal people among whom I work, I own a reliable vehicle, I can buy fuel when I need it, I always have food in the house, I am allowed to run up an account at the store. These are indicators of wealth. Sometimes, as I weave my evasive course through a web of subtle and overt demands, carrying only small change in my pockets, walking instead of driving so my car is not commandeered as a taxi to ferry people home with their shopping, making continual small adjustments and compromises against my better judgement, I catch a glimpse of the truly provisional nature of people's lives. When I buy diesel at $2.20 a litre, when I pay $5 for a carton of soy milk that would cost me half that in a southern supermarket, I appreciate the mirage-like nature of money in this world. I understand why the fortnightly pension cheque is converted to cash and lost in a card game an hour later. Paul Virilio, in *The Aesthetics of Disappearance* (MIT Press, 1991), says "number games, like lotto or the lottery, with their disproportionate winnings, connote disobedience to society's laws, exemption from taxes, immediate redressment of poverty".

If I was of an academic turn of mind, I would be tempted to pursue a thesis on the role and meaning of money in Aboriginal communities. There is no apparent logic to its availability. Acquiring it is a serious preoccupation, with none of the social prohibitions that disguise the same preoccupation in non-Aboriginal society. It is easy to become cynical at the manoeuvring to prove traditional links to mining land and thus access to royalties. It is easy to be appalled by the ruthlessness with which elderly painters are milked by their extended family, or to be exhausted by the relentless pursuit of payment for the smallest snippet of cultural knowledge.

These are the cross-cultural tensions nobody talks about, except in those *gardiya* enclaves within the communities, as one tries to find ways to dissipate the frustrations and misunderstandings. I found an explanation that took much of my own cultural distaste out of the equation when I made an analogy between hunting and gathering for food and hunting and gathering for money. It may not persuade others, but it works for me. One has only to listen to accounts of traditional itineraries to notice the preoccupation with food. Desert society evolved in the boom and bust economy of one of the hardest environments on the planet, and survival was predicated on the efficiency with which its resources could be utilised. My theory – not entirely frivolous – is that the same energy once spent on getting food is now spent on getting money.

To be white is to be seen to have mysterious access to money. Sometimes I think we are perceived by the Aboriginal people as money guards, standing at the door to vaults full of wealth and doling out pocket money to them while we take all we want for ourselves. The government supply lines that support remote communities are poorly understood by the recipients. In the tightening political environment, there is a growing emphasis on accountability and effective governance, with a number of training programs and workshops designed to assist communities. Earlier this year I was co-opted to assist in the trial of one such program.

"The Australian Governance Story" has been designed in response to a request from Aboriginal communities to explain how government works in Australia. Its purpose is to give the people an overview of where they fit into the larger structures of government, where the money that supports their existence comes from, and their rights and responsibilities in managing these funds and services.

Over the years of my involvement with the community, I have deliberately avoided the Gordian knot of bureaucracy, working instead on cultural mapping projects to record the stories and knowledge people still hold about their country. A fortuitous encounter with a deeply committed and imaginative public servant called Kerrie, one of those people without whom the really hard challenges would never be attempted, resulted in us throwing ideas around about how our different enterprises might assist one another. My brief assignment as a public servant was an experiment, to see whether my work could be married to the daily business of people learning to manage their communities effectively. My reasons for taking it on were self-interested. I try to spend several months of every year in this place, and it is a constant financial struggle to find ways of doing so.

This is how I find myself with the task of explaining "The Australian Governance Story" to the community members and persuading people to attend a workshop – a proposition that more or less cancels itself out. I am up against the deeply embedded suspicion of and resistance to white government-driven agendas, even when those agendas are in response to requests and proposals from the communities themselves.

The workshop is planned for July, the time of year when the congestion of visitors is at its most intense. One of the major disadvantages of belonging to a disadvantaged minority, particularly one that is central to our sense of national identity, is the relentless stream of government officials whose job it is to assess and redress those disadvantages. On any given day between May and September (after the wet season and before it gets too hot, which happens to coincide with the southern winter), a number of spanking white four-wheel drives, doors decorated with logos, will be parked in the dusty quadrangle outside the office, while the government officials they have brought compete for the attention of the community residents. It's not uncommon to find a disconsolate government rep hanging about with a satchel of information and no one to deliver it to.

In any small community, there are a limited number of people who take on the responsibility for its social and practical maintenance. This is especially true of an Aboriginal community. Whether the issue is governance or childcare or aged care, social security, substance abuse, sexual health, store committees, education and training, tourism development, environmental management, fire control, dogs, housing or garbage management, it is the same seven or eight people who are in demand. Meeting fatigue is endemic. Burnout is a recognised syndrome among white staff in communities, but little notice is given to the same phenomenon among the Aboriginal people. When the pressure gets too much, they simply disappear for extended periods.

A three-day workshop is a big ask for people on whom the daily functioning of the community rests. It is a fine line I have to negotiate between the requirements of the government agency (I will call it ACRO) and the potential workshop participants. There are bureaucratic formalities to be met – numbers, names, the demographics of age, gender, literacy and language, signed agreements from participants that they will attend and complete the workshop.

This last requirement presents particular difficulties. It is as likely to scare people away as it is to commit them to coming. Signed pieces of paper are whitefella business, implicit with danger. I know that I can count on the core group of older women with whom I usually work, unless family business intervenes. They will come because I ask them to, because over the years we have established a relationship of mutual trust and exchange. But family business takes precedence, and signed papers will not alter that. Among the younger, overburdened community members, the risk of getting them to sign up lies in giving them too much time to plan their escape.

I re-read the list of selection criteria that applies to my temporary position as an Australian public servant: At "no. 4 – Innovates" I find what I am looking for: "able to develop solutions that are outcomes focused and informed by a strategic perspective". I interpret this to mean get bums on seats by whatever means necessary.

Since Rebecca has discovered that we have the same-sized feet, she has been humbugging me relentlessly for the slip-on shoes I wear, unimpressed by my refusal on the grounds that they are the only shoes I've brought with me.

"What am I supposed to do, go barefoot?"

She looks pointedly at her own bare hard-soled feet and says nothing.

"You're a blackfella, you go barefoot all the time. I have to wear shoes, my feet are too soft."

She throws me a grin that is knowing, charming and manipulative. "I got some old ones you can have."

"I don't want your old shoes. I'm quite happy with these." I beg a cigarette from her. My resolve not to smoke is folding, as it always does within a few weeks of returning to the community.

"Where's that thing you got for not smoking?" She's referring to the nicotine inhaler I've been sucking on since I arrived. I take it out of my pocket and show it to her.

"Doesn't work?"

"Not under pressure."

"Buy me a packet of cigarettes."

I agree to do this. That way I can beg one from her whenever I need to.

Rebecca is smart and literate, one of the people in constant demand to interpret the two worlds to one another. She fits the profile of the target workshop participant perfectly.

"You can have my shoes if you promise to come to the workshop."

"That's, what do you call it … coercion."

"Fuck off. Do you want the shoes or not?"

"Okay, I'll come. Can I have them now?"

"No way. After the workshop. And you have to come all three days."

She gives me a deep, resentful frown, one of her stock array of expressions, all bordering on parody, which crack into broad grins of amusement at the absurdities we are obliged to play out. The self-satisfied crocodile grin appears; she has established that the shoes are negotiable. Whether she comes to the workshop or not, we both know which foot the shoe is going to end up on.

Enlisting men was always going to be difficult. So many of the arenas in which their identities as men are formulated have been undermined. The radar alert for coercion is set at a hair-trigger. In any case, there are very few young and middle-aged men in the community, a fair proportion of them being in jail for various misdemeanours and crimes, mostly alcohol related.

My key target is Patrick, a man of standing in the community and a member of one of the strong families. He is a short, square, suspicious man with a flaring temper, and has just returned from a stint in prison for cutting someone with a tomahawk. A few days ago I gave him and his wife a lift back to the community from a broken-down car. Later that evening, I encountered him with his son and brother-in-law trying to get the same vehicle going, and loaned them my torch and tools. I have also loaned him jerry cans of fuel on several occasions.

"Patrick, I need you to come to this workshop. It's to teach people about how the government works, to help you to look after the community properly."

Patrick's expression is sceptical, mildly amused. Most of what is important in the encounter is unspoken. There is genuine liking here, and also an understanding that the situation is improvised, because neither of us has more than a bare glimpse into the other's thinking processes.

"You're strong. People respect you. If you come, some of the other men will come too."

The appeal to his vanity works. I get him to sign the paper. We both know that this is no guarantee that he will attend the workshop. What it does mean is that he will put in an appearance and that this will help to swing a few of the men and boys at least to consider attending.

Payment is an issue. People are used to being paid for attending meetings. For those on the work-for-the-dole scheme, the hours spent in the workshop can be claimed, but for the rest there is nothing I can offer except the suggestion that it's in their own interests to participate. This does not wash with Fatima, who has the profile and character of a Roman potentate.

"You *gardiya*," she says, "always coming and telling us what to do. You want us to come to meetings and then you won't pay us."

Attack is the best form of defence with Fatima, who is one of the community powerbrokers. "Listen, if you were white you'd be expected to pay for a workshop like this, not be paid to come."

She leans her bulk back in the chair and smirks, satisfied that she's made me say something she can hold against me later.

"Anyway, it's about how to manage things yourself, so you don't have to put up with *gardiya* telling you what to do."

"You shouldn't get upset, Napuru. I'll come, just to help you out."

And so it goes for the weeks leading up to the arrival of the training team. Kerrie wants a guarantee of twenty participants, preferably the younger, more literate members of the community. I tell her I can't guarantee anything, but I'm doing my best. Rebecca checks every day that the deal with the shoes is still on.

I receive a list of questions from the trainers:

- Do people understand what it means to be a COAG site?
- Do DOTARS, DEWR, ICC and OIPC have regional reps?
- What is the current status of SRAs in the community?
- Do people have an understanding of how the CDEP changes will affect them?
- Will they come under an RAE?
- How will it impact on NAHS, HACC and FACS?
- Who is the local RSP?
- Is the IPA funded by DEH or DIA?
- What is the role of the KLC? Does KALACC come under the same umbrella?

- Has anyone in the community accessed the ISBF?
- Should one approach KLRC or KIC for interpretive services?

With the help of Rebecca and her sister Julie, I decode most of this curious document.

When the training duo arrives I am mending a flat tyre. They are called Bob and Deborah, and have been refining and delivering workshops to Aboriginal organisations for many years. They are experienced, good-humoured, flexible and tough. In the face of their professionalism I feel awkward and incompetent.

Kerrie and her ACRO team arrive the next morning. Things look moderately promising. The weather isn't too cold and most people have stayed in the community in spite of it being school holidays. This has also made it possible to hold the workshop in the school library, which is comfortable, well resourced and away from the distractions of the community. It is also potentially intimidating for people who don't usually sit at desks, but there's no better alternative. I have a list of seventeen possible participants, about half of whom I can be confident will turn up.

The workshop is due to start at nine. At eight-thirty I begin my rounds. There's a recognised protocol to this, which is to drive your vehicle as close as possible to people's houses and keep your hand on the horn until someone appears. After a few circuits I've roused most of the community and extracted promises that they will come down to the school after they've been to the shop. No one shows any enthusiasm. At nine I do another round and catch Fatima trying to climb into the Indigenous Protected Area (IPA) troop carrier, which is taking a group of young rangers away to a training workshop. I work her over with shameless emotional manipulation, payback for the many times she's done it to me.

"How can you do this, after you promised me? I thought I could trust you. This makes me really upset."

She casts a backward glance at the troopie, which is too crowded to fit her in, and pats me on the arm. "Don't worry, Napuru. I was going to look after these kids but you need me, so I'll come with you."

By ten-thirty about twenty-five people have wandered down to the school to see what's going on. The trainers give their introduction and we break for morning tea, after which the numbers drop to sixteen. Patrick has put in his promised appearance, lurking just inside the door and ducking outside after half an hour for a cigarette. I join him.

"What do you think?"

He shakes his head. "That stuff make my head hurt." He finishes his cigarette, gives me a nod and leaves.

After lunch the numbers are down to nine. By my reckoning the dropout ratio is one-third per session, which doesn't bode well for tomorrow. But the afternoon session becomes animated. Bob and Deborah know their stuff. They get people to unpick the network of organisations that service the community. Rebecca and Julie spearhead the group of women who reveal a sound grasp of the organisational network, which is astonishingly complicated. I am in sympathy with Patrick – it makes my head hurt too.

The challenge on day two is to get people to the workshop before the Tanami bus comes through on its bi-weekly run into Halls Creek. I collect them in twos and threes and drop them at the school. Half of them circle around behind the toilet block and beat me through the gate. They wave as I drive past, and someone calls out "Taxi", at which they all hoot with laughter.

I drive to Fatima's house to see whether she is coming today. Yesterday there was a nasty domestic incident involving her youngest daughter, who collapsed after being beaten by her husband and has been flown out on the doctor plane. This incident accounted for most of the absentees from the afternoon session. There's no response to my horn, but I see the curtain flicker in the front room. In attempting to get out of the car, I discover that the door lock is jammed. Fatima appears in the doorway to watch me climbing out of the window.

"What you doing, Napuru?"

"I can't open the door."

"You should get that fixed." She gets into the car. "What we doing today?"

On the way to the workshop, several of my previous passengers flag me down for a lift back to the school. They inform me that the Tanami bus has broken down and there's no run to town this week.

I am impressed by the training team, who adjust seamlessly to the changing dynamics of the group, and keep everyone fully engaged. The day is spent outlining the structure of the federal government and the lines of communication from the community through to the various departments responsible for delivering services. Most people are not aware that there is both a state and a federal government. The most pertinent piece of information they absorb is that the budget is passed by law, and that once a certain amount of money has been designated it can't be altered, and must be delivered through the appropriate channels. At the community level, money is an arbitrary and unpredictable resource, so the notion that it is a finite and regulated commodity is novel. The trainers tell them that the money is provided

## Blow-ins on the cold desert wind

by taxpayers. "Your money," they say. This bothers me, since I know that no one in the community apart from the white staff pays tax, although I appreciate the need for people to feel empowered. It's another of those irreconcilable contradictions.

At the end of the day, everyone agrees to come at nine the next morning. They say I don't need to drive around and pick them up, although they enjoy seeing me climb in and out of my car window.

"You should get that door fixed, Napuru."

That evening, on the downward haul, there's an air of hilarity among the workshop team. I remark that I feel like a hapless victim of fate, and we discuss the need for more hap to deal with events like this. This leads to reflections on being gormless and feckless. The next morning, the team leaders are sporting name tags that say Hap, Feck and Gorm.

At eight-thirty the wailing begins and my stomach drops. Someone has died, and I feel the fear we all live with that it will be someone you know and love. Life is so precarious here, death frequent and sudden. But it is Wendy's sister who has died in Derby, a woman whose life has been violent and troubled for many years. I join the group of people offering condolences, and sit with Wendy while the older women join her in the protocols of sorry business. So much for the nine o'clock start. It's out of my hands now; people will decide their own priorities.

Evelyn comes by to tell me she is going out with her family to kill a bullock. She says she will keep some rib bones for me, indicating that she feels I need to be compensated for her withdrawal from the workshop. She's learned as much as she wants to know about the "guvment". Her own concerns are closer to home, in the refined and complex politics of family and country. Rebecca has also dropped out with the excuse that she has to get organised to travel to her father-in-law's funeral. She wants to know if she can still have my shoes. We negotiate a debrief on the workshop when she gets back.

By ten o'clock there are ten people in the library. The new name tags of the training team members pass without comment. After all, people here go by names such as Rimikus, Spieler and Blah Blah. There is an air of empowerment among the stayers. They carry out enthusiastic role-plays of how to present a request to their state or federal minister. They have a far better grasp than I do of the labyrinthine structures at the lower levels of bureaucracy, which I have come to appreciate bear some resemblance to their own convoluted family and political structures. At the end of the day they are pleased and happy with what they have learned, and eager for follow-up sessions. The training team has a substantial list of adjustments to implement from the trial. Everyone but me seems to think that something has been achieved.

The next day, Bessie comes to the office and asks me to ring Peter Costello to ask him about funding for her outstation. I find the number of the Treasurer's office and tell her to ring him herself. Monica appears with a photocopied paper which shows the line of funding support for the Indigenous Protected Area.

"You can help me?"

"What for?"

She shows me the paper. "This for money in't it?"

"Only for the IPA."

She throws the paper in the bin.

Julie comes in and asks me when I'm going to pay her for her work as interpreter for the workshop.

"That's ACRO's business. They haven't paid me either. Where's that list telling us who to ring up?"

Fatima comes in and parks herself portentously in the chair beside my desk.

"Napuru, you know I'm always working to help people, old people and young people together and *gardiya* too. I should get paid for that."

Evelyn comes to tell me she's got some rib bones for me in the freezer at her daughter's house.

During a lull, I lock the office and make my escape. The community is quiet; today there are no visitors from the other world. The cold desert wind that seems to rise in agitation at the influx of too many outsiders has dropped, and the day is clear and sunny. I climb through the car window into the driver's seat, avoiding the broken mirror stem where the rear-vision mirror has been pulled off by a child doing chin-ups.

"You should fix that door, Napuru," someone calls out. "It looks like an Aboriginal car." Fatima appears at the passenger door with her shopping.

"You can give me a lift home, Napuru?"

In the car she says: "That was a good meeting. We should have more like that." ∎

---

Kim Mahood is an artist and an author. Her *Craft for a Dry Lake* (Random House) won the 2001 NSW Premier's Prize for Non-fiction.

# Don't miss a word ....

"What we have here is, first and foremost, fine writing: creative, challenging and moving."

FRANK O'SHEA,
CANBERRA TIMES

"For what it's worth, I think Griffith REVIEW has developed into one of the very best journals in the country. I'd put it on the shortest of shortlists."

PHILLIP ADAMS, JOURNALIST
AND COMMENTATOR

**Bring your collection up to date now.**

Past editions of Griffith REVIEW are available from ABC Centres and Shops and all good booksellers!

**Shop online at:**
www.abcshop.com.au
www.coop-bookshop.com.au